THE ETHICS OF BELIEF DEBATE

ᴁR

American Academy of Religion
Academy Series

Editors
Charley Hardwick
James O. Duke

Number 41
THE ETHICS OF BELIEF DEBATE
Edited by
Gerald D. McCarthy

THE ETHICS OF BELIEF DEBATE

Edited by
Gerald D. McCarthy

Scholars Press
Atlanta, Georgia

THE ETHICS OF BELIEF DEBATE

Edited by
Gerald D. McCarthy

© 1986
The American Academy of Religion

Library of Congress Cataloging in Publication Data

The Ethics of belief debate.–

  (Studies in religion ; 41)
  Bibliography: p.
  1. Belief and doubt—Moral and ethical aspects—
Addresses, essays, lectures. 2. Theism—Addresses,
essays, lectures. 3. Knowledge, Theory of (Religion)—
Addresses, essays, lectures. I. McCarthy, Gerald,
1945–   . II. Series: Studies in religion (American
Academy of Religion); no. 41.
BD215.E84 1986   170   85-19568
ISBN 0-89130-892-X (alk. paper)
ISBN 0-89130-893-8 (pbk. : alk. paper)

Printed in the United States of America
on acid-free paper

TABLE OF CONTENTS

RETROSPECTIVE ESSAYS

For
Eileen and Michael McCarthy
and
Michael and Eric Darrah

who interrupted the preparation of this volume just often
enough that I never forgot what really counts.

THE AUTHORS

William K. Clifford (1845–1879), distinguished mathematician and philosopher, was elected a fellow of Trinity College, Cambridge in 1868 and in 1870 was appointed professor of applied mathematics at University College, London. His election to a fellowship in the Royal Society at age 29 (1874) testifies to his reputation. Originally attracted to High Church principles, he lost his faith when he encountered Darwin and Darwinism. His major papers are collected in *The Common Sense of the Exact Sciences*, ed. Karl Pearson (1885); *Lectures and Essays*, ed. F. Pollock (1879); and *Mathematical Papers*, ed. H. J. Smith (1882). An early and briefer version of "The Ethics of Belief" was read to the Metaphysical Society on April 11, 1876. The version that is reprinted in this volume appeared in the *Contemporary Review* (1877).

St. George Jackson Mivart (1827–1900) studied at King's College, London and, upon his conversion to Roman Catholicism in 1844, at St. Mary's College, Oscott. He distinguished himself as a scientist and was a member of the Royal Institution and a fellow of the Zoological Society and the Linnean Society. In 1869 he was elected to membership in the Royal Society. He also wrote extensively on philosophical and theological matters in the hope of mediating between Roman Catholicism and modern thought and restoring the philosophical bases of Roman Catholicism. His theological liberalism, however, brought him into conflict with his church and he was excommunicated in 1890. In addition to authoring scientific papers and monographs, he was a prolific essayist and many of these are collected in *Essays and Criticism* (1889), *Essays on Religion and Literature* (1874), and *Lessons from Nature as Manifested in Mind and Matter* (1876). "What is the Good of Truth?" was read to the Metaphysical Society on June 13, 1876 and forms the partial basis for his paper, "Force, Energy and Will" that appeared in the *Nineteenth Century* (1878) and to which James F. Stephen responded in his paper "On the Utility of Truth."

Sir James Fitzjames Stephen (1829–1894) was born into a prominent Evangelical family. His father, James Stephen, was a member of the Clapham sect and wished his son to obtain a clerical degree. Despite his father's preference, and after a somewhat indifferent academic career, the younger Stephen became one of England's outstanding lawyers and codifiers of legal theory and theories of evidence. To supplement his income as a young lawyer, he began writing articles on social and political matters for the *Saturday Review, Cornhill Magazine*, and the *Pall Mall Gazette* and continued the practice throughout his life. His major works are *Liberty, Equality, Fraternity* (1873), *A Digest of the Laws of Evidence* (1876), and *A History of the Criminal Law of England* (1878). "On the Utility of Truth," an answer to Mivart's paper, was read to the Metaphysical Society on February 11, 1879. "On Certitude in Religious Assent," a response to Ward's "Certitude in Religious Assent," appeared in *Fraser's Magazine* in January, 1872.

John Stuart Mill (1806–1873) was Victorian England's most influential philosopher, writing on logic, epistemology, metaphysics, economics, political and moral philosophy, and religion. His *System of Logic* and *An Examination of Sir William Hamilton's Philosophy* were perhaps the century's most elaborate and sustained attacks on "intuitionism." His works are too numerous to list here; however, in addition to the above, his most influential books are his *Autobiography* (1873), *Utilitarianism* (1863), *On Liberty* (1859) and *Three Essays on Religion* (1874). The selection in this volume is from the conclusion of his essay, "Theism," included in *Three Essays on Religion*.

William James (1842–1910) received his medical degree from Harvard in 1869 and, from 1873, taught anatomy and physiology, psychology and philosophy there. His lecture, "Philosophical Conceptions and Practical Results" (1908), is generally considered to mark the beginning of pragmatism as an explicit movement. His major works include *The Varieties of Religious Experience* (1902), *Principles of Psychology* (1890), *The Will to Believe and Other Essays in Popular Philosophy* (1897), *Pragmatism: A New Name for Some Old Ways of Thinking* (1907), *The Meaning of Truth: A Sequel to "Pragmatism"* (1909) and *A Pluralistic Universe* (1909). "The Will to Believe" originally appeared in the book bearing that title.

John Henry Newman (1801–1890) matriculated in 1816 at Trinity College, Oxford and was elected a fellow of Oriel College, Oxford in 1823. Raised an Anglican but with Evangelical influences, he took Holy Orders in that Church in 1824. Throughout his life he was an ardent foe of "Liberalism" and was the intellectual leader of the Oxford Movement. For his authorship of *Tract 90* of *Tracts for the Times* he received an official censure. In 1845 he became a Roman Catholic and in 1847 was ordained a priest in that Church. Viewed with suspicion by conservative Roman Catholics, he lived much of his life in that communion "under a cloud." In 1879 he was vindicated and Pope Leo XIII created him a cardinal. His most influential works are *Sermons, Chiefly in the Theory of Religious Belief, Preached Before the University of Oxford* (1843), *An Essay on the Development of Christian Doctrine* (1845), *Apologia Pro Vita Sua* (1861) and *An Essay in Aid of a Grammar of*

Assent (1870). The selections in this volume are taken from C. F. Harrold's edition of the *Grammar of Assent* (New York, 1947), pp. 120–125, 130–137, 219–223, 240–260, and 268–273.

Leslie Stephen (1832–1904) was the brother of Sir James F. Stephen. He was elected a fellow of Trinity College, Cambridge in 1854 and subsequently ordained a priest in the Church of England. Troubled by religious doubts, he resigned his fellowship in 1862 and by 1865 he had lost all religious belief. Perhaps his outstanding achievement is his editing of the *Dictionary of National Biography*. He alone wrote 387 of the biographies. His important historical studies are *History of English Thought in the Eighteenth Century* (1876), *The English Utilitarians* (1900), and *English Thought and Society in the Eighteenth Century* (1904). His better known essays are collected in *An Agnostic's Apology and Other Essays* (1893) and *Essays in Freethinking and Plainspeaking* (1873). "Belief and Evidence" was read to the Metaphysical Society on June 12, 1877.

Richard H. Hutton (1826–1897) was educated at University College and at the universities of Heidelberg and Berlin. Born into a distinguished Unitarian family, he dissented from several Unitarian positions and, under the influence of F. D. Maurice and F. W. Robertson, came to accept the main principles and beliefs of the Anglican Church. From 1861 until shortly before his death he was the editor of the *Spectator*. This assured him a place of prominence in British intellectual life. His major essays are collected in *Essays Theological and Literary* (1871), and *Aspects of Religious and Scientific Thought*, ed. Elizabeth M. Roscoe (1899). "On the Relation of Evidence to Conviction," a reply to Leslie Stephen's "Belief and Evidence," was read to the Metaphysical Society on November 13, 1877.

William George Ward (1812–1882) was elected a fellow of Balliol College in 1834 but his support of *Tract 90* in 1841 cost him his fellowship. In 1844 he was censured by the Vice Chancellor of Oxford for certain ideas expressed in his *Ideal of the Christian Church in Comparison with Existing Practice*. A friend (but later sometimes adversary) of Newman, he became a Roman Catholic in 1845. In 1851 he was appointed lecturer in moral philosophy and professor of dogmatic theology at St. Edmund's College. He was the editor of the *Dublin Review* from 1863 until 1878. Perhaps the leading mid-century critic of empiricism and utilitarianism, in its pages he carried on extensive controversies with John Stuart Mill and Sir James F. Stephen. His major philosophical writings have been collected in *Essays in the Philosophy of Theism*, ed. Wilfrid Ward (1884). "The Philosophy of the Theistic Controversy" and "Certitude in Religious Assent" originally appeared in the *Dublin Review* (1882 and 1871, respectively) and "The Reasonable Basis of Certitude" in the *Nineteenth Century* (1878).

Henry Sidgwick (1838–1900) attended Rugby and Trinity College, Cambridge and was appointed a fellow at Trinity in 1859. Troubled by religious doubts, he resigned his fellowship in 1869 because he felt that he could no longer honestly subscribe to the Thirty-Nine Articles, as fellows were required to do. When religious tests were dropped he was reappointed to his fellowship. His interests and writings covered many fields but he is best known for *The Methods of Ethics* (1874) in which he attempted to solve the controversy between utilitarians and intuitionists. His other works include *Outlines of the History of Ethics* (1886), *Principles of Political Economy* (1883) and *Philosophy, Its Scope and Relations* (1902). "Incoherence of empirical Philosophy" was read to the Metaphysical Society on January 14, 1879. A slightly different version was published in *Mind* (1882). The former version of the paper is reprinted in this volume.

Van A. Harvey received his Ph.D. from Yale University and did post-doctoral work at Marburg and Oxford. He has taught at Princeton University, Southern Methodist University and the University of Pennsylvania. He is currently chair of the Department of Religious Studies at Stanford University. He is the author of scores of articles, *A Handbook of Theological Terms* (1964), and *The Historian and the Believer* (1966). He is currently working on a book dealing with projection theories of religion. "The Ethics of Belief Reconsidered" originally appeared in *The Journal of Religion* in 1979 and is reprinted here with the kind permission of the author and of the University of Chicago Press.

George I. Mavrodes received his Ph.D. from the University of Michigan where he is currently Professor of Philosophy. He has taught at Princeton University, Carleton College, Kenyon College and has been a fellow of the Calvin College Center for Christian Scholarship. He is the author of more than fifty articles and of *Belief in God: A Study in the Epistemology of Religion* (1970). His most recent article is "Jerusalem and Athens Revisited" in *Faith and Rationality*, ed. P. Plantinga and N. Wolterstorff (1983).

James F. Ross received his Ph.D. from Brown University and is currently Professor of Philosophy at the University of Pennsylvania. He has been a fellow at the Institute for Advanced Study, a Guggenheim Scholar and an Associate Member of Darwin College, Cambridge. He is the author of many articles and *Philosophical Theology* (1969), *An Introduction to the Philosophy of Religion* (1970) and *Portraying Analogy* (1982).

ACKNOWLEDGMENTS

My gratitude is owed to many people. Van Harvey, James Livingston and John Esposito were there when needed with advice and support. James Ross and George Mavrodes were kind enough to write their valuable essays and were thoughtful enough to meet some difficult deadlines. Mr. D. S. Porter of the Bodleian Library made microfilm copies of the papers of the Metaphysical Society available to me and James Mahoney, librarian of the College of the Holy Cross (Worcester, Massachusetts), supervised the printing of them. Finally, but certainly not least, Mary Cerasuolo, Bea Charette and Olive Berg typed the manuscript, made countless corrections (of my mistakes) and remained good-humored throughout the process.
Clark University
Worcester, Massachusetts
Fall, 1984

INTRODUCTION

From the time of St. Paul's polemic against the "wisdom of this world" in his first letter to the Corinthians until the present day, the relationship between the Christian faith and standards of rationality has been a subject of constant scrutiny and debate. This work presents an important moment in the history of that debate. As James Ross reminds us in his essay, many of the partners to the Victorian contribution to the history of that debate shared common, though often hidden, psychological and epistemological assumptions that were not taken for granted at other times and by other thinkers. Hence this was but a moment in the debate. And yet it was an important moment, important because of the quality of the controversialists, because of the centrality of the issues they raised and because their concerns are still very much our own.[1]

The purpose of an introduction to a book such as this is to introduce and not to pronounce. The attempt to resolve the issues raised here is best left to the reader. In what follows, therefore, I shall simply underscore several of the central issues that arise in the different papers and attempt to indicate the social and intellectual milieu out of which this discussion emerged.

I

The first, and perhaps most obvious, question is whether there ought to be or even can be an "Ethics of Belief." The most sustained arguments for such an "Ethics" in this volume come from William Clifford and Van Harvey. Both argue on social and cultural grounds that the ongoing success of our culture demands that we respect each other enough to tell each other only the truth. This commitment to truth, in turn, demands that we adopt a self-consciously critical attitude towards our beliefs and the procedures we employ in adopting them, criticizing them, supporting them and rejecting them. Only the adoption of such an attitude will enable us to discharge our truth-telling obligations.

In the other hand, St. George Jackson Mivart, Richard H. Hutton. John H. Newman, William George Ward and William James contend that such a rule is infeasible or, if feasible, is not justifiable on either social or rational

---

[1] See, for example, the influential discussions of Van A. Harvey, *The Historian and the Believer* (New York, 1966) and David Tracy, *The Analogical Imagination* (New York, 1981), pp. 3–98.

grounds. All five offer putative counter-examples to the "Ethics of Belief," questioning both its epistemic plausibility and its beneficence. They ask: can we really expect *everyone* to adopt such an attitude? Or, more radically, can we really expect *anyone* to adopt it? A negative answer to either of these questions would raise serious doubts about the very possibility of such an "Ethics."

The complexities that surface in these discussions open up another set of issues. Even if it is granted that there is a moral dimension to our acts of belief, the question arises as to when such moral principles might apply. Would they apply to all our believings, as Clifford seems to think? Or just to some subset of our believings? William James and John Stuart Mill argue that there are some cases in which we are either allowed (Mill) or even forced (James) to go beyond the requirements established by the proponents of an "Ethics of Belief." Newman, Ward and Henry Sidgwick take a further step and argue that, unless we are to be sceptics, there *must* be a class of beliefs to which these requirements do not apply. Van Harvey examines this latter claim in the context of contemporary analytic philosophy (especially Wittgenstein) and attempts to restate the argument for an "Ethics of Belief" in such a way as to meet this objection. What all these arguments point to is the need for an exploration of the role that the context of some believings plays in the responsible adoption and discarding of beliefs. Such an exploration might clarify the role that the will and/or the emotions play in belief. James Ross (drawing on Augustine and Aquinas) and George I. Mavrodes (drawing on James) contend that these features are overlooked by Clifford, *et al*.

These considerations direct our attention to a third issue. Mavrodes and Ward both note that, in the standard presentation of the rules for moral believing, there are really two principles enunciated. One, traceable to Locke and Hume, requires that we *proportion* the confidence that we invest in our beliefs to the evidence that we have for them. (Mavrodes calls this a "proportionality rule" and Ward "equationism.") The second, traceable to Clifford, demands that we assent to only those propositions for which we have sufficient evidence. (Mavrodes calls this a "threshold rule.") In reading these essays, the attentive reader will want to determine whether the criticisms raised against the "Ethics of Belief" (for example, by Newman, James, or Ross) are applicable to both these principles or just one, leaving the other untouched.

The issue of certitude also occupies a prominent place in the conversation. Implicit in the essays by William Clifford and James F. and Leslie Stephen is a conviction that all human beliefs are fallible and that they should therefore be held with a greater or lesser degree of tentativeness depending on the evidence upon which they rest. In the next section of this introduction I will examine the reasons why they thought this was so. However, both Ward and Newman contest this vigorously. They argue that such a position would be destructive of religious belief (this much might have been willingly conceded by some of their opponents) and that, as a matter of fact, the ordinary certitudes of common life, certitudes that do not conform to the cognitive-ethical norms of the "Ethics of Belief" and yet are held by all reasonable men, reveal the inadequacy of both the "Ethics of Belief" and its commitment to fallibilism.

Finally, no statement of the rules or principles of an "Ethics of Belief" has much impact until it is joined to some definite epistemological and psychological theory so that the epistemic notions crucial to it (e.g., belief, evidence, assurance, sufficient warrant, etc.) are unpacked and analyzed. The standard empiricist account, first formulated in the seventeenth century and later elaborated by Mill in his *Logic* might best be represented by a scale. The task of the responsible believer is to accumulate all the relevant evidence *pro* and *con* a specific belief and then adopt it or reject it (or vary the conviction with which it is held or rejected) depending on which way and how far the scale tilts. The disinterestedness of such an approach would have seemed "comic" to Kierkegaard and is strenuously rejected by several of our authors. For example, the above formulation leaves entirely unanswered the question of what sorts of evidence are to be placed on the scales. It was precisely on this point that the "empiricists" (Clifford, Mill and the Stephens) and the "intuitionists" (especially Ward) disagreed and this disagreement provides much of the energy in the papers that follow.[2] The "empiricists" argued that allowing "intuitions" to influence the balance of the scale led only to intellectual sloth, obscurantism and false beliefs.[3] The "intuitionists" retorted that the confining of evidence to sense-data and experience reducible in some way to sense data led only to scepticism, thus ruling out the very knowledge that the "Ethics of Belief" purported to protect.

There are two other lines of attack against the "empiricist" position that develop. As we have seen above, James, Ross and Mill argue that, in certain cases (perhaps many), the scale model is psychologically unsound and epistemologically bogus. They argue that we neither can nor should be as disinterested in certain sorts of beliefs as this model suggests and that the will and the emotions are legitimate factors to take into consideration when we decide to believe or disbelieve. Newman's approach is that the whole model is naive and fails to do justice to the subtle workings of the human mind in its pursuit of truth. The process is so complex, says Newman, that any attempt to construct a scale of this sort is bound to falsify our cognitive procedures.

[2] The importance of this diagreement is noted by Archbishop Manning in his paper, "A Diagnosis and a Prescription," read to the Metaphysical Society on June 10, 1873. The course of the argument is competently surveyed by James Livingston in *The Ethics of Belief: An Essay on the Victorian Religious Conscience* (Tallahassee, 1974), pp. 17–35.

[3] How intensely this was felt can be seen in Mill's *Autobiography*, reprinted in *The Essential Works of John Stuart Mill*, ed. M. Lerner (New York, 1961), pp. 133–134 and 159–161.

Such are, I believe, the central issues that confronted the participants in this debate. They are not the only issues, of course, but I think that the others all cluster around these. At any rate, I hope that I have provided something of a guide to the conversation that follows.

II

At no time in the history of ideas does a debate such as this one emerge without parentage. The antecedents of this debate are particularly complex inasmuch as they reach across three centuries of religious, social, intellectual and political change. In spite of this complexity and at the risk of a degree of oversimplification, I believe that a cursory glance at the historical and intellectual background of the issues under consideration will enable us to appreciate more fully just what was involved in these discussions.

In the previous section our first question concerned why there should be an "Ethics of Belief" at all. Three factors contributed to the development of the position enunciated most elaborately by John Locke.[4]

The first was the humanistic and social goals of the research program developed by Francis Bacon in *The Great Instauration*, the *Novum Organon*, and *The Advancement of Learning*. In these works Bacon argued at length that material, human and social progress had been retarded for centuries by false philosophies that pandered to human credulity, superstition and what he called the "Idols of the Mind," and he expressed his hope that his experimental logic would liberate the human intellect so that mankind could assume its rightful heritage of domination over nature.[5] Indeed, in his view, a methodologically proper cultivation of the Arts and Sciences would lead to results of almost eschatological proportions, i.e., the domination of nature by man would annul the losses incurred at the time of the Biblical Fall.[6]

But the achievement of this happy of affairs requires a radical disciplining of the intellect, for the mind, if left to its own desires and the daily habits of life, will be possessed by the "vainest phantoms".[7] The pervasiveness of the "Idols" of the Tribe, Cave, Marketplace and Theatre[8] and

[4] The classical statement, cited in several of the essays in this volume, is contained in *An Essay Concerning Human Understanding*, ed. A. C. Fraser (New York, 1959), II, 429–430. "How a man may know whether he be so [a lover of truth] in earnest, is worth inquiry: and I think there is one unerring mark of it, viz. The not entertaining any proposition with greater assurance than the proofs it is built upon will warrant." Other statements of this position can be found in *The Conduct of the Understanding*, in *The Works of John Locke* (London, 1823), III, 228–231, 265–258 and 278.

[5] See, for example, *The Novum Organon*, trans. G. W. Kitchin (Oxford, 1855), pp. 5–10 and 57.

[6] *Ibid.*, p. 306.

[7] *Ibid.*, p. 5

[8] *Ibid.*, pp. 19–36. See also *The Great Instauration*, ed. J. Weinberger (Arlington Heights, 1980), pp. 25–26 and *The Advancement of Learning*, ed. W. Wright (Oxford, 1885), pp. 161–184

the all-too-human tendencies towards laziness, credulity and superstition give plausibility to the sceptic's argument that knowledge is impossible. Nevertheless, the sceptic is mistaken. However, he has a valuable lesson to teach; in fact, if Bacon had to choose between the sceptic and the dogmatist, he would choose the sceptic since the dogmatist suppresses the doubts that are essential to genuine inquiry.[9]

Bacon, however, did not have to choose between scepticism and dogmatism since he claimed to have found the genuine alternative in his experimental logic. The solution to the sceptical enfeeblement of the intellect is not dogmatism but the cultivation and resolution of doubt through the patient application of inductive procedures of inquiry and verification. "It [induction] takes away all levity , temerity and insolvency by copious suggestions of doubts and difficulties and acquainting the mind to balance reasons on both sides, and to turn back the first offers and conceits of the mind and accept nothing but the examined and tried"[10]. It is only by this sort of disciplined cognitive procedure that mankind can progress towards genuine knowledge "for the uses of life."

The cognitive-ethical thrust of Bacon's position is clear. Genuine knowledge and the prospects that it holds are possible only if his procedures for disciplined inquiry are accepted. To fail to do so and for men to indulge their credulities and intellectual foibles would rob mankind of its rightful heritage. Intellectual error begets moral evil. Such arguments for the connection between meliorism and scientific procedure recur frequently in the centuries that follow[11] and, in this volume, find their most explicit statement in Clifford's essay.

The second factor behind the formulation of the "Ethics of Belief" is closely related to the first and is rooted in the problems posed by the scepticism that surfaced in the sixteenth and seventeenth centuries. .The Renaissance retrieval of Greek scepticism and the Reformation's challenge to the authority of the Roman Church raised the problem of truth and certainty in a profound way. The sceptical arguments of Carneades and Pyrrho concerning the fallibility of our senses, memories and reasoning faculties seemed to render all claims to knowledge suspect. The proliferation of churches after the Reformation, each claiming that only its doctrines were true and could be known to be so with certainty, caused thoughtful persons

[9] *Novum Organon*, p. 41; *The Great Instauration*, p. 31: *The Advancement of Learning*, p. 126.

[10] *The Advancement of Learning*, p. 67.

[11] The literature on this subject is enormous. Two useful surveys are J. B. Bury, *The Idea of Progress* (London, 1924) and Carl Becker, *The Heavenly City of the Eighteenth-Century Philosophers* (New Haven, 1932). Basil Wiley in *The Seventeenth-Century Background* (New York, 1934), pp. 31–40 and 187–188, discusses the topic in the seventeenth century and Walter Houghton treats the Victorian ideas in *The Victorian Frame of Mind* (New York and London, 1957), pp. 33–36. For a further discussion of the Victorian beliefs, see John Bowle and Basil Willey, "Origins and Development of the Idea of Progress," in *Ideas and Beliefs of the Victorians* (New York, 1966), pp. 33–45.

to question whether religious truth could ever be found with any assurance. Roman Catholics appealed to the authority and tradition of their Church, Lutherans appealed to Scripture and Calvinists appealed to the inner testimony of the Holy Spirit as the source of their certainties and each argued that the others' positions led to religious scepticism. The negative arguments that each raised against the others seemed sufficient to cast doubt on all the positions with the result that theological scepticism seemed the most viable alternative. Given the arguments, the proper choice between dogmatic certainty and scepticism seemed clear[12].

However, perhaps these alternatives do not exhaust the possibilities. In England, William Chillingsworth searched for an alternative to the theological impasse in his *The Religion of Protestants—A Safe Way to Salvation*[13]. In this work he rejected the alternative between scepticism and dogmatism and claimed that the sort of certainty demanded by the dogmatists was unachievable and gave unwarranted plausibility to the sceptic's arguments. This however, did not mean that the sceptics were correct. There are, he argued, different sorts of certainty, each appropriate to different subject matters and to search for the certainty appropriate to (e.g.) mathematics in religious inquiry would be unnecessary and futile. There is an intermediate grade of certainty, appropriate to religion and common life, *moral certainty*. While this is not absolute and infallible, it is sufficient *for practical purposes* to exclude the possibility of error. It is the certainty that a reasonable person who has dispassionately examined all the evidence available can come to, and is sufficient that he can act on it without fear or hesitation.

Coupled with this is a theory of degrees of evidence and belief. Below the level of moral certainty, there is a variety of grades of evidence and a corresponding variety of grades of belief. The thoughtful inquirer is the one who is careful to proportion the degree of his belief to the degree of the evidence available. Thus the authority that breaks the sceptical impasse is neither authoritative tradition, nor Scripture nor the inner testimony of the Holy Spirit. It is reason, but reason shaped by common sense and chastened by scepticism[14].

This theological position was rapidly secularized and provided the developing natural sciences with a model for inquiry and a criterion of knowledge. The members of the newly established Royal Society consciously

[12] This literature is competently discussed by Richard Popkin in *The History of Scepticism from Erasmus to Descartes* (New York, 1964), pp. 1–43.

[13] A brief discussion of Chillingsworth and of the tradition he established is found in Popkin, pp. 150–151. Much more elaborate treatments are given by Henry Lee Leeuwen, *The Problem of Certainty in English Thought* (The Hague, 1963) and Barbara Shapiro, *Probability and Certainty in Seventeenth-Century England* (Princeton, 1983).

[14] Mark Pattison in "Tendencies of Religious Thought in England, 1688–1750," in *Essays and Reviews* (London, 1860), pp. 328–329 gives an elegant description of the dialectical development of this position.

adopted the cognitive procedures established by Chillingsworth and Bacon[15]. In fact, a new intellectual style had been established, one which would dominate the arts and sciences during the latter part of the seventeenth and the eighteenth centuries.

> . . . the model scientist was the admittedly imperfect and fallible "reasonable man" who collected and examined data and the propositions and hypotheses derived from them as calmly and impartially as humanly possible. He employed his rational faculties to weigh, judge, and evaluate observed sense data, experiments, and testimony dealing with natural phenomena. He engaged in a certain amount of speculation and hypothesis construction, but was careful not to attribute certainty to his intellectual construction. He was prepared calmly and judiciously to evaluate the contributions of others in terms of probability and degrees of certainty. He avoided both skepticism and dogmatism, and was, above all, open-minded. He expected diversity of opinion and the gradual improvement of natural knowledge. The "new philosopher" and natural scientist represent a new intellectual type that can be contrasted profitably with the ancient philosopher, as well as with his early seventeenth-century and Continental counterpart.[16]

This emphasis on fallibility and tentativeness brings us to the last of the factors that shaped the rationale behind the "Ethics of Belief," perhaps the most pressing of all, the need for civil peace and religious toleration.

England, like the rest of Europe, had been savaged by the religious conflicts that followed the Reformation. The tensions between Anglicans and Roman Catholics under the Tudors and between Puritans and Anglicans during the Commonwealth and the Restoration had been consistently simmering and had finally erupted in the Civil War of 1642–1646 and the Revolution of 1688. These years saw a proliferation of religious sects and an intensity of religious feeling that threatened to destroy England. The horror that this inspired in many is evidenced in Joseph Glanvill's scathing description of the "enthusiasms" of that era as "those sickly conceits and enthusiastic dreams and unsound doctrines that have poisoned our air, and infatuated the minds of men, and exposed religion to the scorn of infidels, and divided the Church, and disturbed the peace of mankind, and involved the nation in so much blood and so many ruins" [17].

The alternative to all of this had to be something that could bind men together rather than divide them. That common factor was reason and the procedures of rational inquiry that had been developed. This commitment to reasonableness took two forms. First, there was a search for the true essen-

---

[15] These developments are discussed in Shapiro, pp. 15–73 and Van Leeuwen, pp. 49–120.

[16] Shapiro, p. 66.

[17] Joseph Glanville, *A Seasonable Recommendation and Defense of Reason in the Affairs of Religion, against Infidelity, Skepticism, and Fanaticisms of All Sorts* (London, 1670), p. 1.

tials of religion, essentials that reasonable men of good faith could agree on. Second, there was a commitment to toleration. Since rational men were above all aware that their powers of reason were limited and that they were unable to achieve an infallible grasp of the truth, it was obvious to them that they had an obligation to hold their religious opinions reasonably and not attempt to force them on anyone else. This idea of religious toleration, developed by the Socinians, Arminians and the Latitudinarian Divines of the sixteenth and early seventeenth centuries, found its most articulate expression in Milton's *Areopagitica* and *Treatise of Civil Powers in Ecclesiastical Causes* and Locke's *Letters Concerning Toleration*. The last work provided the theoretical justification for the Toleration Act of 1689 and subsequent attempts to ameliorate the condition of Dissenters, Roman Catholics, Jews, and even, contrary to Locke's explicit intentions, atheists.

Essentially, Locke's argument is rooted in the fallibilism that we saw operating in the theories of Bacon and Chillingsworth. Since religious truth is so complex that no one can be sure that he possesses it *in toto*, only God can judge what is true or false in these matters. The attitude of human beings, therefore, ought to be one of charity, rather than one of zeal to extirpate error. Furthermore, since final truth is not something in our possession but is something to be achieved, we ought to allow the free play of non-dangerous opinions so that the full truth will eventually emerge[18].

Thus, Locke's attack on "Enthusiasm" in the course of which he formulated the description of the "lover of truth" that was to be so influential in the subsequent discussion of the "Ethics of Belief." was not motivated exclusively by epistemological concerns. Seen against the background of *The Reasonableness of Christianity* and the *Letters Concerning Toleration*, the attack reveals its ethical motivation. In Locke's view, the recognition of the limitations of the human intellect and the adoption of the cognitive norms laid down in *An Essay Concerning Human Understanding* were essential for restoring peace and civil harmony to England.

In the seventeenth and eighteenth centuries, therefore, a variety of thinkers sought for a form of religious belief that all reasonable men could assent to and that would be socially cohesive rather than divisive. This, plus the hope for material progress and prosperity, provided the ethical basis for the cognitive norms that they laid down. And, to a certain degree, they succeeded in establishing a viable epistemological and religious position. The compromise between scepticism and religion represented by the Deist and Latitudinarian movements reflected a harmony between reason and religion and between science and theology that was satisfactory to many. It

---

[18] See John Locke, *A Letter Concerning Toleration* (Indianapolis, 1950), pp. 15, 25, 31 and 50. The influence of Locke's arguments is evident from the fact that they are substantially repeated by John Stuart Mill some 170 years later. See *On Liberty*, in *The Essential Works of John Stuart Mill*, pp. 268–304.

seemed that both religious scepticism and dogmatic "enthusiasm" had been defeated by reason.

And yet, even a quick glance at this volume shows that this compromise was short-lived. In the century following, both Deism and the cognitive-ethical norms codified by Locke came under increasing attack on both religious and philosophical grounds. Furthermore, the developments in nineteenth-century scientific and historical research rendered the Deist position increasingly fragile and finally untenable.

The religious attack came from a variety of quarters—orthodox Anglican, Evangelical, Tractarian and Romantic. What all had in common was a conviction that the religion that derived from the rationalist movement had forfeited essential Christian doctrines and was too lifeless and too cold to satisfy genuine religious needs. Law, Butler, Wilberforce, Wesley, Newman, Keble, and Coleridge, each in his own way and with differing theological presuppositions, argued that the religion of reason was insufficient to satisfy the heart (and the head) and that it was incapable of stirring men to genuine Christian lives.

The chief theological complaint of Deism's critics was that its emphasis on reason and the religion of reason forced it to either neglect or disparage the truth of Revelation. Some, for example William Law, argued that the Deists had overestimated reason's capacities and that, in fact, reason was not competent to deal with divine matters.[19] Others, more hospitable to reason's claims, such as Joseph Butler, criticized the Deists for failing to see that the objections that they raised against Revealed Religion could be used with equal force against their rationalist version of the religion of Nature.[20]

Both arguments were partially successful in stemming the Deist tide. And yet it was a costly victory since the arguments they brought to bear against the Deists had equal force against their own convictions. Many of their sceptical arguments against the Deists were picked up by later agnostics sceptical of all religious claims. By pushing the Deist compromise out of the intellectual picture, they set the stark alternatives that were to shape the nineteenth-century debate: scepticism, fideism and the appeal to the intuitions or the heart.[21]

Perhaps more than any other figure, it was David Hume who mapped out the consequences of the Deist controversy. In his work, the scepticism

---

[19] See *The Case of Reason*, in *The Collected Works of William Law* (London, 1892), Vol. II.

[20] Joseph Butler, *The Analogy of Religion, Natural and Revealed, to the Constitution and Course of Nature*, ed. E. C. Mossner (New York, 1961), pp. 125–259. The history of the Deist controversy is admirably traced by Leslie Stephen, *History of English Thought in the Eighteenth Century* (New York and London, 1902), I, 74–343 and by E. C. Mossner, *Bishop Butler and the Age of Religion* (New York, 1936). *Deism and Natural Religion*, ed. E. G. Waring (New York, 1967), contains a good sampling of the writings of the Deists and their critics.

[21] See Stephen, I, 170–172; II, 383–435 and Mossner, pp. 151–155.

that rational religion and the "Ethics of Belief" were intended to mitigate resurfaced with a vengeance. *The Natural History of Religion* attacked the Deist *consensus gentium* argument that its minimal religious convictions represented the original (and true) religion of mankind. "On Miracles" developed Tillotson's attack on ecclesiastical miracles (advanced by Roman Catholics in defense of their ecclesiastical claims) and turned it into an attack against the evidential value of *all* miracles (including the Biblical miracles). Finally, his *Dialogues Concerning Natural Religion* exploded simultaneously the philosophical bases of both rational theism and fideism. The over-all conclusion of the *Dialogues* was that all religious disputes are essentially verbal and that the beliefs that the Deist and the fideist hold are religiously indistinguishable from those of the sceptic.[22] From Hume's time on, the battle between sceptic and believer was to be fought on more radical terrain.

No less influential was his drawing out of the sceptical implications of the marriage between the "Ethics of Belief" and Lockean empiricism. While on one level assenting to Locke's cognitive-ethical norms, he argued that their rigorous application invalidated not only superstition and "enthusiasm" but also many treasured common-sense beliefs as well, e.g., the belief in the reality of the external world,[23] the enduring nature of the personal self[24] and the uniformity of nature.[25] The melancholy conclusion of Book I of his *Treatise of Human Nature* stands in stark contrast to the optimism generated by Bacon's research program and Locke's "plain, historical method."

> The intense view of these manifold contradictions and imperfections in human reason has so wrought upon me, and heated my brain, that I am ready to reject all belief and reasoning, and can look upon no opinion even as more probable and likely than another. Where am I, or what? From what causes do I derive my existence, and to what condition shall I return? Whose favour shall I count, and whose anger must I dread? What beings surround me? and on whom have I any influence, or who have any influence on me? I am confounded with all these questions, and begin to fancy myself in the most deplorable condition imaginable, inviron'd with the deepest darkness, and utterly deprived of the use of every member and faculty.[26]

Interestingly, Hume's arguments influenced both sides of the "Ethics of Belief" debate. His trenchant criticisms of the rational basis of theistic belief,

---

[22] David Hume, *Dialogues Concerning Natural Religion*, ed. Nelson Pike (Indianapolis and New York, 1970), pp. 40–41 and 110–114.

[23] *A Treatise of Human Nature*, ed. E. C. Mossner (Baltimore, 1969), pp. 239–243 and 261–264.

[24] *Ibid.*, pp. 299–311.

[25] *Ibid.*, pp. 137–138; *An Enquiry Concerning Human Understanding*, reprinted in *The Empiricists* (Garden City, New York, 1961), pp. 329–330.

[26] *Treatise*, p. 316.

the trustworthiness of miracle stories and the moral and social utility of religious belief shaped the agnostic criticisms of Mill, Clifford and the Stephens. I think that it is safe to say that, because of Hume, the minimalist beliefs of the Deists were no longer a serious intellectual option for many mid-Victorian thinkers.[27] The argument had taken on a more radical character than it had in the eighteenth century. On the other hand, his tracing of the sceptical implications of traditional empiricism and his appeal to Nature, the instincts, the imagination and "common sense" to mitigate his scepticism supplied Newman, Sidgwick and Ward with the philosophical ammunition to attack the empiricists and to construct their own epistemological positions.[28]

In an ironic mood Hume once remarked that when sceptical doubts pressed too heavily upon him, he would retire to the companionship of his friends and a game of backgammon.[29] Such a retreat was generally unavailable to the Victorians. Walter Houghton, in his deft portrait of *The Victorian Frame of Mind*, has vividly described the pain and anxiety that Victorians felt because of their loss of confidence and religious belief.[30] When Clifford wrote that his was the generation that had seen "the spring sun shine out of an empty heaven, to light up a soulless earth"; and had felt "with utter loneliness that the Great Companion is dead,"[31] he was speaking not only for himself but for Froude, Eliot, Tennyson, Arnold and many others of his generation.

Hume's easy-going response to scepticism was unavailable to the Victorians for several reasons. First, The Victorian era was a time of rapid social, intellectual and political change. Economic change, technological innovation, and political experimentation all contributed to a renewal of Benthamism that raised radical questions about old values and institutions. Foremost among those institutions whose role and value was questioned was

[27] This is not to deny that there was a liberal religious option in the Victorian era. The Broad Church party, represented (among others) by Thomas Arnold, Julius Hare, the contributors to *Essays and Reviews*, James Martineau and F. D. Maurice, in many ways was that option. However, this school of thought had its philosophical roots in Coleridge's criticism of common-sense "reason" as a means of apprehending religious truth and so was sharply separated from the liberals of the eighteenth century. Mark Pattison gives a good illustration of how members of the Broad Church party criticized the rationalists.

[28] There is no doubt that Ward's arguments benefitted from Hume's analysis of the sceptical implications of traditional empiricism. Where Hume and Ward differ is that the latter assigns far more cognitive value to "intuition" than Hume does to "instinct." J. M. Cameron's "Newman and Hume," in *The Night Battle* (London, 1962) argues that the epistemological strategies of Newman and Hume are strikingly similar. The same point is made with respect to the arguments of Hume and Butler by A. Jeffner, *Butler and Hume on Religion* (Stockholm, 1966).

[29] *Treatise*, p. 316.

[30] Pp. 54–109, 218–262 and 394–430. For a similar analysis of this mood, see Gertrude Himmelfarb, *Victorian Minds* (New York, 1968), pp. 274–313.

[31] W. K. Clifford, *Lectures and Essays*, ed. Leslie Stephen and Frederick Pollock (London, 1879), II, 247, cited in Houghton, p. 85.

the Church.[32] In such a time of crisis, when the social fabric and, for many, the meaningfulness of life was called into question, the sceptic's doubts were not so easily dissipated. This volume displays some of the different strategies that were employed to deal with those doubts and none of them were as lighthearted as Hume's.

Second, between Hume's time and that of the Victorians, an Evangelical revival had swept over England—both inside and outside the Established Church. This revival, with its emphasis on introspection, honest self-appraisal and moral seriousness, spread its influence far beyond its original ecclesiastical scope and shaped the moral temper of the Victorian age as a whole.[33] Believers and nonbelievers alike inherited its fervor and, regardless of their theological disagreements, pursued the debate with a common intensity. For either side to have reacted as Hume did would have been, in their eyes, an immoral evasion of an all-important issue.[34]

Finally, the intellectual climate of the Victorian era gave to the "Ethics of Belief" debate an ominous tone that it had not previously had. In the seventeenth and eighteenth centuries, the cognitive-ethical norms of the rationalists and the efforts of most scientists had been directed towards combatting religious "enthusiasts," refuting sceptics (particularly Hobbes) and constructing and defending a rational core of religious beliefs. But in the nineteenth century, the rules of the game were changed and the stakes raised. It was no longer this or that theological doctrine that came under the rationalists' critical gaze but the very fundamentals of the classical religious world-view, fundamentals that had been accepted as proven by the seventeenth- and eighteenth-century rationalists.

Noel Annan has usefully separated what he calls "three strands" of Victorian unbelief: the political, the moral and the scientific-historical.[35] The

---

[32] Much of the first volume of Owen Chadwick's *The Victorian Church* (New York, 1966) is devoted to a discussion of these questions and the Whig-Tory debate on the proper role of the Church in society. See especially chapters I, II, IV and VII.

[33] Useful discussions of the Evangelicals can be found in Chadwick, pp. 370–421 and 440–455; B. M. G. Reardon, *Religious Thought in the Victorian Age* (London and New York, 1971), pp. 23–30; Charles Smyth, "The Evangelical Discipline," in *Ideas and Beliefs of the Victorians*, pp. 97–104; Gordon Rupp, "Evangelicalism of the Nonconformists," *ibid.*, pp. 105–112 and G. Best, "Evangelicalism and the Victorians," in *The Victorian Crisis of Faith*, ed. A. Symondson (London, 1970), pp. 37–56. The Evangelical influence on the larger culture is traced by Himmelfarb, pp. 278–289 and Houghton, pp. 222–262.

[34] The words of Noel Annan are appropriate in this context. "But let us never forget the moral and intellectual work of the Victorian rationalists. We should remember that they were opposing the bigotry and uncritical prejudice of their times. To all criticisms they would have replied that we must always form our beliefs on the best evidence available and that merely to believe what we want to believe and to appeal to the 'heart' or to 'intuition' is to give in to a temptation and acquire a frame of mind which may be very dangerous when applied to politics. Victorian rationalism was a faith, like any other kind of belief—a faith built on what were regarded as probabilities. The Agnostics in a sense, were a new non-conformist sect." "Three Strands of Unbelief," in *Ideas and Beliefs of the Victorians*, p. 155.

[35] *Ibid.*, pp. 150–56.

criticisms and questions raised in each of these strands can be found in earlier writers (particularly Hume), but the social and intellectual changes of the nineteenth century gave them a force that they had not previously had in England.

The oldest strand, the political, has its roots in the antireligious polemics of Tom Paine and surfaces in the resurgent Benthamism of the *Westminster Review* and the Chartist movement. Influential primarily among the working classes and its pamphleteers, this strand criticised the socially dysfunctional character of religious otherworldliness and the financial and social privileges of the Established Church. Both, it was argued, were inherently socially conservative and a hindrance to the achievement of a just society.[36] Thus, the social and moral utility of religion could no longer be assumed.

The second strand, related to the first in its moral concerns, is ironically related to the moralism of the Evangelical revival. To several eminent Victorians (e.g., Francis Newman, George Eliot and J. A. Froude) certain key traditional Christian doctrines such as predestination, original sin, the vicarious atonement and the eternal punishment of hell were sub-ethical. When they looked at these doctrines with their refined moral senses, they were repelled by what they considered to be their moral crudity.[37] Furthermore, the demand for a *sacrificium intellectus* in the Reformation doctrine of *sola fide* required, in their eyes, an immoral abandonment of the truth. There were some Victorians who felt that, even if Christianity were not true, at least it was morally elegant and a force for social stability. However, there were many others who denied even this, thus calling into question Christianity's claim to be a vehicle of moral (even if not scientific and historical) truth.[38]

The final strand, most attended to by Victorian scholars, is the unbelief that had its source in scientific and historical criticisms of Christian beliefs. In the early nineteenth century, geological investigations had begun to cast critical doubts on the literal truth of the natural history contained in the book of Genesis. Later researches in biology (the theory of evolution) and physics (the theory of the conservation of energy) deepened these doubts. These scientific developments, coupled with a philosophical commitment to the universal applicability of natural laws and a scepticism towards supernatural

[36] This sort of criticism is treated more fully by Owen Chadwick, "The Established Church Under Attack," in Symondson, pp. 91–106 and Edward Royle, *Victorian Infidels* (Manchester, 1974).

[37] See Howard Murphy, "The Ethical Revolt Against Christian Orthodoxy in Early Victorian England," *The American Historical Review*, LX, 3 (April, 1955), 800–817.

[38] This argument was particularly dangerous to liberal interpretations of Christianity that asserted that, although its doctrines need not be taken as literally true, their worth lay in their moral impact. How important this issue was to the Victorians can be ascertained from John Stuart Mill's attack on Mansel's theory that moral (as well as other) predicates apply only equivocally to God. See *An Examination of Sir William Hamilton's Philosophy*, in *The Collected Works of John Stuart Mill* (Toronto, 1979), IX, 98–108.

events, called into serious question not only the literal truth of the Bible and its status as a divinely inspired document but also the classical doctrine of God's Particular Providence and His intervention in human affairs. How sensitive Victorian believers were to this issue is evidenced by the almost frantic reaction, legal and theological, to theological reformers such as Bishop Colenso and the contributors to *Essays and Reviews* who granted the validity of the contemporary scientific world-view and attempted to state Christian doctrines in a way that did not conflict with it.[39]

Perhaps the most devastating shock came from the publication of Charles Darwin's *Origin of Species* and *The Descent of Man*[40] Not only did Darwin's work tell against the Biblical account of the creation of man and extend radically the realm of natural causation, but, by apparently reckoning man among the animals, it threatened his unique status within the natural world. Furthermore, his seemingly non-teleological vision of nature, a nature "red in tooth and claw," appeared to make a mockery of Divine Providence and Benevolence. If the existence of occasional evil had forced Hume to question the moral character of the Deity,[41] Darwin's world-view threatened the moral structure of the whole universe. It is a long road from Paley's benevolent watchmaker to whatever might superintend the ceaseless struggle for survival.

All these factors, taken together, pushed the debate over religion and its place in social and intellectual life to fundamental questions and this, in turn, made the discussion about the "Ethics of Belief" more intense than it had been in the past. Most of the participants in the discussion felt that, if religion were measured by Locke's and Clifford's standards and their theories of knowledge, it would lose the battle with scientific materialism and agnosticism. The stakes in the discussion were acknowledged by all to be high.

Much of this discussion took place at the meetings of the Metaphysical Society and many of the papers that are printed in this volume were originally read to that Society. With the exception of Mill, James, and Newman, all the Victorian essayists were members and participated actively in its meetings. So, before passing to the papers themselves, a brief word about the Society is in order[42].

[39] For a treatment of the controversy surrounding Biblical scholarship in general and *Essays and Reviews* in particular, see Chadwick, II, 40–111; Reardon, pp. 321–359 and Basil Willey, *More Nineteenth-Century Studies* (New York, 1956), pp. 137–185.

[40] The literature on this topic is voluminous. Brief discussions can be found in Chadwick, II, 1–35; Reardon, pp. 285–298 and Robert M. Young, "The Impact of Darwin on Conventional Thought," in Symondson, pp. 13–36. Fuller treatments are given by Loren Eisley, *Darwin's Century* (New York, 1958); C. C. Gillespie, *Genesis and Geology* (New York, 1959) and Gertrude Himmelfarb, *Darwin and the Darwinian Revolution* (London, 1959).

[41] *Dialogues Concerning Natural Religion*, pp. 86–96.

[42] The fullest description of the history and character of the Metaphysical Society is given by Alan Brown, *The Metaphysical Society* (New York, 1947). R. H. Hutton's "The Metaphysical Society: A Reminiscence," *Nineteenth Century*, VIII (August, 1885), 177–196 gives a charming account of a typical meeting.

In November of 1868, James Knowles, later the influential editor of the *Nineteenth Century*, was entertaining his old headmaster, Charles Pritchard, and the Poet Laureate, Alfred Tennyson. The subject of the conversation turned to theology and, in the course of it, Knowles suggested that a society be formed to continue the discussion and to attempt to unite warring theological factions to counteract scientific materialism. Knowles contracted various religious leaders to form such a society but Dean Stanley and James Martineau argued that such a society should include scientists and materialists as well as religious believers. Knowles agreed and thus its character was changed from a theological society to a philosophical one.

From April 21, 1869 until November 16, 1880, the Metaphysical Society met almost monthly. At its meetings controversial papers were read and discussed in an atmosphere of absolute candour and liberty of expression. The papers ranged over a variety of topics from euthanasia to the evidence for the Resurrection of Christ. And yet there is a common thread that has been well described by Alan Brown: "The history of the Society is a long unfolding of one argument, constantly elaborated, modified and re-directed, an argument which can perhaps be stated as: 'What must a man believe? What can a man believe?'"[43]

Even a quick glance at the membership list of the Society shows the varied and distinguished character of its members. What follows is only a partial listing. There were statesmen (Gladstone), ecclesiastical figures (Archbishop Manning and the Archbishop of York), politicians (Lord Arthur Russell), theologians (F. D. Maurice, James Martineau and W. G. Ward), philosophers (Henry Sidgwick and A. C. Fraser), historians (Froude and Pattison), editors and critics (Hutton, Leslie Stephen, Morley and Ruskin), natural scientists (Huxley, Mivart, and Tyndall), mathematicians (Clifford and Sylvester), physicians (Acland and Clark) and lawyers (Fitzjames Stephen and Pollock). The influence of its members is perhaps best evidenced by the fact that ten of them were editors of Victorian England's most prestigious journals. Among these were the *Contemporary Review* (Alford and Knowles), the *Nineteenth Century* (Knowles), the *Spectator* (Hutton), *Fraser's* (Froude), *Macmillan's* (Grove), the *Dublin Review* (Ward), *Cornhill* (L. Stephen), the *Fortnightly* (Morley) and, later on, *Mind* (Robertson). After the Society disbanded, its debates were carried on in the pages of these journals and at the meetings of the still-influential Aristotelian Society.

In the selection and ordering of the papers in this book, I have attempted to recreate the discussions of the Metaphysical Society. Limitations of space (and questions of relevance) permitted the printing of only a small fraction of the ninety-four papers that were presented to it. Since the discussion was also carried on in journals and books, I have gone beyond the Society's papers to include some relevant articles and chapters. To preserve the nineteenth-century flavor of the essays, they appear in this volume as

[43] Brown, p. 33.

they were originally printed. I have left unaltered idiosyncracies of style, grammatical usage, and methods of documentation. Many of these essays were written in direct response to other essays (see the biographical remarks on the authors on pages ix–xii) and I have attempted to preserve the continuity of the conversation. This, I hope, will enable the reader to get a sense of the direction and energy of the debate. The retrospective essays of Harvey, Mavrodes, and Ross, in turn, testify to the discussion's continuing importance as well as carry it forward.

THE VICTORIAN DEBATE

THE ETHICS OF BELIEF
William K. Clifford

I.—THE DUTY OF INQUIRY

A shipowner was about to send to sea an emigrant-ship. He knew that she was old, and not over-well built at the first; that she had seen many seas and climes, and often had needed repairs. Doubts had been suggested to him that possibly she was not seaworthy. These doubts preyed upon his mind, and made him unhappy; he thought that perhaps he ought to have her thoroughly overhauled and refitted, even though this should put him to great expense. Before the ship sailed, however, he succeeded in overcoming these melancholy reflections. He said to himself that she had gone safely through so many voyages and weathered so many storms, that it was idle to suppose she would not come safely home from this trip also. He would put his trust in Providence, which could harldy fail to protect all these unhappy families that were leaving their fatherland to seek for better times elsewhere. He would dismiss from his mind all ungenerous suspicions about the honesty of builders and contractors. In such ways he acquired a sincere and comfortable conviction that his vessel was thoroughly safe and seaworthy; he watched her departure with a light heart, and benevolent wishes for the success of the exiles in their strange new home that was to be; and he got his insurance-money when she went down in mid-ocean and told no tales.

What shall we say of him? Surely this, that he was verily guilty of the death of those men. It is admitted that he did sincerely believe in the soundness of his ship; but the sincerity of his conviction can in nowise help him, because *he had no right to believe on such evidence as was before him*. He had acquired his belief not by honestly earning it in patient investigation, but by stifling his doubts. And although in the end he may have felt so sure about it that he could not think otherwise, yet inasmuch as he had knowingly and willingly worked himself into that frame of mind, he must be held responsible for it.

Let us alter the case a little, and suppose that the ship was not unsound after all; that she made her voyage safely, and many others after it. Will that diminish the guilt of her owner? Not one jot. When an action is once done, it is right or wrong for ever; no accidental failure of its good or evil fruits can possibly alter that. The man would not have been innocent, he would only have been not found out. The question of right or wrong has to do with the origin of his belief, not the matter of it; not what it was, but how he got it; not whether it turned out to be true or false, but whether he had a right to believe on such evidence as was before him.

There was once an island in which some of the inhabitants professed a religion teaching neither the doctrine of original sin nor that of eternal punishment. A suspicion got abroad that the professors of this religion had made use of unfair means to get their doctrines taught to children. They were accused of wresting the laws of their country in such a way as to remove children from the care of their natural and legal guardians; and even of stealing them away and keeping them concealed from their friends and relations. A certain number of men formed themselves into a society for the purpose of agitating the public about this matter. They published grave accusations against individual citizens of the highest position and character, and did all in their power to injure these citizens in the exercise of their professions. So great was the noise they made, that a Commission was appointed to investigate the facts; but after the Commission had carefully inquired into all the evidence that could be got, it appeared that the accused were innocent. Not only had they been accused on insufficient evidence, but the evidence of their innocence was such as the agitators might easily have obtained, if they had attempted a fair inquiry. After these disclosures the inhabitants of that country looked upon the members of the agitating society, not only as persons whose judgment was to be distrusted, but also as no longer to be counted honourable men. For although they had sincerely and "conscientiously" believed in the charges they made, yet *they had no right to believe on such evidence as was before them*. Their sincere convictions, instead of being honestly earned by patient inquiring, were stolen by listening to the voice of prejudice and passion.

Let us vary this case also, and suppose, other things remaining as before, that a still more accurate investigation proved the accused to have been really guilty. Would this make any difference in the guilt of the accusers? Clearly not; the question is not whether their belief was true or false, but whether they entertained it on wrong grounds. They would no doubt say, "Now you see that we were right after all; next time perhaps you will believe us." And they might be believed, but they would not thereby become honourable men. They would not be innocent, they would only be not found out. Every one of them, if he chose to examine himself *in foro conscientiæ*, would know that he had acquired and nourished a belief, when he had no right to believe on such evidence as was before him; and therein he would know that he had done a wrong thing.

It may be said, however, that in both of these supposed cases it is not the belief which is judged to be wrong, but the action following upon it. The shipowner might say, "I am perfectly certain that my ship is sound, but still I feel it my duty to have her examined, before trusting the lives of so many people to her." And it might be said to the agitator, "However convinced you were of the justice of your cause and the truth of your convictions, you ought not to have made a public attack upon any man's character until you had examined the evidence on both sides with the utmost patience and care."

In the first place, let us admit that, so far as it goes, this view of the case is right and necessary; right, because even when a man's belief is so fixed that he cannot think otherwise, he still has a choice in regard to the action suggested by it, and so cannot escape the duty of investigating on the ground of the strength of his convictions; and necessary, because those who are not yet capable of controlling their feelings and thoughts must have a plain rule dealing with overt acts.

But this being premised as necessary, it becomes clear that it is not sufficient, and that our previous judgment is required to supplement it. For it is not possible so to sever the belief from the action it suggests as to condemn the one without condemning the other. No man holding a strong belief on one side of a question, or even wishing to hold a belief on one side, can investigate it with such fairness and completeness as if he were really in doubt and unbiassed; so that the existence of a belief, not founded on fair inquiry, unfits a man for the performance of this necessary duty.

Nor is that truly a belief at all which has not some influence upon the actions of him who holds it. He who truly believes that which prompts him to an action has looked upon the action to lust after it, he has committed it already in his heart. If a belief is not realized immediately in open deeds it is stored up for the guidance of the future. It goes to make a part of that aggregate of beliefs which is the link between sensation and action at every moment of all our lives, and which is so organized and compacted together that no part of it can be isolated from the rest, but every new addition modifies the structure of the whole. No real belief, however trifling and fragmentary it may seem, is ever truly insignificant; it prepares us to receive more of its like, confirms those which resembled it before, and weakens others; and so gradually it lays a stealthy train in our inmost thoughts, which may some day explode into overt action, and leave its stamp upon our character for ever.

And no one man's belief is in any case a private matter which concerns himself alone. Our lives are guided by that general conception of the course of things which has been created by society for social purposes. Our words, our phrases, our forms and processes and modes of thought, are common property, fashioned and perfected from age to age; an heirloom, which every succeeding generation inherits as a precious deposit and a sacred trust, to be handed on to the next one, not unchanged, but enlarged and purified, with some clear marks of its proper handiwork. Into this, for good or ill, is woven every belief of every man who has speech of his fellows. An awful privilege, and an awful responsibility, that we should help to create the world in which posterity will live.

In the two supposed cases which have been considered, it has been judged wrong to believe on insufficient evidence, or to nourish belief by suppressing doubts and avoiding investigation. The reason of this judgment is not far to seek; it is that in both these cases the belief held by one man was of great importance to other men. But forasmuch as no belief held by one man, however seemingly trivial the belief, and however obscure the believer, is ever actually insignificant or without its effect on the fate of mankind, we have no choice but to extend our judgment to all cases of belief whatever. Belief, that sacred faculty, which prompts the decisions of our will, and knits into harmonious working all the compacted energies of our being, is ours not for ourselves but for humanity. It is rightly used on truths which have been established by long experience and waiting toil, and which have stood in the fierce light of free and fearless questioning. Then it helps to bind men together, and to strengthen and direct their common action. It is desecrated when given to unproved and unquestioned statements, for the solace and private pleasure of the believer; to add a tinsel splendour to the plain straight road of our life, and display a bright mirage beyond it; or even to drown the common sorrows of our kind by a self-deception which allows them not only to cast down, but also to degrade us. Whoso would deserve well of his fellows in this matter will guard the purity of his belief with a very fanaticism of jealous care, lest at any time it should rest on an unworthy object, and catch a stain which can never be wiped away.

It is not only the leader of men, statesman, philosopher, or poet, that owes this bounden duty to mankind. Every rustic who delivers in the village alehouse his slow, infrequent sentences, may help to kill or keep alive the fatal superstitions which clog his race. Every hard-worked wife of an artisan may transmit to her children beliefs which shall knit society together, or rend it in pieces. No simplicity of mind, no obscurity of station, can escape the universal duty of questioning all that we believe.

It is true that this duty is a hard one, and the doubt which comes out of it is often a very bitter thing. It leaves us bare and powerless where we thought that we were safe and strong. To know all about anything is to know how to deal with it under all circumstances. We feel much happier and more secure when we think we know precisely what to do, no matter what happens, than when we have lost our way and do not know where to turn. And if we have supposed ourselves to know all about anything, and to be capable of doing what is fit in regard to it, we naturally do not like to find that we are really ignorant and powerless, that we have to begin again at the beginning, and try to learn what the thing is and how it is to be dealt with—if indeed anything can be learnt about it. It is the sense of power attached to a sense of knowledge that makes men desirous of believing, and afraid of doubting.

This sense of power is the highest and best of pleasures when the belief on which it is founded is a true belief, and has been fairly earned by investigation. For then we may justly feel that it is common property, and holds good for others as well as for ourselves. Then we may be glad, not that *I* have learned secrets by which I am safer and stronger, but that *we men* have got mastery over more of the world; and we shall be strong, not for ourselves, but in the name of Man and in his strength. But if the belief has been accepted on insufficient evidence, the pleasure is a stolen one. Not only does it deceive ourselves by giving us a sense of power which we do not really possess, but it is sinful, because it is stolen in defiance of our duty to mankind. That duty is, to guard ourselves from such beliefs as from a pestilence, which may shortly master our own body and then spread to the rest of the town. What would be thought of one who, for the sake of a sweet fruit, should deliberately run the risk of bringing a plague upon his family and his neighbours?

And, as in other such senses, it is not the risk only which has to be considered; for a bad action is always bad at the time when it is done, no matter what happens afterwards. Every time we let ourselves believe for unworthy reasons, we weaken our powers of self-control, of doubting, of judicially and fairly weighing evidence. We all suffer severely enough from the maintenance and support of false beliefs and the fatally wrong actions which they lead to, and the evil born when one such belief is entertained is great and wide. But a greater and wider evil arises when the credulous character is maintained and supported, when a habit of believing for unworthy reasons is fostered and made permanent. If I steal money from any person, there may be no harm done by the mere transfer of possession; he may not feel the loss, or it may prevent him from using the money badly. But I cannot help doing this great wrong towards Man, that I make myself dishonest. What hurts society is not that it should lose its property, but that it should become a den of thieves; for then it must cease to be society. This is why we ought not to do evil that good may come; for at any rate this great evil has come, that we have done evil and are made wicked thereby. In like manner, if I let myself believe anything on insufficient evidence, there may be no great harm done by the mere belief; it may be true after all, or I may never have occasion to exhibit it in outward acts. But I cannot help doing this great wrong towards Man, that I make myself credulous. The danger to society is not merely that it should believe wrong things, though that is great enough; but that it should become credulous, and lose the habit of testing things and inquiring into them; for then it must sink back into savagery.

The harm which is done by credulity in a man is not confined to the fostering of a credulous character in others, and consequent support of false beliefs. Habitual want of care about what I believe leads to habitual want of care in others about the truth of what is told to me. Men speak the truth to one another when each reveres the truth in his own mind and in the other's mind; but how shall my friend revere the truth in my mind when I myself am careless about it, when I believe things because I want to believe them, and because they are comforting and pleasant? Will he not learn to cry, "Peace," to me, when there is no peace? By such a course I shall surround myself with a thick atmosphere of falsehood and fraud, and in that I must live. It may matter little to me, in my cloud-castle of sweet illusions and darling lies; but it matters much to Man that I have made my neighbours ready to deceive. The credulous man is father to the liar and the cheat; he lives in the bosom of this his family, and it is no marvel if he should become even as they are. So closely are our duties knit together, that whoso shall keep the whole law, and yet offend in one point, he is guilty of all.

To sum up: it is wrong always, everywhere, and for any one, to believe anything upon insufficient evidence.

If a man, holding a belief which he was taught in childhood or persuaded of afterwards, keeps down and pushes away any doubts which arise about it in his mind, purposely avoids the reading of books and the company of men that call in question or discuss it, and regards as impious those questions which cannot easily be asked without disturbing it; the life of that man is one long sin against mankind.

If this judgment seems harsh when applied to those simple souls who have never known better, who have been brought up from the cradle with a horror of doubt, and taught that their eternal welfare depends on *what* they believe; then it leads to the very serious question, *Who hath made Israel to sin?*

It may be permitted me to fortify this judgment with the sentence of Milton *—

> "A man may be a heretic in the truth; and if he believe things only because his pastor says so, or the assembly so determine, without knowing other reason, though his belief be true, yet the very truth he holds becomes his heresy."

And with this famous aphorism of Coleridge†—

> "He who begins by loving Christianity better than Truth, will proceed by loving his own sect or Church better than Christianity, and end in loving himself better than all."

Inquiry into the evidence of a doctrine is not to be made once for all, and then taken as finally settled. It is never lawful to stifle a doubt; for either it can be honestly answered by means of the inquiry already made, or else it proves that the inquiry was not complete.

"But," says one, "I am a busy man; I have no time for the long course of study which would be necessary to make me in any degree a competent judge of certain questions, or even able to understand the nature of the arguments." Then he should have no time to believe.

II.—THE WEIGHT OF AUTHORITY

Are we then to become universal sceptics, doubting everything, afraid always to put one foot before the other until we have personally tested the

---

* Areopagitica.
† Aids to Reflection.

firmness of the road? Are we to deprive ourselves of the help and guidance of that vast body of knowledge which is daily growing upon the world, because neither we nor any other one person can possibly test a hundredth part of it by immediate experiment or observation, and because it would not be completely proved if we did? Shall we steal and tell lies because we have had no personal experience wide enough to justify the belief that it is wrong to do so?

There is no practical danger that such consequences will ever follow from scrupulous care and self-control in the matter of belief. Those men who have most nearly done their duty in this respect have found that certain great principles, and these most fitted for the guidance of life, have stood out more and more clearly in proportion to the care and honesty with which they were tested, and have acquired in this way a practical certainty. The beliefs about right and wrong which guide our actions in dealing with men in society, and the beliefs about physical nature which guide our actions in dealing with animate and inanimate bodies, these never suffer from investigation; they can take care of themselves, without being propped up by "acts of faith," the clamour of paid advocates, or the suppression of contrary evidence. Moreover there are many cases in which it is our duty to act upon probabilities, although the evidence is not such as to justify present belief; because it is precisely by such action, and by observation of its fruits, that evidence is got which may justify future belief. So that we have no reason to fear lest a habit of conscientious inquiry should paralyze the actions of our daily life.

But because it is not enough to say, "It is wrong to believe on unworthy evidence," without saying also what evidence is worthy, we shall now go on to inquire under what circumstances it is lawful to believe on the testimony of others; and then, further, we shall inquire more generally when and why we may believe that which goes beyond our own experience, or even beyond the experience of mankind.

In what cases, then, let us ask in the first place, is the testimony of a man unworthy of belief? He may say that which is untrue either knowingly or unknowingly. In the first case he is lying, and his moral character is to blame; in the second case he is ignorant or mistaken, and it is only his knowledge or his judgment which is in fault. In order that we may have the right to accept his testimony as ground for believing what he says, we must have reasonable grounds for trusting his *veracity*, that he is really trying to speak the truth so far as he knows it; his *knowledge*, that he has had opportunities of knowing the truth about this matter; and his *judgment*, that he has made a proper use of those opportunities in coming to the conclusion which he affirms.

However plain and obvious these considerations may be, so that no man of ordinary intelligence, reflecting upon the matter, could fail to arrive at them, it is nevertheless true that a great many persons do habitually disregard them in weighing testimony. Of the two questions, equally important to the trustworthiness of a witness, "Is he dishonest?" and "May he be mistaken?" the majority of mankind are perfectly satisfied if *one* can, with some show of probability, be answered in the negative. The excellent moral character of a man is alleged as ground for accepting his statements about things which he cannot possibly have known. A Mohammedan, for example, will tell us that the character of his Prophet was so noble and majestic that it commands the reverence even of those who do not believe in his mission. So admirable was his moral teaching, so wisely put together the great social machine which he created, that his precepts have not only been accepted by a great portion of mankind, but have actually been obeyed. His institutions have on the one hand rescued the negro from savagery, and on the other hand have taught civilization to the advancing West; and although the races which held the highest forms of his faith, and most fully embodied his mind and thought, have all been conquered and swept away by barbaric tribes, yet the history of their marvellous attainments remains as an imperishable glory to Islam. Are we to doubt the word of a man so great and so good? Can we suppose that this magnificent genius, this splendid moral hero, has lied to us about the most solemn and sacred matters? The testimony of Mohammed is clear, that there is but one God, and that he, Mohammed, is his prophet; that if we believe in him we shall enjoy everlasting felicity, but that if we do not we shall be damned. This testimony rests on the most awful of foundations, the revelation of heaven itself; for was he not visited by the angel Gabriel, as he fasted and prayed in his desert cave, and allowed to enter into the blessed fields of Paradise? Surely God is God, and Mohammed is the Prophet of God.

What should we answer to this Mussulman? First, no doubt, we should be tempted to take exception against his view of the character of the Prophet and the uniformly beneficial influence of Islam: before we could go with him altogether in these matters it might seem that we should have to forget many terrible things of which we have heard or read. But if we chose to grant him all these assumptions, for the sake of argument, and because it is difficult both for the faithful and for infidels to discuss them fairly and without passion; still we should have something to say which takes away the ground of his belief, and therefore shows that it is wrong to entertain it. Namely this: the character of Mohammed is excellent evidence that he was honest and spoke the truth so far as he knew it; but it is no evidence at all that he knew what the truth was. What means could he have of knowing that the form which appeared to him to be the angel Gabriel was not a hallucination, and that his apparent visit to Paradise was not a dream? Grant that he himself was fully persuaded and honestly believed that he had the guidance of heaven, and was the vehicle of a supernatural revelation; how could he know that this strong conviction was not a mistake? Let us put ourselves in his place; we shall find that the more completely we endeavour to realize what passed through his mind, the more clearly we shall perceive that the Prophet could have had no adequate ground for the belief in his own inspiration. It is most probable that he himself never doubted of the matter, or thought of asking the question; but we are in the position of those to whom the question has been asked, and who are bound to answer it. It is known to medical observers that solitude and want of food are powerful means of producing delusion and of fostering a tendency to mental disease. Let us suppose, then, that I, like Mohammed, go into desert places to fast and pray; what things can happen to me which will give me the right to believe that I am divinely inspired? Suppose that I get information, apparently from a celestial visitor, which upon being tested is found to be correct. I cannot be sure, in the first place, that the celestial visitor is not a figment of my own mind, and that the information did not come to me, unknown at the time to my consciousness, through some subtle channel of sense. But if my visitor were a real visitor, and for a long time gave me information which was found to be trustworthy, this would indeed be good ground for trusting him in the future as to such matters as fall within human powers of verification; but it would not be ground for trusting his testimony as to any other matters. For although his tested character would justify me in believing that he spoke the truth so far as he knew, yet the same question would present itself—what ground is there for supposing that he knows?

Even if my supposed visitor had given me such information, subsequently verified by me, as proved him to have means of knowledge about verifiable matters far exceeding my own; this would not justify me in believing what he said about matters that are not at present capable of verification by man. It would be ground for interesting conjecture, and for the hope that, as the fruit of our patient inquiry, we might by-and-by attain to such a means of verification as should rightly turn conjecture into belief. For belief belongs to man, and to the guidance of human affairs: no belief is real unless it guide our actions, and those very actions supply a test of its truth.

But, it may be replied, the acceptance of Islam as a system is just that action which is prompted by belief in the mission of the Prophet, and which will serve for a test of its truth. Is it possible to believe that a system which has succeeded so well is really founded upon a delusion? Not only have individual saints found joy and peace in believing, and verified those spiritual experiences which are promised to the faithful, but nations also have been raised from savagery or barbarism to a higher social state. Surely we are at liberty to say that the belief has been acted upon, and that it has been verified.

It requires, however, but little consideration to show that what has really been verified is not at all the supernal character of the Prophet's mission, or the trustworthiness of his authority in matters which we ourselves cannot test; but only his practical wisdom in certain very mundane things. The fact that believers have found joy and peace in believing gives us the right to say that the doctrine is a comfortable doctrine, and pleasant to the soul; but it does not give us the right to say that it is true. And the question which our conscience is always asking about that which we are tempted to believe is not "Is it comfortable and pleasant?" but "Is it true?" That the Prophet preached certain doctrines, and predicted that spiritual comfort would be found in them, proves only his sympathy with human nature and his knowledge of it; but it does not prove his superhuman knowledge of theology.

And if we admit for the sake of argument (for it seems that we cannot do more) that the progress made by Moslem nations in certain cases was really due to the system formed and sent forth into the world by Mohammed; we are not at liberty to conclude from this that he was inspired to declare the truth about things which we cannot verify. We are only at liberty to infer the excellence of his moral precepts, or of the means which he devised for so working upon men as to get them obeyed, or of the social and political machinery which he set up. And it would require a great amount of careful examination into the history of those nations to determine which of these things had the greater share in the result. So that here again it is the Prophet's knowledge of human nature, and his sympathy with it, that are verified; not his divine inspiration, or his knowledge of theology.

If there were only one Prophet, indeed, it might well seem a difficult and even an ungracious task to decide upon what points we would trust him, and on what we would doubt his authority; seeing what help and furtherance all men have gained in all ages from those who saw more clearly, who felt more strongly, and who sought the truth with more single heart than their weaker brethren. But there is not only one Prophet; and while the consent of many upon that which, as men, they had real means of knowing and did know, has endured to the end, and been honourably built into the great fabric of human knowledge; the diverse witness of some about that which they did not and could not know remains as a warning to us that to exaggerate the prophetic authority is to misuse it, and to dishonour those who have sought only to help and further us after their power. It is hardly in human nature that a man should quite accurately gauge the limits of his own insight; but it is the duty of those who profit by his work to consider carefully where he may have been carried beyond it. If we must needs embalm his possible errors along with his solid achievements, and use his authority as an excuse for believing what he cannot have known, we make of his goodness an occasion to sin.

To consider only one other such witness: the followers of Buddha have at least as much right to appeal to individual and social experience in support of the authority of the Eastern saviour. The special mark of his religion, it is said, that in which it has never been surpassed, is the comfort and consolation which it gives to the sick and sorrowful, the tender sympathy with which it soothes and assuages all the natural griefs of men. And surely no triumph of social morality can be greater or nobler than that which has kept nearly half the human race from persecuting in the name of religion. If we are to trust the accounts of his early followers, he believed himself to have come upon earth with a divine and cosmic mission to set rolling the wheel of the law. Being a prince, he emptied himself of his kingdom, and of his free will became acquainted with misery, that he might learn how to meet and subdue it. Could such a man speak falsely about solemn things? And as for his knowledge, was he not a man miraculous, with powers more than man's? He was born of woman without the help of man; he rose into the air and was transfigured before his kinsmen; at last he went up bodily into heaven from the top of Adam's Peak. Is not his word to be believed in when he testifies of heavenly things?

If there were only he, and no other, with such claims! But there is Mohammed with his testimony; we cannot choose but listen to them both. The Prophet tells us that there is one God, and that we shall live for ever in joy or misery, according as we believe in the Prophet or not. The Buddha says that there is no God, and that we shall be annihilated by-and-by if we are good enough. Both cannot be infallibly inspired; one or the other must have been the victim of a delusion, and thought he knew that which he really did not know. Who shall dare to say which? and how can we justify ourselves in believing that the other was not also deluded?

We are led, then, to these judgments following. The goodness and greatness of a man do not justify us in accepting a belief upon the warrant of his authority, unless there are reasonable grounds for supposing that he knew the truth of what he was saying. And there can be no grounds for supposing that a man knows that which we, without ceasing to be men, could not be supposed to verify.

If a chemist tells me, who am no chemist, that a certain substance can be made by putting together other substances in certain proportions and sub-jecting them to a known process, I am quite justified in believing this upon his authority, unless I know anything against his character or his judgment. For his professional training is one which tends to encourage veracity and the honest pursuit of truth, and to produce a dislike of hasty conclusions and slovenly investigation. And I have reasonable ground for supposing that he knows the truth of what he is saying, for although I am no chemist, I can be made to understand so much of the methods and processes of the science as makes it conceivable to me that, without ceasing to be man, I might verify the statement. I may never actually verify it, or even see any experiment which goes towards verifying it; but still I have quite reason enough to justify me in believing that the verification is within the reach of human appliances and powers, and in particular that it has been actually performed by my informant. His result, the belief to which he has been led by his inquiries, is valid not only for himself but for others; it is watched and tested by those who are working in the same ground, and who know that no greater service can be rendered to science than the purification of accepted results from the errors which may have crept into them. It is in this way that the result becomes common property, a right object of belief, which is a social affair and matter of public business. Thus it is to be observed that his authority is valid because there are those who question it and verify it; that it is precisely this process of examining and purifying that keeps alive among investigators the love of that which shall stand all possible tests, the sense of public responsibility as of those whose work, if well done, shall remain as the enduring heritage of mankind.

But if my chemist tells me that an atom of oxygen has existed unaltered in weight and rate of vibration throughout all time, I have no right to believe this on his authority, for it is a thing which he cannot know without ceasing to be man. He may quite honestly believe that this statement is a fair inference from his experiments, but in that case his judgment is at fault. A very simple consideration of the character of experiments would show him that they never can lead to results of such a kind; that being themselves only approximate and limited, they cannot give us knowledge which is exact and universal. No eminence of character and genius can give a man authority enough to justify us in believing him when he makes statements implying exact or universal knowledge.

Again, an Arctic explorer may tell us that in a given latitude and longitude he has experienced such and such a degree of cold, that the sea was of such a depth, and the ice of such a character. We should be quite right to believe him in the absence of any stain upon his veracity. It is conceivable that we might, without ceasing to be men, go there and verify his statement; it can be tested by the witness of his companions, and there is adequate ground for supposing that he knows the truth of what he is saying. But if an old whaler tells us that the ice is three hundred feet thick all the way up to the Pole, we shall not be justified in believing him. For although the statement may be capable of verification by man, it is certainly not capable of verification by *him,* with any means and appliances which he has possessed; and he must have persuaded himself of the truth of it by some means which does not attach any credit to his testimony. Even if, therefore, the matter affirmed is within the reach of human knowledge, we have no right to accept it upon authority unless it is within the reach of our informant's knowledge.

What shall we say of that authority, more venerable and august than any individual witness, the time-honoured tradition of the human race? An atmosphere of beliefs and conceptions has been formed by the labours and struggles of our forefathers, which enables us to breathe amid the various and complex circumstances of our life. It is around and about us and within us; we cannot think except in the forms and processes of thought which it supplies. Is it possible to doubt and to test it? and if possible, is it right?

We shall find reason to answer that it is not only possible and right, but our bounden duty; that the main purpose of the tradition itself is to supply us with the means of asking questions, of testing and inquiring into things; that if we misuse it, and take it as a collection of cut-and-dried statements, to be accepted without further inquiry, we are not only injuring ourselves here, but by refusing to do our part towards the building up of the fabric which shall be inherited by our children, we are tending to cut off ourselves and our race from the human line.

Let us first take care to distinguish a kind of tradition which especially requires to be examined and called in question, because it especially shrinks from inquiry. Suppose that a medicine-man in Central Africa tells his tribe that a certain powerful medicine in his tent will be propitiated if they kill their cattle; and that the tribe believe him. Whether the medicine was propitiated or not, there are no means of verifying, but the cattle are gone. Still the belief may be kept up in the tribe that propitiation has been effected in this way; and in a later generation it will be all the easier for another medicine-man to persuade them to a similar act. Here the only reason for belief is that everybody has believed the thing for so long that it must be true. And yet the belief was founded on fraud, and has been propagated by credulity. That man will undoubtedly do right, and be a friend of men, who shall call it in question and see that there is no evidence for it, help his neighbours to see as he does, and even, if need be, go into the holy tent and break the medicine.

The rule which should guide us in such cases is simple and obvious enough: that the aggregate testimony of our neighbours is subject to the same conditions as the testimony of any one of them. Namely, we have no right to believe a thing true because everybody says so, unless there are good grounds for believing that some one person at least has the means of knowing what is true, and is speaking the truth so far as he knows it. However many nations and generations of men are brought into the witness-box, they cannot testify to anything which they do not know. Every man who has accepted the statement from somebody else, without himself testing and verifying it, is out of court; his word is worth nothing at all. And when we get back at last to the true birth and beginning of the statement, two serious questions must be disposed of in regard to him who first made it: was he mistaken in thinking that he *knew* about this matter, or was he lying?

This last question is unfortunately a very actual and practical one, even to us at this day and in this country. We have no occasion to go to La Salette, or to Central Africa, or to Lourdes, for examples of immoral and debasing superstition. It is only too possible for a child to grow up in London surrounded by an atmosphere of beliefs fit only for the savage, which have in our own time been founded in fraud and propagated by credulity.

Laying aside, then, such tradition as is handed on without testing by successive generations, let us consider that which is truly built up out of the common experience of mankind. This great fabric is for the guidance of our thoughts, and through them of our actions, both in the moral and in the material world. In the moral world, for example, it gives us the conceptions of right in general, of justice, of truth, of beneficence, and the like. These are given as conceptions, not as statements or propositions; they answer to certain definite instincts, which are certainly within us, however they came there. That it is right to be beneficent is matter of immediate personal experience; for when a man retires within himself and there finds something, wider and more lasting than his solitary personality, which says, "I want to do right," as well as, "I want to do good to man," he can verify by direct observation that one instinct is founded upon and agrees fully with the other. And it is his duty so to verify this and all similar statements.

The tradition says also, at a definite place and time, that such and such actions are just, or true, or beneficent. For all such rules a further inquiry is necessary, since they are sometimes established by an authority other than that of the moral sense founded on experience. Until recently, the moral tradition of our own country—and indeed of all Europe—taught that it was beneficent to give money indiscriminately to beggars. But the questioning of this rule, and investigation into it, led men to see that true beneficence is that which helps a man to do the work which he is most fitted for, not that which keeps and encourages him in idleness; and that to neglect this distinction in the present is to prepare pauperism and misery for the future. By this testing and discussion, not only has practice been purified and made more beneficent, but the very conception of beneficence has been made wider and wiser. Now here the great social heirloom consists of two parts: the instinct of beneficence, which makes a certain side of our nature, when predominant, wish to do good to men; and the intellectual conception of beneficence, which we can compare with any proposed course of conduct and ask "Is this beneficent or not?" By the continual asking and answering of such questions the conception grows in breadth and distinctness, and the instinct becomes strengthened and purified. It appears then that the great use of the conception, the intellectual part of the heirloom, is to enable us to ask questions; that it grows and is kept straight by means of these questions; and if we do not use it for that purpose we shall gradually lose it altogether, and be left with a mere code of regulations which cannot rightly be called morality at all.

Such considerations apply even more obviously and clearly, if possible, to the store of beliefs and conceptions which our fathers have amassed for us in respect of the material world. We are ready to laugh at the rule of thumb of the Australian, who continues to tie his hatchet to the side of the handle, although the Birmingham fitter has made a hole on purpose for him to put the handle in. His people have tied up hatchets so for ages: who is he that he should set himself up against their wisdom? He has sunk so low that he cannot do what some of them must have done in the far distant past—call in question an established usage, and invent or learn something better. Yet here, in the dim beginning of knowledge, where science and art are one, we find only the same simple rule which applies to the highest and deepest growths of that cosmic Tree; to its loftiest flower-tipped branches as well as to the profoundest of its hidden roots; the rule, namely, that what is stored up and handed down to us is rightly used by those who act as the makers acted, when they stored it up; those who use it to ask further questions, to examine, to investigate; who try honestly and solemnly to find out what is the right way of looking at things and of dealing with them.

A question rightly asked is already half answered, said Jacobi; we may add that the method of solution is the other half of the answer, and that the actual result counts for nothing by the side of these two. For an example let us go to the telegraph, where theory and practice, grown each to years of discretion, are marvellously wedded for the fruitful service of men. Ohm found that the strength of an electric current is directly proportional to the strength of the battery which produces it, and inversely as the length of the wire along which it has to travel. This is called Ohm's law; but the result, regarded as a statement to be believed, is not the valuable part of it. The first half is the question: what relation holds good between these quantities? So put, the question involves already the conception of strength of current, and of strength of battery, as quantities to be measured and compared; it hints clearly that these are the things to be attended to in the study of electric currents. The second half is the method of investigation; how to measure these quantities, what apparatus are required for the experiment, and how are they to be used? The student who begins to learn about electricity is not asked to believe in Ohm's law; he is made to understand the question, he is placed before the apparatus, and he is taught to verify it. He learns to do things, not to think he knows things; to use instruments and to ask questions, not to accept a traditional statement. The question which required a genius to ask it rightly is answered by a tiro. If Ohm's law were suddenly lost and forgotten by all men, while the question and the method of solution remained, the result could be rediscovered in an hour. But the result by itself, if known to a people who could not comprehend the value of the question or the means of solving it, would be like a watch in the hands of a savage who could not wind it up, or an iron steamship worked by Spanish engineers.

In regard, then, to the sacred tradition of humanity, we learn that it consists, not in propositions or statements which are to be accepted and believed on the authority of the tradition, but in questions rightly asked, in conceptions which enable us to ask further questions, and in methods of answering questions. The value of all these things depends on their being tested day by day. The very sacredness of the precious deposit imposes upon us the duty and the responsibility of testing it, of purifying and enlarging it to the utmost of our power. He who makes use of its results to stifle his own doubts, or to hamper the inquiry of others, is guilty of a sacrilege which centuries shall never be able to blot out. When the labours and questionings of honest and brave men shall have built up the fabric of known truth to a glory which we in this generation can neither hope for nor imagine; in that pure and holy temple he shall have no part nor lot, but his name and his works shall be cast out into the darkness of oblivion for ever.

III.—THE LIMITS OF INFERENCE

The question, in what cases we may believe that which goes beyond our experience, is a very large and delicate one, extending to the whole range of scientific method, and requiring a considerable increase in the application of it before it can be answered with anything approaching to completeness. But one rule, lying on the threshold of the subject, of extreme simplicity and vast practical importance, may here be touched upon and shortly laid down.

A little reflection will show us that every belief, even the simplest and most fundamental, goes beyond experience when regarded as a guide to our actions. A burnt child dreads the fire, because it believes that the fire will burn it to-day just as it did yesterday; but this belief goes beyond experience, and assumes that the unknown fire of to-day is like the known fire of yesterday. Even the belief that the child was burnt yesterday goes beyond *present* experience, which contains only the memory of a burning, and not the burning itself; it assumes, therefore, that this memory is trustworthy, although we know that a memory may often be mistaken. But if it is to be used as a guide of action, as a hint of what the future is to be, it must assume something about that future, namely, that it will be consistent with the supposition that the burning really took place yesterday; which is going beyond experience. Even the fundamental "I am," which cannot be doubted, is no guide to action until it takes to itself "I shall be," which goes beyond experience. The question is not, therefore, "May we believe what goes beyond experience?" for this is involved in the very nature of belief; but "How far and in what manner may we add to our experience in forming our beliefs?"

And an answer, of utter simplicity and universality, is suggested by the example we have taken: a burnt child dreads the fire. We may go beyond experience by assuming that what we do not know is like what we do know; or, in other words, we may add to our experience on the assumption of a uniformity in nature. What this uniformity precisely is, how we grow in the knowledge of it from generation to generation, these are questions which for the present we lay aside, being content to examine two instances which may serve to make plainer the nature of the rule.

From certain observations made with the spectroscope, we infer the existence of hydrogen in the sun. By looking into the spectroscope when the sun is shining on its slit, we see certain definite bright lines; and experiments made upon bodies on the earth have taught us that when these bright lines are seen, hydrogen is the source of them. We assume, then, that the unknown bright lines in the sun are like the known bright lines of the laboratory, and that hydrogen in the sun behaves as hydrogen under similar circumstances would behave on the earth.

But are we not trusting our spectroscope too much? Surely, having found it to be trustworthy for terrestrial substances, where its statements can be verified by man, we are justified in accepting its testimony in other like cases; but not when it gives us information about things in the sun, where its testimony cannot be directly verified by man?

Certainly, we want to know a little more before this inference can be justified; and fortunately we do know this. The spectroscope testifies to exactly the same thing in the two cases; namely, that light-vibrations of a certain rate are being sent through it. Its construction is such that if it were wrong about this in one case it would be wrong in the other. When we come to look into the matter, we find that we have really assumed the matter of the sun to be like the matter of the earth, made up of a certain number of distinct substances; and that each of these, when very hot, has a distinct rate of vibration, by which it may be recognized and singled out from the rest. But this is the kind of assumption which we are justified in using when we add to our experience. It is an assumption of uniformity in nature, and can only be checked by comparison with many similar assumptions which we have to make in other such cases.

But is this a true belief, of the existence of hydrogen in the sun? Can it help in the right guidance of human action?

Certainly not, if it is accepted on unworthy grounds, and without some understanding of the process by which it is got at. But when this process is taken in as the ground of the belief, it becomes a very serious and practical matter. For if there is no hydrogen in the sun, the spectroscope—that is to say, the measurement of rates of vibration—must be an uncertain guide in recognizing different substances; and consequently it ought not to be used in chemical analysis—in assaying, for example—to the great saving of time, trouble, and money. Whereas the acceptance of the spectroscopic method as trustworthy has enriched us not only with new metals, which is a great thing, but with new processes of investigation, which is vastly greater.

For another example, let us consider the way in which we infer the truth of an historical event—say the siege of Syracuse in the Peloponnesian war. Our experience is that manuscripts exist which are said to be and which call themselves manuscripts of the history of Thucydides; that in other manuscripts, stated to be by later historians, he is described as living during the time of the war; and that books, supposed to date from the revival of learning, tell us how these manuscripts had been preserved and were then acquired. We find also that men do not, as a rule, forge books and histories without a special motive; we assume that in this respect men in the past were like men in the present; and we observe that in this case no special motive was present. That is, we add to our experience on the assumption of a uniformity in the characters of men. Because our knowledge of this uniformity is far less complete and exact than our knowledge of that which obtains in physics, inferences of the historical kind are more precarious and less exact than inferences in many other sciences.

But if there is any special reason to suspect the character of the persons who wrote or transmitted certain books, the case becomes altered. If a group of documents give internal evidence that they were produced among people who forged books in the names of others, and who, in describing events, suppressed those things which did not suit them, while they amplified such as did suit them; who not only committed these crimes, but gloried in them as proofs of humility and zeal; then we must say that upon such documents no true historical inference can be founded, but only unsatisfactory conjecture.

We may, then, add to our experience on the assumption of a uniformity in nature; we may fill in our picture of what is and has been, as experience gives it us, in such a way as to make the whole consistent with this uniformity. And practically demonstrative inference—that which gives us a right to believe in the result of it—is a clear showing that in no other way than by the truth of this result can the uniformity of nature be saved.

No evidence, therefore, can justify us in believing the truth of a statement which is contrary to, or outside of, the uniformity of nature. If our experience is such that it cannot be filled up consistently with uniformity, all we have a right to conclude is that there is something wrong somewhere; but the possibility of inference is taken away; we must rest in our experience, and not go beyond it at all. If an event really happened, which was not a part of the uniformity of nature, it would have two properties; no evidence could give the right to believe it to any except those whose actual experience it was; and no inference worthy of belief could be founded upon it at all.

Are we then bound to believe that nature is absolutely and universally uniform? Certainly not; we have no right to believe anything of this kind. The rule only tells us that in forming beliefs which go beyond our experience, we may make the assumption that nature is practically uniform so far as we are concerned. Within the range of human action and verification, we may form, by help of this assumption, actual beliefs; beyond it, only those hypotheses which serve for the more accurate asking of questions.

To sum up:—

We may believe what goes beyond our experience, only when it is inferred from that experience by the assumption that what we do not know is like what we know.

We may believe the statement of another person, when there is reasonable ground for supposing that he knows the matter of which he speaks, and that he is speaking the truth so far as he knows it.

It is wrong in all cases to believe on insufficient evidence; and where it is presumption to doubt and to investigate, there it is worse than presumption to believe.

WHAT IS THE GOOD OF TRUTH?
St. George Jackson Mivart

By the question, "What is the good of Truth?" I mean, how far and why is truth desirable, and what postulates are needed before we can affirm that truth is necessarily a good?

Some of my esteemed club-fellows, such as Professor Tyndall amongst others, who do not appear to entirely agree with me on all points, often surprise me by the great warmth with which they advocate "Truth," as if it was manifestly at all times necessarily a good. I think I have even detected a disposition to bear somewhat hardly upon sceptics like myself, who feel that, after all, something may, on their hypothesis, perhaps be said on the other side.

I therefore gladly take this opportunity of laying some of my doubts before the Club, feeling that surely here, if anywhere, I may have them resolved, to my very great contentment.

Those present will probably agree in affirming that truth is desirable. But what do we mean by "truth," and what by "desirable?"

Now, I suppose by "truth" is meant merely the "general laws of Nature," and not particular truths, as it is manifest that on no hypothesis can a knowledge of "truth," in this extreme sense, be always desirable.

The utility of informing Pitt on his death-bed of the battle of Austerlitz can, it seems to me, be apparent only to a stronger supporter of vivisection than even I can claim to be, nor probably would any one affirm that to tell a dying man with no property to dispose of that the children he loved were not really his would be a *praiseworthy* action. Of course, I do not suppose that my friends who are so zealous for truth would go to this extreme, and yet the language used has sometimes been so strong as almost to justify the inference that they would do so, and to imply the latent existence of a sort of superstitious awe, as if truth was something almost supernatural. Yet "truth" is but a relation of conformity between mind and objective existence, and if objective existence happens to be itself *undesirable*, it seems to me that such conformity might sometimes be also undesirable.

But granting that by "Truth" is meant scientific truth only—a knowledge of the facts of Nature and her laws—what is meant by "desirable?" *That is surely desirable which each man desires, and I suppose most men desire their own well-being and that of those they care for, and I can easily imagine cases in which the knowledge of scientific truths, such as those of toxicology, might not be thought desirable by some people, even for the sharers of their bed and board.*

But it will probably be replied, that "desirable" means "desirable for the human race," and we may therefore proceed at once upon the amiable fiction that the desire of most men is the welfare of mankind, and that there are very many good enough to sympathise with our much-esteemed *confrère*, Mr. Harrison, in really caring about remote generations, existing in æons of time after they, if his philosophy is right, have faded into what Science, as opposed to Rhetoric, must, instead of "infinite azure," call "very finite mud."

According to the conscious-automaton hypothesis, a knowledge of truth or falsehood, being a state of consciousness, must be indifferent, since it can have no influence upon action, but is a mere concomitant. *Can we, then, be sure that a knowledge of all the facts of Nature will necessarily be conducive to the welfare of mankind?*

Now, it seems to me that to be able to affirm this, we need the theistic postulate. Without this, I find myself quite unable to acquiesce in such a dictum. Without this, we have no certain ground for affirming that the objective world and its laws are good, while there is much apparent evidence the other way. As a naturalist, I cannot but think, that apart from the postulate referred to, Nature presents many blots, or to say the least, very doubtful puzzles?

I have never yet met with even a good suggestion as to the beneficial action of the descent of the *testis* in our own frame, that fruitful source of hernia and other evils. Probably the members of the Metaphysical Club would themselves hardly have arranged that snakes should feed as they do, or designed the somewhat one-sided beneficence of the wasp *Sphex*.

As to ourselves, it is surely conceivable that it may be with the race as with the individual, and that the environment may be so conditioned as to make the extinction of the one, as of the other, merely a question of time; and such, I take it, would be the anticipation of most evolutionists. *If, then, a complete mental conformity to the environment, a thorough knowledge of actually existing circumstances, may be prejudicial to the individual, and accelerate his extinction (and such cases might be easily imagined, had not many a suicide demonstrated the fact), I should like to be made sure that it could never be so to the race. I think that all sides must admit that certain nations seem to have been strengthened by the acceptance of a falsehood as truth.* England was strengthened by the movement of the sixteenth century, and Spain by its Catholicism in the fourteenth and fifteenth centuries, and if a sanguine temperament leads us to join in the exclamation, *Magna est veritas, et prævalebit!* I think experience will not altogether refuse its sanction to the contrary proclamation, *Magnum est mendacinon, et prævaluit.* If the views of my friends of the opposite school were correct, and freedom and responsibility were but unmeaning words, it seems to me a grave question, whether a general knowledge of the fact would be desirable.

That degree of civilisation and social amelioration which has been attained has been attained on the supposition of their reality; may not, then, retrogression accompany the overthrow of such belief? *Would not the universal realisation of "determinism" tend to paralyse effort on critical occasions? My own experience convinces me that it often would. Moreover, since the belief in responsibility has been hitherto generally accepted and acted on, this fact alone constitutes a sufficient proof, for those with whom I am arguing, that the delusion was beneficial for the race, since they must admit that otherwise it could never have arisen through the survival of the fittest.*

Now, Mr. Herbert Spencer freely allows that a nation may get free of its faith too early for its own safety. Why is it certain that it may not be the same with the whole human race?

If the doubts here expressed are well founded, there would surely be much truth in the saying attributed to Voltaire, *Si Dieu n'existait pas, il faudrait l'inventer*, and it appears to me that the philanthropist who declines the postulate here advocated should pause before propagating what he deems to be truth.

It may, to say the least, be far more philanthropic in such a one, instead of seeking to tear down systems the congruity of which with human welfare experience has demonstrated, to select from amongst what he deems the mythologies of his day that which he considers most calculated to promote human happiness, and to, more or less, energetically support it.

For those, however, who accept the postulate, there is, of course, no difficulty; and they can freely affirm that however perplexing the aspect of the Universe, it must yet be good, and the most complete knowledge of its truth desirable for mankind. But I should be most glad to be made sure that we can, in no case, have anything to fear from what is deemed "truth" by the opponents of the postulate; and I have, therefore, ventured to intrude these doubts upon the indulgent hearing of this metaphysical tribunal.

ON THE UTILITY OF TRUTH
James Fitzjames Stephen

Our Secretary having asked me to get him out of a difficulty, by writing something which the Society could discuss, I haved tried to do so, at very short notice indeed. This must be my excuse for the imperfection and want of system which I fear will be found in these remarks.

A paper called, "Force, Energy, and Will," by Mr. Mivart, published in the *Nineteenth Century* for May last, contains the following passages. I do not think their detachment from their context does their author injustice:—

"It seems to me demonstrable that without Theism, we have no certain ground for affirming the necessary universal goodness of Truth, for without Theism we have no certain ground for affirming that the objective world and its laws are good, whilst there is much apparent evidence the other way." (p. 946.)

"If the doubts here expressed are well founded, there would surely be much widsom in the saying attributed to Voltaire,—'Si Dieu n'existait pas, il faudrait l'inventer;' and it appears to me that the philanthropist who declines the postulate" (I understand this to mean the postulate that there is a God) "here advocated, should pause before propagating his negative convictions. It may, to say the least, be far more philanthropic in such a one, instead of seeking to tear down systems the congruity of which with human welfare experience has demonstrated, to select from amongst what he deems the mythologies of his day that which he considers the most calculated to promote human happiness, and to more or less energetically support it." (p. 947.) After quoting passages in which Mr. Bain and Mr. Mill speak of Truth as being valuable on the ground of its utility, Mr. Mivart adds:—"As to the general utility of Truth, there can, of course, be no question, any more than that the love of it ought to be an all-powerful sentiment. But I go further than this, and in common with all those who accept the Theistic postulate, can *logically* as well as heartily affirm that however perplexing the aspect of the Universe, it must yet be good, and the most complete knowledge of its truth desirable for mankind."

I propose to make a few observations on these views. In a part of Mr. Mivart's paper which precedes the passages quoted (p. 945), *he argues that on no hypothesis can a knowledge of Truth, in the extreme sense of a knowledge of all facts whatever, be desirable. No one (whether he believed in God or not) would think it necessary to pain the feelings of a dying man by*

telling him bad news, or to instruct a murderer in the properties of poisons.
The question, then, is confined to Truth in a wider sense, to what Mr. Mivart
calls "the general laws of Nature." I dislike the phrase, but let it pass.
Practically, his view appears to me to come to this:—A true general conception of the universe, as far as it is known to me, is advantageous if we
assume the existence of God, but not otherwise. The reason given is that
"without Theism, we have no certain ground for affirming that the objective
world and its laws are good." *This appears to involve the notion that no
knowledge can be good, unless the thing known is good. Surely this is a
mistake. It is quite as important to know things bad in themselves, as to know
things good in themselves,—nay, it is generally more important.* The knowledge of evil, may enable you to avoid it. The knowledge of good may, under
circumstances, be superfluous. If we were all in perfect health during our
whole lives, the most pressing reason for the study of human physiology
would be removed. The knowledge of disease is valuable, not although, but
because disease is an evil. The knowledge of our physical constitution would
be mere matter of curiosity, if we all had absolutely perfect health, and were
exempt from injury. Be this as it may, however, what difference can "the
Theistic postulate" make in the matter? Mr. Mivart's view on the subject
must be gathered from the juxtaposition of two passages in his article:—
"Truth is but a relation of conformity between mind and objective existence,
and if objective existence happens to be itself undesirable, can moral conformity to it be always the reverse?" (The conformity, by the way, is not
moral, but intellectual; a man who studies the Plague in order to cure it,
surely is not in any relation of "moral conformity" to it.) "Those who accept
the Theistic postulate can logically, as well as heartily, affirm that however
perplexing the aspect of the universe, it must yet be good, and the most
complete knowledge of its truth desirable for mankind."

I am quite unable to understand this. The knowledge of the manner in
which cholera is propagated is bad *prima facie*, because cholera is bad, but
believe in God (or if Mr. Mivart prefers it, accept the Theistic hypothesis),
and then both the cholera, and the knowledge of its mode of procedure,
become good. *I would propose the following questions to Mr. Mivart:—1. Is
the knowledge of the manner in which cholera is propagated of any other use
to a believer in God, than that it enables him to avoid or cure, and teach
others to avoid or cure, the cholera? 2. Is not this knowledge equally
beneficial for these purposes to Atheists? 3. If so, how can the value of truth
in this matter be affected by a belief in God; and if not in this matter, why in
any other matter? 4. If a belief in God "makes objective existence desirable,"
does it make the cholera desirable? If Yes, why is knowledge of the means by
which the cholera may be avoided desirable? If No, how does "the Theistic
postulate" make any truth desirable which would not be desirable on the
Atheistic postulate?*

One very strong case occurs to my mind as to the importance of the knowledge of an alleged "objective existence in itself undesirable." The Roman Catholic Catechism says that the wicked will live for ever in the flames of hell. This can hardly be called objectively desirable, upon any hypothesis or postulate, but surely it is important to be known, if it is true; and this, I presume, Mr. Mivart would hardly deny. But if it is important that the truth of the doctrine should be known, assuming it to be true, how can it be otherwise than important that its falsehood should be known, if it is false, or its doubtfulness, if it is doubtful? Mr. Mivart's view seems to lead to the strange result that unless you believe in God, you have no interest in knowing the truth about Hell. To me, the converse doctrine that unless you believe in hell, it is a matter of comparative indifference whether or not the world was made by God, appears much more plausible. I must, however, fairly confess that I am, for the reasons already given, so completely puzzled by Mr. Mivart's logic, that I do not propose to attempt to follow it any further.

I must, however, make a few remarks upon his suggestion that an Atheist ought to select from what he deems the "mythologies of his day that which he considers the most calculated to support human happiness, and more or less energetically support it." How, he asks, can any one who regards such conduct as grossly immoral reconcile that opinion with the belief that morals are based upon utility? "If that is moral which 'tends to increase the happiness of men,' how can that be 'immoral' which, ex hypothesi, has that very tendency?"

In order to answer this question fairly, we must assume that a man is convinced that the progress of knowledge has made the existence of God highly improbable; that physical science shows no traces of the existence of such a Being; that history explains the steps by which a belief in his existence grew up; and that it also discloses a state of things, past and present, which it is hardly possible to reconcile, without the most violent and unproved assumptions, with the belief that the state of things in which we live was designed and is overruled by a Conscious Being, of Supreme Intelligence and Goodness.

A man who seriously and deliberately holds this view ought, says, Mr. Mivart, to choose what he regards as the most beneficent of the existing mythologies, and support it, because such conduct will promote human happiness. In what manner—assuming, for the sake of the argument, the truth of Atheism—would this enormous falsehood promote human happiness? In the first place, it is a plain matter of fact that no one can play fast and loose with truth. To accustom yourself to lying on one subject, is like accustoming yourself to indulging any other vice, under some special restriction. It is morally impossible to maintain that restriction. A man who deliberately, systematically, and "more or less energetically" lied on subjects of this transcendent importance, would inevitably become false in everything. I should not trust such a man's word on any common matter. I am sure Mr. Mivart himself would feel that any one offered him a deadly insult who

said, "I believe you have taken your own advice. I don't support you are
foolish enough really to believe the religion you profess. I have no doubt you
are a sensible Atheist, selecting from amongst what you deem the mythologies of the day that which you consider the most calculated to promote
human happiness. I understand and applaud you." But though such would,
of course, be Mr. Mivart's feelings in the case supposed, they would be
inconsistent with his theory; at least, his indignation ought to be limited to
being suspected of Atheism. He ought to feel complimented rather than
otherwise by the suggestion that, being an Atheist, he had at least the sense
and modesty to be besides a systematic liar.

*The supposed Atheist, however, would not only immolate his own moral
character on the shrine of general benevolence. It is difficult to see what
object he would gain by it for others. If there is no God and no future state,
what good do mankind at large get by believing in them?* Which of the
"mythologies of the day" is so obviously beneficial, apart from its truth, that a
man ought to convert his whole life into one huge lie, and try to make his
neighbours see history, science, political economy, politics, law, morals,
literature—every subject which interests men as such—in a false light, for
the sake of bolstering it up? If the doctrine that "the wicked shall live for ever
in the flames of hell" is false, if it is false that any real advantage is to be
obtained by confession to a priest, if all the spiritual authority as to faith and
morals claimed by the Pope and his clergy is a mere fiction, can any one
assert that they are, nevertheless, so pre-eminently beneficient, that in
order to believe them it is worth while to make nearly everything else more
or less incredible? Not to insist on this, take the cardinal doctrines of all
doctrines more or less common to all Christians, the doctrine of a good
God,—the doctrine of the Sermon on the Mount. If these doctrines are false,
are they useful? *To me, it appears that the utility of each depends on its
truth.* If the world in which we live was made by a good God, the way in
which we ought to look at it, and take its good and evil, will be different from
that in which we ought to look at it if we have no reason to hold that opinion.
If all men are brothers, and if another life is to redress the defects of this life,
much may be endured and many things may be undertaken which it would
be weak to endure and foolish to undertake, if the world has come to be what
it is by the operation of a prolonged struggle for existence in which the
weakest goes to the wall. If Jesus Christ was mistaken in saying that we are all
the children of one Father, it seems to me that he cannot have been right in
saying, "Blessed are the poor in spirit," "Blessed are the meek," "Blessed
are they that mourn," and the like. And how mankind are to be benefited by
keeping up one fundamental error for the sake of the minor errors which
spring from it, I do not understand.

The falsehood which Mr. Mivart thinks a benevolent Atheist ought to tell
might, perhaps be beneficial to those who have got the good things of life,
because it might tend to keep the poor and wretched quiet, in the hope that

Lazarus would in time change places with Dives, but this possible accidental advantage to the rich ought not to be described as a tendency to increase the happiness of mankind at large.

It is to me matter of surprise to find Christians, and especially Roman Catholics, taking the view put forward by Mr. Mivart. There is hardly any topic on which eminent writers have been so fond of insisting as the antithesis between the Christian and the worldly point of view. That Christianity imposes restraints on human nature; that it exalts much which the world despises, and abases much which the world exalts; that it treats as splendid vices many things which would by common standards be regarded as virtues, and as supernatural virtues much which would otherwise be looked upon as morbid, are the common-places of preachers of all Churches. Asceticism in all its forms is one broad illustration of this side of Christianity. How can it be regarded as useful, if Christianity is altogether false? and how can a man who believes it to be false, suppose that he is benefiting the world by supporting an unnatural state of mind founded on a delusion? What should we think of a man who falsely pretended to believe in Confucius, for fear the women of China should let their feet grow to their natural size?

I cannot, however, think that even if a person did believe that Christianity was both beneficial and false, he ought to support it. *I quite agree in the doctrine that Truth is valuable, not as an end in itself, but as a means to ends; but I think that it is an indispensable means to all the ends which collectively make up human happiness, and the supposition that it can ever be advantageous to mankind on a large scale, and in the long-run, to believe in a falsehood which affects important parts of their conduct, appears to me as unlikely as that the relations of space or number will alter.*

Mr. Mivart himself admits, as every one must, that as to the general utility of Truth there can be no question. I believe that the alleged exceptions to the general rule are not really exceptions. Most of them are cases in which it would be more correct to say that an imperfect statement of truth is better than none. For instance, language corresponds very imperfectly with facts. Truth, in particular cases, can only be hinted at or conveyed by metaphors or parables. In some instances, exaggerated statements must be made, in order to attract attention; but in all these cases it is more correct to say that truth, imperfectly expressed, is beneficial, than to say that falsehood is beneficial. I do not know that any one has ever maintained that deliberate, intentional falsehood, on a subject of general interest and great importance, is, or can be, beneficial, except in regard to religion; and this has usually been maintained by unbelievers. It is an entirely new experience to me to meet with a man who at once affirms his creed to be true, and says that people who conscientiously reject it ought to pretend to believe it.

One remark in conclusion. Mr. Mivart speaks with something like a sneer of "our friends who are so zealous for Truth." He says, "The language used has sometimes been so strong as . . . to imply the existence of a sort of superstitious awe, as if Truth was something almost supernatural." I must own that I do not think any language can be too strong upon this subject. I think that people ought to feel an awe, deep and genuine, and not in the least superstitious, upon the subject of Truth. I think that the temptation to lie, and that the temptation to believe that a falsehood is a short cut to some desirable end, is the strongest, the most subtle, the most universal of all temptations. It is the temptation to which every cheat, and thief, and forger, and coiner gives way, and it is quite as strong in other shapes amongst people far too respectable to steal or forge. To see the truth and to speak the truth are operations of the greatest difficulty. They can be performed only by constant care, and a persevering determination to shun neither danger, nor labour, nor discredit. The doctrine that this is the path to all that is worth having, and that apparent exceptions to it are temptations to be withstood, is a hard one to learn, and like other moral doctrines resting on expediency, it requires faith; and it is the consciousness of the difficulty of keeping it steadily in view, and of acting upon it under all circumstances, that makes me look with indignation on attempts to weaken it, by appropriating it to theological ends.

THEISM
John Stuart Mill

From the result of the preceding examination of the evidences of Theism, and (Theism being presupposed) of the evidences of any Revelation, it follows that the rational attitude of a thinking mind towards the supernatural, whether in natural or in revealed religion, is that of scepticism as distinguished from belief on the one hand, and from atheism on the other: including, in the present case, under atheism, the negative as well as the positive form of disbelief in a God, viz., not only the dogmatic denial of his existence, but the denial that there is any evidence on either side, which for the most practical purposes amounts to the same thing as if the existence of a God had been disproved. If we are right in the conclusions to which we have been led by the preceding inquiry there is evidence, but insufficient for proof, and amounting only to one of the lower degrees of probability. The indication given by such evidence as there is, points to the creation, not indeed of the universe, but of the present order of it by an Intelligent Mind, whose power over the materials was not absolute, whose love for his creatures was not his sole actuating inducement, but who nevertheless desired their good. The notion of a providential government by an omnipotent Being for the good of his creatures must be entirely dismissed. Even of the continued existence of the Creator we have no other guarantee than that he cannot be subject to the law of death which affects terrestrial beings, since the conditions that produce this liability wherever it is known to exist are of his creating. That this Being, not being omnipotent, may have produced a machinery falling short of his intentions, and which may require the occasional interposition of the Maker's hand, is a supposition not in itself absurd nor impossible, though in none of the cases in which such interposition is believed to have occurred is the evidence such as could possibly prove it; it remains a simple possibility, which those may dwell on to whom it yields comfort to suppose that blessings which ordinary human power is inadequate to attain, may come not from extraordinary human power, but from the bounty of an intelligence beyond the human, and which continuously cares for man. The possibility of a life after death rests on the same footing—of a boon which this powerful Being who wishes well to man, may have the power to grant, and which if the message alleged to have been sent by him was really sent, he has actually promised. The whole domain of the supernatural is thus removed from the region of Belief into that of simple Hope; and in that, for anything we can see, it is likely always to remain; for we can hardly anticipate either that any positive evidence will be acquired of the direct agency of Divine Benevolence in human destiny, or that any reason will be discovered for considering the realization of human hopes on that subject as beyond the pale of possibility.

It is now to be considered whether the indulgence of hope, in a region of imagination merely, in which there is no prospect that any probable grounds of expectation will ever be obtained, is irrational, and ought to be discouraged as a departure from the rational principle of regulating our feelings as well as opinions strictly by evidence.

This is a point which different thinkers are likely, for a long time at least, to decide differently, according to their individual temperament. The principles which ought to govern the cultivation and the regulation of the imagination—with a view on the one hand of preventing it from disturbing the rectitude of the intellect and the right direction of the actions and will, and on the other hand of employing it as a power for increasing the happiness of life and giving elevation to the character—are a subject which has never yet engaged the serious consideration of philosophers, though some opinion on it is implied in almost all modes of thinking on human character and education. And, I expect, that this will hereafter be regarded as a very important branch of study for practical purposes, and the more, in proportion as the weakening of positive beliefs respecting states of existence superior to the human, leaves the imagination of higher things less provided with material from the domain of supposed reality. To me it seems that human life, small and confined as it is, and as, considered merely in the present, it is likely to remain even when the progress of material and moral improvement may have freed it from the greater part of its present calamities, stands greatly in need of any wider range and greater height of aspiration for itself and its destination, which the exercise of imagination can yield to it without running counter to the evidence of fact; and that it is a part of wisdom to make the most of any, even small, probabilities on this subject, which furnish imagination with any footing to support itself upon. And I am satisfied that the cultivation of such a tendency in the imagination, provided it goes on *pari passu* with the cultivation of severe reason, has no necessary tendency to pervert the judgment; but that it is possible to form a perfectly sober estimate of the evidences on both sides of a question and yet to let the imagination dwell by preference on those possibilities, which are at once the most comforting and the most improving, without in the least degree overrating the solidity of the grounds for expecting that these rather than any others will be the possibilities actually realized.

Though this is not in the number of the practical maxims handed down by tradition and recognized as rules for the conduct of life, a great part of the happiness of life depends upon the tacit observance of it. What, for instance, is the meaning of that which is always accounted one of the chief blessings of life, a cheerful disposition? What but the tendency, either from constitution or habit, to dwell chiefly on the brighter side both of the present and of the future? If every aspect, whether agreeable or odious of every thing, ought to occupy exactly the same place in our imagination which it fills in fact, and therefore ought to fill in our deliberate reason, what we call a cheerful disposition would be but one of the forms of folly, on a par except in agreeableness with the opposite disposition in which the gloomy and painful view of all things is habitually predominant. But it is not found in practice that those who take life cheerfully are less alive to rational prospects of evil or danger and more careless of making due provision against them, than other people. The tendency is rather the other way, for a hopeful disposition gives a spur to the faculties and keeps all the active energies in good working order. When imagination and reason receive each its appropriate culture they do not succeed in usurping each other's prerogatives. It is not necessary for keeping up our conviction that we must die, that we should be always brooding over death. It is far better that we should think no further about what we cannot possibly avert, than is required for observing the rules of prudence in regard to our own life and that of others, and fulfilling whatever duties devolve upon us in contemplation of the inevitable event. The way to secure this is not to think perpetually of death, but to think perpetually of our duties, and of the rule of life. The true rule of practical wisdom is not that of making all the aspects of things equally prominent in our habitual contemplations, but of giving the greatest prominence to those of their aspects which depend on, or can be modified by, our own conduct. In things which do not depend on us, it is not solely for the sake of a more enjoyable life that the habit is desirable of looking at things and at mankind by preference on their pleasant side; it is also in order that we may be able to love them better and work with more heart for their improvement. To what purpose, indeed, should we feed our imagination with the unlovely aspect of persons and things? All *unnecessary* dwelling upon the evils of life is at best a useless expenditure of nervous force: and when I say unnecessary I mean all that is not necessary either in the sense of being unavoidable, or in that of being needed for the performance of our duties and for preventing our sense of the reality of those evils from becoming speculative and dim. But if it is often waste of strength to dwell on the evils of life, it is worse than waste to dwell habitually on its meannesses and basenesses. It is necessary to be aware of them; but to live in their contemplation makes it scarcely possible to keep up in oneself a high tone of mind. The imagination and feelings become tuned to a lower pitch; degrading instead of elevating associations become connected with the daily objects and incidents of life, and give their colour to the thoughts, just as associations of sensuality do in those who indulge freely in that sort of contemplations. Men have often felt what it is to have had their imaginations corrupted by one class of ideas, and I think they must have felt with the same kind of pain how the poetry is taken out of the things fullest of it, by mean associations, as when a beautiful air that had been associated with highly poetical words is heard sung with trivial and vulgar ones. All these things are said in mere illustration of the principle that in the regulation of the imagination literal truth of facts is not the only thing to be considered. Truth is the province of reason, and it is by the cultivation of the rational faculty that provision is made for its being known always, and thought of as often as is required by duty and the circumstances of human life. But when the reason is strongly cultivated, the imagination may safely follow its own end, and do its best to make life pleasant and lovely inside the castle, in reliance on the fortifications raised and maintained by Reason round the outward bounds.

On these principles it appears to me that the indulgence of hope with regard to the government of the universe and the destiny of man after death, while we recognize as a clear truth that we have no ground for more than a hope, is legitimate and philosophically defensible. The beneficial effect of such a hope is far from trifling. It makes life and human nature a far greater thing to the feelings, and gives greater strength as well as greater solemnity to all the sentiments which are awakened in us by our fellow-creatures and by mankind at large. It allays the sense of that irony of Nature which is so painfully felt when we see the exertions and sacrifices of a life culminating in the formation of a wise and noble mind, only to disappear from the world when the time has just arrived at which the world seems about to begin reaping the benefit of it. The truth that life is short and art is long is from of old one of the most discouraging parts of our condition; this hope admits the possibility that the art employed in improving and beautifying the soul itself may avail for good in some other life, even when seemingly useless for this. But the benefit consists less in the presence of any specific hope than in the enlargement of the general scale of the feelings; the loftier aspirations being no longer in the same degree checked and kept down by a sense of the insignificance of human life—by the disastrous feeling of 'not worth while.' The gain obtained in the increased inducement to cultivate the improvement of character up to the end of life, is obvious without being specified.

There is another and a most important exercise of imagination which, in the past and present, has been kept up principally by means of religious belief and which is infinitely precious to mankind, so much so that human excellence greatly depends upon the sufficiency of the provision made for it. This consists of the familiarity of the imagination with the conception of a morally perfect Being, and the habit of taking the approbation of such a Being as the *norma* or standard to which to refer and by which to regulate our own characters and lives. This idealization of our standard of excellence in a Person is quite possible, even when that Person is conceived as merely imaginary. But religion, since the birth of Christianity, has inculcated the belief that our highest conceptions of combined wisdom and goodness exist in the concrete in a living Being who has his eyes on us and cares for our good. Through the darkest and most corrupt periods Christianity has raised this torch on high—has kept this object of veneration and imitation before the eyes of man. True, the image of perfection has been a most imperfect, and, in many respects a perverting and corrupting one, not only from the low moral ideas of the times, but from the mass of moral contradictions which the deluded worshipper was compelled to swallow by the supposed necessity of complimenting the Good Principle with the possession of infinite power. But it is one of the most universal as well as of the most surprising characteristics of human nature, and one of the most speaking proofs of the low stage to which the reason of mankind at large has ever yet advanced, that they are capable of overlooking any amount of either moral or intellectual contradictions and receiving into their minds propositions utterly inconsistent with one another, not only without being shocked by the contradiction, but without preventing both the contradictory beliefs from producing a part at least of their natural consequences in the mind. Pious men and women have gone on ascribing to God particular acts and a general course of will and conduct incompatible with even the most ordinary and limited conception of moral goodness, and have had their own ideas of morality, in many important particulars, totally warped and distorted, and notwithstanding this have continued to conceive their God as clothed with all the attributes of the highest ideal goodness which their state of mind enabled them to conceive, and have had their aspirations towards goodness stimulated and encouraged by that conception. And, it cannot be questioned that the undoubting belief of the real existence of a Being who realizes our own best ideas of perfection, and of our being in the hands of that Being as the ruler of the universe, gives an increase of force to these feelings beyond what they can receive from reference to a merely ideal conception.

This particular advantage it is not possible for those to enjoy, who take a rational view of the nature and amount of the evidence for the existence and attributes of the Creator. On the other hand, they are not encumbered with the moral contradictions which beset every form of religion which aims at justifying in a moral point of view the whole government of the world. They are, therefore, enabled to form a far truer and more consistent conception of Ideal Goodness, than is possible to any one who thinks it necessary to find ideal goodness in an omnipotent ruler of the world. The power of the Creator once recognized as limited, there is nothing to disprove the supposition that his goodness is complete and that the ideally perfect character in whose likeness we should wish to form ourselves and to whose supposed approbation we refer our actions, may have a real existence in a Being to whom we owe all such good as we enjoy.

Above all, the most valuable part of the effect on the character which

Christianity has produced by holding up in a Divine Person a standard of excellence and a model for imitation, is available even to the absolute unbeliever and can never more be lost to humanity. For it is Christ, rather than God, whom Christianity has held up to believers as the pattern of perfection for humanity. It is the God incarnate, more than the God of the Jews or of Nature, who being idealized has taken so great and salutary a hold on the modern mind. And whatever else may be taken away from us by rational criticism, Christ is still left; a unique figure, not more unlike all his precursors than all his followers, even those who had the direct benefit of his personal teaching. It is of no use to say that Christ as exhibited in the Gospels is not historical and that we know not how much of what is admirable has been superadded by the tradition of his followers. The tradition of followers suffices to insert any number of marvels, and may have inserted all the miracles which he is reputed to have wrought. But who among his disciples or among their proselytes was capable of inventing the sayings ascribed to Jesus or of imagining the life and character revealed in the Gospels? Certainly not the fishermen of Galilee; as certainly not St. Paul, whose character and idiosyncrasies were of a totally different sort; still less the early Christian writers in whom nothing is more evident than that the good which was in them was all derived, as they always professed that it was derived, from the higher source. What *could* be added and interpolated by a disciple we may see in the mystical parts of the Gospel of St. John, matter imported from Philo and the Alexandrian Platonists and put into the mouth of the Saviour in long speeches about himself such as the other Gospels contain not the slightest vestige of, though pretended to have been delivered on occasions of the deepest interest and when his principal followers were all present; most prominently at the last supper. The East was full of men who could have stolen any quantity of this poor stuff, as the multitudinous Oriental sects of Gnostics afterwards did. But about the life and sayings of Jesus there is a stamp of personal originality combined with profundity of insight, which if we abandon the idle expectation of finding scientific precision where something very different was aimed at, must place the Prophet of Nazareth, even in the estimation of those who have no belief in his inspiration, in the very first rank of the men of sublime genius of whom our species can boast. When this pre-eminent genius is combined with the qualities of probably the greatest moral reformer, and martyr to that mission, who ever existed upon earth, religion cannot be said to have made a bad choice in pitching on this man as the ideal representative and guide of humanity; nor, even now, would it be easy, even for an unbeliever, to find a better translation of the rule of virtue from the abstract into the concrete, than to endeavour so to live that Christ would approve our life. When to this we add that, to the conception of the rational sceptic, it remains a possibility that Christ actually was what he supposed himself to be—not God, for he never made the smallest pretension to that character and would probably have thought such a

pretension as blasphemous as it seemed to the men who condemned him—
but a man charged with a special, express and unique commission from God
to lead mankind to truth and virtue; we may well conclude that the influences of religion on the character which will remain after rational criticism
has done its utmost against the evidences of religion, are well worth preserving, and that what they lack in direct strength as compared with those of a
firmer belief, is more than compensated by the greater truth and rectitude of
the morality they sanction.

Impressions such as these, though not in themselves amounting to what
can properly be called a religion, seem to me excellently fitted to aid and
fortify that real, though purely human religion, which sometimes calls itself
the Religion of Humanity and sometimes that of Duty. To the other induce-
ments for cultivating a religious devotion to the welfare of our fellow-creatures as an obligatory limit to every selfish aim, and an end for the direct
promotion of which no sacrifice can be too great, it superadds the feeling that
in making this the rule of our life, we may be co-operating with the unseen
Being to whom we owe all that is enjoyable in life. One elevated feeling this
form of religious idea admits of, which is not open to those who believe in the
omnipotence of the good principle in the universe, the feeling of helping
God—of requiting the good he has given by a voluntary co-operation which
he, not being omnipotent, really needs, and by which a somewhat nearer
approach may be made to the fulfilment of his purposes. The conditions of
human existence are highly favourable to the growth of such a feeling
inasmuch as a battle is constantly going on, in which the humblest human
creature is not incapable of taking some part, between the powers of good
and those of evil, and in which every even the smallest help to the right side
has its value in promoting the very slow and often almost insensible progress
by which good is gradually gaining ground from evil, yet gaining it so visibly
at considerable intervals as to promise the very distant but not uncertain final
victory of Good. To do something during life, on even the humblest scale if
nothing more is within reach, towards bringing this consummation ever so
little nearer, is the most animating and invigorating thought which can
inspire a human creature; and that it is destined, with or without supernatural sanctions, to be the religion of the Future I cannot entertain a doubt. But
it appears to me that supernatural hopes, in the degree and kind in which
what I have called rational scepticism does not refuse to sanction them, may
still contribute not a little to give to this religion its due ascendancy over the
human mind.

THE WILL TO BELIEVE.[1]
William James

In the recently published Life by Leslie Stephen of his brother, Fitz-James, there is an account of a school to which the latter went when he was a boy. The teacher, a certain Mr. Guest, used to converse with his pupils in this wise: "Gurney, what is the difference between justification and sancti-fication?—Stephen, prove the omnipotence of God!" etc. In the midst of our Harvard freethinking and indifference we are prone to imagine that here at your good old orthodox College conversation continues to be somewhat upon this order; and to show you that we at Harvard have not lost all interest in these vital subjects, I have brought with me to-night something like a sermon on justification by faith to read to you,—I mean an essay in justifica-tion *of* a defence of our right to adopt a believing attitude in religious matters, in spite of the fact that our merely logical intellect may not have been coerced. 'The Will to Believe,' accordingly, is the title of my paper.

I have long defended to my own students the lawfulness of voluntarily adopted faith; but as soon as they have got well imbued with the logical spirit, they have as a rule refused to admit my contention to be lawful philosophically, even though in point of fact they were personally of the time chock-full of some faith or other themselves. I am all the while, however, so profoundly convinced that my own position is correct, that your invitation has seemed to me a good occasion to make my statements more clear. Perhaps your minds will be more open that those with which I have hitherto had to deal. I will be as little technical as I can, though I must begin by setting up some technical distinctions that will help us in the end.

I.

Let us give the name of *hypothesis* to anything that may be proposed to our belief; and just as the electricians speak of live and dead wires, let us speak of any hypothesis as either *live* or *dead*. A live hypothesis is one which appeals as a real possibility to him to whom it is proposed. If I ask you to believe in the Mahdi, the notion makes no electric connection with your nature,—it refuses to scintillate with any credibility at all. As an hypothesis it

[1] An Address to the Philosophical Clubs of Yale and Brown Universities. Published in the New World, June, 1896.

is completely dead. To an Arab, however (even if he be not one of the Mahdi's followers), the hypothesis is among the mind's possibilities: it is alive. This shows that deadness and liveness in an hypothesis are not intrinsic properties, but relations to the individual thinker. They are measured by his willingness to act. The maximum of liveness in an hypothesis means willingness to act irrevocably. Practically, that means belief; but there is some believing tendency wherever there is willingness to act at all.

Next, let us call the decision between two hypotheses an *option*. Options may be of several kinds. They may be—1, *living* or *dead;* 2, *forced* or *avoidable;* 3, *momentous* or *trivial;* and for our purposes we may call an option a *genuine* option when it is of the forced, living, and momentous kind.

1. A living option is one in which both hypotheses are live ones. If I say to you: "Be a theosophist or be a Mohammedan," it is probably a dead option, because for you neither hypothesis is likely to be alive. But if I say: "Be an agnostic or be a Christian," it is otherwise: trained as you are, each hypothesis makes some appeal, however small, to your belief.

2. Next, if I say to you: "Choose between going out with your umbrella or without it," I do not offer you a genuine option, for it is not forced. You can easily avoid it by not going out at all. Similarly, if I say, "Either love me or hate me," "Either call my theory true or call it false," your option is avoidable. You may remain indifferent to me, neither loving nor hating, and you may decline to offer any judgment as to my theory. But if I say, "Either accept this truth or go without it," I put on you a forced option, for there is no standing place outside of the alternative. Every dilemma based on a complete logical disjunction, with no possibility of not choosing, is an option of this forced kind.

3. Finally, if I were Dr. Nansen and proposed to you to join my North Pole expedition, your option would be momentous; for this would probably be your only similar opportunity, and your choice now would either exclude you from the North Pole sort of immortality altogether or put at least the chance of it into your hands. He who refuses to embrace a unique opportunity loses the prize as surely as if he tried and failed. *Per contra,* the option is trivial when the opportunity is not unique, when the stake is insignificant, or when the decision is reversible if it later prove unwise. Such trivial options abound in the scientific life. A chemist finds an hypothesis live enough to spend a year in its verification: he believes in it to that extent. But if his experiments prove inconclusive either way, he is quit for his loss of time, no vital harm being done.

It will facilitate our discussion if we keep all these distinctions well in mind.

II.

The next matter to consider is the actual psychology of human opinion. When we look at certain facts, it seems as if our passional and volitional nature lay at the root of all our convictions. When we look at others, it seems as if they could do nothing when the intellect had once said its say. Let us take the latter facts up first.

Does it not seem preposterous on the very face of it to talk of our opinions being modifiable at will? Can our will either help or hinder our intellect in its perceptions of truth? Can we, by just willing it, believe that Abraham Lincoln's existence is a myth, and that the portraits of him in McClure's Magazine are all of some one else? Can we, by any effort of our will, or by any strength of wish that it were true, believe ourselves well and about when we are roaring with rheumatism in bed, or feel certain that the sum of the two one-dollar bills in our pocket must be a hundred dollars? We can *say* any of these things, but we are absolutely impotent to believe them; and of just such things is the whole fabric of the truths that we do believe in made up,—matters of fact, immediate or remote, as Hume said, and relations between ideas, which are either there or not there for us if we see them so, and which if not there cannot be put there by any action of our own.

In Pascal's Thoughts there is a celebrated passage known in literature as Pascal's wager. In it he tries to force us into Christianity by reasoning as if our concern with truth resembled our concern with the stakes in a game of chance. Translated freely his words are these: You must either believe or not believe that God is—which will you do? Your human reason cannot say. A game is going on between you and the nature of things which at the day of judgment will bring out either heads or tails. Weigh what your gains and your losses would be if you should stake all you have on heads, or God's existence: if you win in such case, you gain eternal beatitude; if you lose, you lose nothing at all. If there were an infinity of chances, and only one for God in this wager, still you ought to stake your all on God; for though you surely risk a finite loss by this procedure, any finite loss is reasonable, even a certain one is reasonable, if there is but the possibility of infinite gain. Go, then, and take holy water, and have masses said; belief will come and stupefy your scruples,—*Cela vous fera croire et vous abêtira.* Why should you not? At bottom, what have you to lose?

You probably feel that when religious faith expresses itself thus, in the language of the gaming-table, it is put to its last trumps. Surely Pascal's own personal belief in masses and holy water had far other springs; and this celebrated page of his is but an argument for others, a last desperate snatch at a weapon against the hardness of the unbelieving heart. We feel that a faith in masses and holy water adopted wilfully after such a mechanical calculation would lack the inner soul of faith's reality; and if we were ourselves in the place of the Deity, we should probably take particular pleasure in cutting off believers of this pattern from their infinite reward. It is evident that unless there be some pre-existing tendency to believe in masses and holy water, the option offered to the will by Pascal is not a living option. Certainly no Turk ever took to masses and holy water on its account; and even to us Protestants these means of salvation seem such foregone impossibilities that Pascal's logic, invoked for them specifically, leaves us unmoved. As well might the Mahdi write to us, saying, "I am the Expected One whom God has created in his effulgence. You shall be infinitely happy if you confess me; otherwise you shall be cut off from the light of the sun. Weigh, then, your infinite gain if I am genuine against your finite sacrifice if I am not!" His logic would be that of Pascal; but he would vainly use it on us, for the hypothesis he offers us is dead. No tendency to act on it exists in us to any degree.

The talk of believing by our volition seems, then, from one point of view, simply silly. From another point of view it is worse than silly, it is vile. When one turns to the magnificent edifice of the physical sciences, and sees how it was reared; what thousands of disinterested moral lives of men lie buried in its mere foundations; what patience and postponement, what choking down of preference, what submission to the icy laws of outer fact are wrought into its very stones and mortar; how absolutely impersonal it stands in its vast augustness,—then how besotted and contemptible seems every little sentimentalist who comes blowing his voluntary smoke-wreaths, and pretending to decide things from out of his private dream! Can we wonder if those bred in the rugged and manly school of science should feel like spewing such subjectivism out of their mouths? The whole system of loyalties which grow up in the schools of science go dead against its toleration; so that it is only natural that those who have caught the scientific fever should pass over to the opposite extreme, and write sometimes as if the incorruptibly truthful intellect ought positively to prefer bitterness and unacceptableness to the heart in its cup.

> It fortifies my soul to know
> That, though I perish, Truth is so—

sings Clough, while Huxley exclaims: "My only consolation lies in the reflection that, however bad our posterity may become, so far as they hold by the plain rule of not pretending to believe what they have no reason to believe, because it may be to their advantage so to pretend [the word 'pretend' is surely here redundant], they will not have reached the lowest depth of immorality." And that delicious *enfant terrible* Clifford writes: "Belief is desecrated when given to unproved and unquestioned statements for the solace and private pleasure of the believer. . . . Whoso would deserve well of his fellows in this matter will guard the purity of his belief with a very fanaticism of jealous care, lest at any time it should rest on an unworthy object, and catch a stain which can never be wiped away. . . . If [a] belief has been accepted on insufficient evidence [even though the belief be true, as Clifford on the same page explains] the pleasure is a stolen one. . . . It is sinful because it is stolen in defiance of our duty to mankind. That duty is to guard ourselves from such beliefs as from a pestilence which may shortly master our own body and then spread to the rest of the town. . . . It is wrong always, everywhere, and for every one, to believe anything upon insufficient evidence."

III.

All this strikes one as healthy, even when expressed, as by Clifford, with somewhat too much of robustious pathos in the voice. Free-will and simple wishing do seem, in the matter of our credences, to be only fifth wheels to the coach. Yet if any one should thereupon assume that intellectual insight is what remains after wish and will and sentimental preference have taken wing, or that pure reason is what then settles our opinions, he would fly quite as directly in the teeth of the facts.

It is only our already dead hypotheses that our willing nature is unable to bring to life again. But what has made them dead for us is for the most part a previous action of our willing nature of an antagonistic kind. When I say 'willing nature,' I do not mean only such deliberate volitions as may have set up habits of belief that we cannot now escape from,—I mean all such factors of belief as fear and hope, prejudice and passion, imitation and partisanship, the circumpressure of our caste and set. As a matter of fact we find ourselves believing, we hardly know how or why. Mr. Balfour gives the name of 'authority' to all those influences, born of the intellectual climate, that make hypotheses possible or impossible for us, alive or dead. Here in this room, we all of us believe in molecules and the conservation of energy, in democracy and necessary progress, in Protestant Christianity and the duty of fighting for 'the doctrine of the immortal Monroe,' all for no reasons worthy of the name. We see into these matters with no more inner clearness, and probably with much less, than any disbeliever in them might possess. His unconventionality would probably have some grounds to show for its conclusions; but for us, not insight, but the *prestige* of the opinions, is what makes the spark shoot from them and light up our sleeping magazines of faith. Our reason is quite satisfied, in nine hundred and ninety-nine cases out of every thousand of us, if it can find a few arguments that will do to recite in case our credulity is criticised by some one else. Our faith is faith in some one else's faith, and in the greatest matters this is most the case. Our belief in truth itself, for instance, that there is a truth, and that our minds and it are made for each other,—what is it but a passionate affirmation of desire, in which our social system backs us up? We want to have a truth; we want to believe that our experiments and studies and discussions must put us in a continually better and better position towards it; and on this line we agree to fight out our thinking lives. But if a pyrrhonistic sceptic asks us *how we know* all this, can our logic find a reply? No! certainly it cannot. It is just one volition against another,—we willing to go in for life upon a trust or assumption which he, for his part, does not care to make.[1]

As a rule we disbelieve all facts and theories for which we have no use. Clifford's cosmic emotions find no use for Christian feelings. Huxley belabors the bishops because there is no use for sacerdotalism in his scheme of life.

---

[1] Compare the admirable page 310 in S. H. Hodgson's "Time and Space," London, 1865.

Newman, on the contrary, goes over to Romanism, and finds all sort of reasons good for staying there, because a priestly system is for him an organic need and delight. Why do so few 'scientists' even look at the evidence for telepathy, so called? Because they think, as a leading biologist, now dead, once said to me, that even if such a thing were true, scientists ought to band together to keep it suppressed and concealed. It would undo the uniformity of Nature and all sorts of other things without which scientists cannot carry on their pursuits. But if this very man had been shown something which as a scientist he might *do* with telepathy, he might not only have examined the evidence, but even have found it good enough. This very law which the logicians would impose upon us—if I may give the name of logicians to those who would rule out our willing nature here— is based on nothing but their own natural wish to exclude all elements for which they, in their professional quality of logicians, can find no use.

Evidently, then, our non-intellectual nature does influence our convictions. There are passional tendencies and volitions which run before and others which come after belief, and it is only the latter that are too late for the fair; and they are not too late when the previous passional work has been already in their own direction. Pascal's argument, instead of being powerless, then seems a regular clincher, and is the last stroke needed to make our faith in masses and holy water complete. The state of things is evidently far from simple; and pure insight and logic, whatever they might do ideally, are not the only things that really do produce our creeds.

IV.

Our next duty, having recognized this mixed-up state of affairs, is to ask whether it be simply reprehensible and pathological, or whether, on the contrary, we must treat it as a normal element in making up our minds. The thesis I defend is, briefly stated, this: *Our passional nature not only lawfully may, but must, decide an option between propositions, whenever it is a genuine option that cannot by its nature be decided on intellectual grounds; for to say, under such circumstances, "Do not decide, but leave the question open," is itself a passional decision,—just like deciding yes or no,—and is attended with the same risk of losing the truth.* The thesis thus abstractly expressed will, I trust, soon become quite clear. But I must first indulge in a bit more of preliminary work.

V.

It will be observed that for the purposes of this discussion we are on 'dogmatic' ground,—ground, I mean, which leaves systematic philosophical scepticism altogether out of account. The postulate that there is truth, and that it is the destiny of our minds to attain it, we are deliberately resolving to make, though the sceptic will not make it. We part company with him, therefore, absolutely, at this point. But the faith that truth exists, and that our minds can find it, may be held in two ways. We may talk of the *empiricist* way and of the *absolutist* way of believing in truth. The absolutists in this matter say that we not only can attain to knowing truth, but we can *know when* we have attained to knowing it; while the empiricists think that although we may attain it, we cannot infallibly know when. To *know* is one thing, and to know for certain *that* we know is another. One may hold to the first being possible without the second; hence the empiricists and the absolutists, although neither of them is a sceptic in the usual philosophic sense of the term, show very different degrees of dogmatism in their lives.

If we look at the history of opinions, we see that the empiricist tendency has largely prevailed in science, while in philosophy the absolutist tendency has had everything its own way. The characteristic sort of happiness, indeed, which philosophies yield has mainly consisted in the conviction felt by each successive school or system that by it bottom-certitude had been attained. "Other philosophies are collections of opinions, mostly false; *my* philosophy gives standing-ground forever,"—who does not recognize in this the key-note of every system worthy of the name? A system, to be a system at all, must come as a *closed* system, reversible in this or that detail, perchance, but in its essential features never!

Scholastic orthodoxy, to which one must always go when one wishes to find perfectly clear statement, has beautifully elaborated this absolutist conviction in a doctrine which it calls that of 'objective evidence.' If, for example, I am unable to doubt that I now exist before you, that two is less than three, or that if all men are mortal then I am mortal too, it is because these things illumine my intellect irresistibly. The final ground of this objective evidence possessed by certain propositions is the *adæquatio intellectûs nostri cum rê*. The certitude it brings involves an *aptitudinem ad extorquendum certum assensum* on the part of the truth envisaged, and on the side of the subject a *quietem in cognitione*, when once the object is mentally received, that leaves no possibility of doubt behind; and in the whole transaction nothing operates but the *entitas ipsa* of the object and the *entitas ipsa* of the mind. We slouchy modern thinkers dislike to talk in Latin,— indeed, we dislike to talk in set terms at all; but at bottom our own state of mind is very much like this whenever we uncritically abandon ourselves: You believe in objective evidence, and I do. Of some things we feel that we are certain: we know, and we know that we do know. There is something that gives a click inside of us, a bell that strikes twelve, when the hands of our mental clock have swept the dial and meet over the meridian hour. The greatest empiricists among us are only empiricists on reflection: when left to their instincts, they dogmatize like infallible popes. When the Cliffords tell us how sinful it is to be Christians on such 'insufficient evidence,' insufficiency is really the last thing they have in mind. For them the evidence is absolutely sufficient, only it makes the other way. They believe so completely in an anti-christian order of the universe that there is no living option: Christianity is a dead hypothesis from the start.

VI.

But now, since we are all such absolutists by instinct, what in our quality of students of philosophy ought we to do about the fact? Shall we espouse and indorse it? Or shall we treat it as a weakness of our nature from which we must free ourselves, if we can?

I sincerely believe that the latter course is the only one we can follow as reflective men. Objective evidence and certitude are doubtless very fine ideals to play with, but where on this moonlit and dream-visited planet are they found? I am, therefore, myself a complete empiricist so far as my theory of human knowledge goes. I live, to be sure, by the practical faith that we must go on experiencing and thinking over our experience, for only thus can our opinions grow more true; but to hold any one of them—I absolutely do not care which—as if it never could be reinterpretable or corrigible, I believe to be a tremendously mistaken attitude, and I think that the whole history of philosophy will bear me out. There is but one indefectibly certain truth, and that is the truth that pyrrhonistic scepticism itself leaves standing,—the truth that the present phenomenon of consciousness exists. That, however, is the bare starting-point of knowledge, the mere admission of a stuff to be philosophized about. The various philosophies are but so many attempts at expressing what this stuff really is. And if we repair to our libraries what disagreement do we discover! Where is a certainly true answer found? Apart from abstract propositions of comparison (such as two and two are the same as four), propositions which tell us nothing by themselves about concrete reality, we find no proposition ever regarded by any one as evidently certain that has not either been called a falsehood, or at least had its truth sincerely questioned by some one else. The transcending of the axioms of geometry, not in play but in earnest, by certain of our contemporaries (as Zöllner and Charles H. Hinton), and the rejection of the whole Aristotelian logic by the Hegelians, are striking instances in point.

No concrete test of what is really true has ever been agreed upon. Some make the criterion external to the moment of perception, putting it either in revelation, the *consensus gentium,* the instincts of the heart, or the systematized experience of the race. Others make the perceptive moment its own test,—Descartes, for instance, with his clear and distinct ideas guaranteed by the veracity of God; Reid with his 'common-sense;' and Kant with his forms of synthetic judgment *a priori*. The inconceivability of the opposite; the capacity to be verified by sense; the possession of complete organic unity or self-relation, realized when a thing is its own other,—are standards which, in turn, have been used. The much lauded objective evidence is never triumphantly there; it is a mere aspiration or *Grenzbegriff*, marking the infinitely remote ideal of our thinking life. To claim that certain truths now possess it, is simply to say that when you think them true and they *are* true, then their evidence is objective, otherwise it is not. But practically one's conviction that the evidence one goes by is of the real objective brand, is only one more subjective opinion added to the lot. For what a contradictory array of opinions have objective evidence and absolute certitude been claimed! The world is rational through and through,—its existence is an ultimate brute fact; there is a personal God,—a personal God is inconceivable; there is an extra-mental physical world immediately known,—the mind can only know its own ideas; a moral imperative exists,—obligation is only the resultant of desires; a permanent spiritual principle is in every one,— there are only shifting states of mind; there is an endless chain of causes,— there is an absolute first cause; an eternal necessity,—a freedom; a purpose,—no purpose; a primal One,—a primal Many; a universal continuity,— an essential discontinuity in things; an infinity,—no infinity. There is this,— there is that; there is indeed nothing which some one has not thought absolutely true, while his neighbor deemed it absolutely false; and not an absolutist among them seems ever to have considered that the trouble may all the time be essential, and that the intellect, even with truth directly in its grasp, may have no infallible signal for knowing whether it be truth or no. When, indeed, one remembers that the most striking practical application to life of the doctrine of objective certitude has been the conscientious labors of the Holy Office of the Inquisition, one feels less tempted than ever to lend the doctrine a respectful ear.

But please observe, now, that when as empiricists we give up the doctrine of objective certitude, we do not thereby give up the quest or hope of truth itself. We still pin our faith on its existence, and still believe that we gain an ever better position towards it by systematically continuing to roll up experiences and think. Our great difference from the scholastic lies in the way we face. The strength of his system lies in the principles, the origin, the *terminus a quo* of his thought; for us the strength is in the outcome, the upshot, the *terminus ad quem*. Not where it comes from but what it leads to is to decide. It matters not to an empiricist from what quarter an hypothesis may come to him: he may have acquired it by fair means or by foul; passion may have whispered or accident suggested it; but if the total drift of thinking continues to confirm it, that is what he means by its being true.

VII.

One more point, small but important, and our preliminaries are done. There are two ways of looking at our duty in the matter of opinion,—ways entirely different, and yet ways about whose difference the theory of knowledge seems hitherto to have shown very little concern. *We must know the truth;* and *we must avoid error*,—these are our first and great command-ments as would-be knowers; but they are not two ways of stating an identical commandment, they are two separable laws. Although it may indeed happen that when we believe the truth *A*, we escape as an incidental consequence from believing the falsehood *B*, it hardly ever happens that by merely disbelieving *B* we necessarily believe *A*. We may in escaping *B* fall into believing other falsehoods, *C* or *D*, just as bad as *B;* or we may escape *B* by not believing anything at all, not even *A*.

Believe truth! Shun error!—these, we see, are two materially different laws; and by choosing between them we may end by coloring differently our whole intellectual life. We may regard the chase for truth as paramount, and the avoidance of error as secondary; or we may, on the other hand, treat the avoidance of error as more imperative, and let truth take its chance. Clifford, in the instructive passage which I have quoted, exhorts us to the latter course. Believe nothing, he tells us, keep your mind in suspense forever, rather than by closing it on insufficient evidence incur the awful risk of believing lies. You, on the other hand, may think that the risk of being in error is a very small matter when compared with the blessings of real knowledge, and be ready to be duped many times in your investigation rather than postpone indefinitely the chance of guessing true. I myself find it impossible to go with Clifford. We must remember that these feelings of our duty about either truth or error are in any case only expressions of our passional life. Biologically considered, our minds are as ready to grind out falsehood as veracity, and he who says, "Better go without belief forever than believe a lie!" merely shows his own preponderant private horror of becom-ing a dupe. He may be critical of many of his desires and fears, but this fear he slavishly obeys. He cannot imagine any one questioning its binding force. For my own part, I have also a horror of being duped; but I can believe that worse things than being duped may happen to a man in this world: so Clifford's exhortation has to my ears a thoroughly fantastic sound. It is like a general informing his soldiers that it is better to keep out of battle forever than to risk a single wound. Not so are victories either over enemies or over nature gained. Our errors are surely not such awfully solemn things. In a world where we are so certain to incur them in spite of all our caution, a certain lightness of heart seems healthier than this excessive nervousness on their behalf. At any rate, it seems the fittest thing for the empiricist phi-losopher.

VIII.

And now, after all this introduction, let us go straight at our question. I have said, and now repeat it, that not only as a matter of fact do we find our passional nature influencing us in our opinions, but that there are some options between opinions in which this influence must be regarded both as an inevitable and as a lawful determinant of our choice.

I fear here that some of you my hearers will begin to scent danger, and lend an inhospitable ear. Two first steps of passion you have indeed had to admit as necessary,—we must think so as to avoid dupery, and we must think so as to gain truth; but the surest path to those ideal consummations, you will probably consider, is from now onwards to take no further passional step.

Well, of course, I agree as far as the facts will allow. Wherever the option between losing truth and gaining it is not momentous, we can throw the chance of *gaining truth* away, and at any rate save ourselves from any chance of *believing falsehood*, by not making up our minds at all till objective evidence has come. In scientific questions, this is almost always the case; and even in human affairs in general, the need of acting is seldom so urgent that a false belief to act on is better than no belief at all. Law courts, indeed, have to decide on the best evidence attainable for the moment, because a judge's duty is to make law as well as to ascertain it, and (as a learned judge once said to me) few cases are worth spending much time over: the great thing is to have them decided on *any* acceptable principle, and got out of the way. But in our dealings with objective nature we obviously are recorders, not makers, of the truth; and decisions for the mere sake of deciding promptly and getting on to the next business would be wholly out of place. Throughout the breadth of physical nature facts are what they are quite independently of us, and seldom is there any such hurry about them that the risks of being duped by believing a premature theory need be faced. The questions here are always trivial options, the hypotheses are hardly living (at any rate not living for us spectators), the choice between believing truth or falsehood is seldom forced. The attitude of sceptical balance is therefore the absolutely wise one if we would escape mistakes. What difference, indeed, does it make to most of us whether we have or have not a theory of the Röntgen rays, whether we believe or not in mind-stuff, or have a conviction about the causality of conscious states? It makes no difference. Such options are not forced on us. On every account it is better not to make them, but still keep weighing reasons *pro et contra* with an indifferent hand.

I speak, of course, here of the purely judging mind. For purposes of discovery such indifference is to be less highly recommended, and science would be far less advanced than she is if the passionate desires of individuals to get their own faiths confirmed had been kept out of the game. See for example the sagacity which Spencer and Weismann now display. On the other hand, if you want an absolute duffer in an investigation, you must, after all, take the man who has no interest whatever in its results: he is the warranted incapable, the positive fool. The most useful investigator, because the most sensitive observer, is always he whose eager interest in one side of the question is balanced by an equally keen nervousness lest he become deceived.[1] Science has organized this nervousness into a regular *technique,* her so-called method of verification; and she has fallen so deeply in love with the method that one may even say she has ceased to care for truth by itself at all. It is only truth as technically verified that interests her. The truth of truths might come in merely affirmative form, and she would decline to touch it. Such truth as that, she might repeat with Clifford, would be stolen in defiance of her duty to mankind. Human passions, however, are stronger than technical rules. "Le cœur a ses raisons," as Pascal says, "que la raison ne connaî pas;" and however indifferent to all but the bare rules of the game the umpire, the abstract intellect, may be, the concrete players who furnish him the materials to judge of are usually, each one of them, in love with some pet 'live hypothesis' of his own. Let us agree, however, that wherever there is no forced option, the dispassionately judicial intellect with no pet hypothesis, saving us, as it does, from dupery at any rate, ought to be our ideal.

The question next arises: Are there not somewhere forced options in our speculative questions, and can we (as men who may be interested at least as much in positively gaining truth as in merely escaping dupery) always wait with impunity till the coercive evidence shall have arrived? It seems *a priori* improbable that the truth should be so nicely adjusted to our needs and powers as that. In the great boarding-house of nature, the cakes and the butter and the syrup seldom come out so even and leave the plates so clean. Indeed, we should view them with scientific suspicion if they did.

IX.

Moral questions immediately present themselves as questions whose solution cannot wait for sensible proof. A moral question is a question not of what sensibly exists, but of what is good, or would be good if it did exist. Science can tell us what exists; but to compare the *worths,* both of what exists and of what does not exist, we must consult not science, but what Pascal calls our heart. Science herself consults her heart when she lays it down that the infinite ascertainment of fact and correction of false belief are the supreme goods for man. Challenge the statement, and science can only repeat it oracularly, or else prove it by showing that such ascertainment and correction bring man all sorts of other goods which man's heart in turn declares. The question of having moral beliefs at all or not having them is decided by our will. Are our moral preferences true or false, or are they only odd biological phenomena, making things good or bad for *us,* but in themselves indifferent? How can your pure intellect decide? If your heart does not *want* a world of moral reality, your head will assuredly never make you believe in one. Mephistophelian scepticism, indeed, will satisfy the head's play-instincts

---

[1]Compare Wilfrid Ward's Essay, "The Wish to Believe," in his *Witnesses to the Unseen,* Macmillan & Co., 1893.

much better than any rigorous idealism can. Some men (even at the student age) are so naturally cool-hearted that the moralistic hypothesis never has for them any pungent life, and in their supercilious presence the hot young moralist always feels strangely ill at ease. The appearance of knowingness is on their side, of *naïveté* and gullibility on his. Yet, in the inarticulate heart of him, he clings to it that he is not a dupe, and that there is a realm in which (as Emerson says) all their wit and intellectual superiority is no better than the cunning of a fox. Moral scepticism can no more be refuted or proved by logic than intellectual scepticism can. When we stick to it that there *is* truth (be it of either kind), we do so with our whole nature, and resolve to stand or fall by the results. The sceptic with his whole nature adopts the doubting attitude; but which of us is the wiser, Omniscience only knows.

Turn now from these wide questions of good to a certain class of questions of fact, questions concerning personal relations, states of mind between one man and another. *Do you like me or not?*—for example. Whether you do or not depends, in countless instances, on whether I meet you half-way, am willing to assume that you must like me, and show you trust and expectation. The previous faith on my part in your liking's existence is in such cases what makes your liking come. But if I stand aloof, and refuse to budge an inch until I have objective evidence, until you shall have done something apt, as the absolutists say, *ad extorquendum assensum meum*, ten to one your liking never comes. How many women's hearts are vanquished by the mere sanguine insistence of some man that they *must* love him! he will not consent to the hypothesis that they cannot. The desire for a certain kind of truth here brings about that special truth's existence; and so it is in innumerable cases of other sorts. Who gains promotions, boons, appointments, but the man in whose life they are seen to play the part of live hypotheses, who discounts them, sacrifices other things for their sake before they have come, and takes risks for them in advance? His faith acts on the powers above him as a claim, and creates its own verification.

A social organism of any sort whatever, large or small, is what it is because each member proceeds to his own duty with a trust that the other members will simultaneously do theirs. Wherever a desired result is achieved by the co-operation of many independent persons, its existence as a fact is a pure consequence of the precursive faith in one another of those immediately concerned. A government, an army, a commercial system, a ship, a college, an athletic team, all exist on this condition, without which not only is nothing achieved, but nothing is even attempted. A whole train of passengers (individually brave enough) will be looted by a few highwaymen, simply because the latter can count on one another, while each passenger fears that if he makes a movement of resistance, he will be shot before any one else backs him up. If we believed that the whole car-full would rise at once with us, we should each severally rise, and train-robbing would never even be attempted. There are, then, cases where a fact cannot come at all unless a preliminary faith exists in its coming. *And where faith in a fact can help create the fact*, that would be an insane logic which should say that faith running ahead of scientific evidence is the 'lowest kind of immorality' into which a thinking being can fall. Yet such is the logic by which our scientific absolutists pretend to regulate our lives!

X.

In truths dependent on our personal action, then, faith based on desire is certainly a lawful and possibly an indispensable thing.

But now, it will be said, these are all childish human cases, and have nothing to do with great cosmical matters, like the question of religious faith. Let us then pass on to that. Religions differ so much in their accidents that in discussing the religious question we must make it very generic and broad. What then do we now mean by the religious hypothesis? Science says things are; morality says some things are better than other things; and religion says essentially two things.

First, she says that the best things are the more eternal things, the overlapping things, the things in the universe that throw the last stone, so to speak, and say the final word. "Perfection is eternal,"—this phrase of Charles Secrétan seems a good way of putting this first affirmation of religion, an affirmation which obviously cannot yet be verified scientifically at all.

The second affirmation of religion is that we are better off even now if we believe her first affirmation to be true.

Now, let us consider what the logical elements of this situation are *in case the religious hypothesis in both its branches be really true*. (Of course, we must admit that possibility at the outset. If we are to discuss the question at all, it must involve a living option. If for any of you religion be a hypothesis that cannot, by any living possibility be true, then you need go no farther. I speak to the 'saving remnant' alone.) So proceeding, we see, first, that religion offers itself as a *momentous* option. We are supposed to gain, even now, by our belief, and to lose by our nonbelief, a certain vital good. Secondly, religion is a *forced* option, so far as that good goes. We cannot escape the issue by remaining sceptical and waiting for more light, because, although we do avoid error in that way *if religion be untrue*, we lose the good, *if it be true*, just as certainly as if we positively chose to disbelieve. It is as if a man should hesitate indefinitely to ask a certain woman to marry him because he was not perfectly sure that she would prove an angel after he brought her home. Would he not cut himself off from that particular angel-possibility as decisively as if he went and married some one else? Scepticism, then, is not avoidance of option; it is option of a certain particular kind of risk. *Better risk loss of truth than chance of error,*—that is your faith-vetoer's exact position. He is actively playing his stake as much as the believer is; he is backing the field against the religious hypothesis, just as the believer is backing the religious hypothesis against the field. To preach scepticism to us as a duty until 'sufficient evidence' for religion be found, is tantamount therefore to telling us, when in presence of the religious hypothesis, that to yield to our fear of its being error is wiser and better than to yield to our hope that it may be true. It is not intellect against all passions, then; it is only intellect with one passion laying down its law. And by what, forsooth, is the supreme wisdom of this passion warranted? Dupery for dupery, what proof is there that dupery through hope is so much worse than dupery through fear? I, for one, can see no proof; and I simply refuse obedience to the scientist's command to imitate his kind of option, in a case where my own stake is important enough to give me the right to choose my own form of risk. If religion be true and the evidence for it be still insufficient, I do not wish, by putting your extinguisher upon my nature (which feels to me as if it had after all some business in this matter), to forfeit my sole chance in life of getting upon the winning side,—that chance depending, of course, on my willing-ness to run the risk of acting as if my passional need of taking the world religiously might be prophetic and right.

All this is on the supposition that it really may be prophetic and right, and that, even to us who are discussing the matter, religion is a live hypoth-esis which may be true. Now, to most of us religion comes in a still further way that makes a veto on our active faith even more illogical. The more perfect and more eternal aspect of the universe is represented in our re-ligions as having personal form. The universe is no longer a mere *It* to us, but a *Thou*, if we are religious; and any relation that may be possible from person to person might be possible here. For instance, although in one sense we are passive portions of the universe, in another we show a curious autonomy, as if we were small active centres on our own account. We feel, too, as if the appeal of religion to us were made on our own active good-will, as if evidence might be forever withheld from us unless we met the hypothesis half-way. To take a trivial illustration: just as a man who in a company of gentlemen made no advances, asked a warrant for every concession, and believed no one's word without proof, would cut himself off by such churlishness from all the social rewards that a more trusting spirit would earn,—so here, one who should shut himself up in snarling logicality and try to make the gods extort his recognition willy-nilly, or not get it at all, might cut himself off forever from his only opportunity of making the gods' acquaintance. This feeling, forced on us we know not whence, that by obstinately believing that there are gods (although not to do so would be so easy both for our logic and our life) we are doing the universe the deepest service we can, seems part of the living essence of the religious hypothesis. If the hypothesis *were* true in all its parts, including this one, then pure intellectualism, with its veto on our making willing advances, would be an absurdity; and some participation of our sympathetic nature would be logically required. I, therefore, for one, cannot see my way to accepting the agnostic rules for truth-seeking, or wilfully agree to keep my willing nature out of the game. I cannot do so for this plain reason, that *a rule of thinking which would absolutely prevent me from acknowledging certain kinds of truth if those kinds of truth were really there, would be an irrational rule*. That for me is the long and short of the formal logic of the situation, no matter what the kinds of truth might materially be.

I confess I do not see how this logic can be escaped. But sad experience makes me fear that some of you may still shrink from radically saying with me, *in abstracto*, that we have the right to believe at our own risk any hypothesis that is live enough to tempt our will. I suspect, however, that if this is so, it is because you have got away from the abstract logical point of view altogether, and are thinking (perhaps without realizing it) of some particular religious hypothesis which for you is dead. The freedom to 'believe what we will' you apply to the case of some patent superstition; and the faith you think of is the faith defined by the schoolboy when he said, "Faith is when you believe something that you know ain't true." I can only repeat that this is misapprehension. *In concreto*, the freedom to believe can only cover living options which the intellect of the individual cannot by itself resolve; and living options never seem absurdities to him who has them to consider. When I look at the religious question as it really puts itself to concrete men, and when I think of all the possibilities which both practically and theoretically it involves, then this command that we shall put a stopper on our heart, instincts, and courage, and *wait*—acting of course meanwhile more or less as if religion were *not* true[1]—till doomsday, or till such time as our intellect and senses working together may have raked in evidence enough,—this command, I say, seems to me the queerest idol ever manufactured in the philosophic cave. Were we scholastic absolutists, there might be more excuse. If we had an infallible intellect with its objective certitudes, we might feel ourselves disloyal to such a perfect organ of knowledge in not trusting to it exclusively, in not waiting for its releasing word. But if we are empiricists, if we believe that no bell in us tolls to let us know for certain when truth is in our grasp, then it seems a piece of idle fantasticality to preach so solemnly our duty of waiting for the bell. Indeed we *may* wait if we will,—I hope you do not think that I am denying that,—but if we do so, we do so at our peril as much as if we believed. In either case we *act*, taking our life in our hands. No

---

[1] Since belief is measured by action, he who forbids us to believe religion to be true, necessarily also forbids us to act as we should if we did believe it to be true. The whole defence of religious faith hinges upon action. If the action required or inspired by the religious hypothesis is in no way different from that dictated by the naturalistic hypothesis, then religious faith is a pure superfluity, better pruned away, and controversy about its legitimacy is a piece of idle trifling, unworthy of serious minds. I myself believe, of course, that the religious hypothesis gives to the world an expression which specifically determines our reactions, and makes them in a large part unlike what they might be on a purely naturalistic scheme of belief.

one of us ought to issue vetoes to the other, nor should we bandy words of abuse. We ought, on the contrary, delicately and profoundly to respect one another's mental freedom: then only shall we bring about the intellectual republic; then only shall we have that spirit of inner tolerance without which all our outer tolerance is soulless, and which is empiricism's glory; then only shall we live and let live, in speculative as well as in practical things.

I began by a reference to Fitz James Stephen; let me end by a quotation from him. "What do you think of yourself? What do you think of the world? . . . These are questions with which all must deal as it seems good to them. They are riddles of the Sphinx, and in some way or other we must deal with them. . . . In all important transactions of life we have to take a leap in the dark. . . . If we decide to leave the riddles unanswered, that is a choice; if we waver in our answer, that, too, is a choice: but whatever choice we make, we make it at our peril. If a man chooses to turn his back altogether on God and the future, no one can prevent him; no one can show beyond reasonable doubt that he is mistaken. If a man thinks otherwise and acts as he thinks, I do not see that any one can prove that *he* is mistaken. Each must act as he thinks best; and if he is wrong, so much the worse for him. We stand on a mountain pass in the midst of whirling snow and blinding mist, through which we get glimpses now and then of paths which may be deceptive. If we stand still we shall be frozen to death. If we take the wrong road we shall be dashed to pieces. We do not certainly know whether there is any right one. What must we do? 'Be strong and of a good courage.' Act for the best, hope for the best, and take what comes. . . . If death ends all, we cannot meet death better."[1]

[1] Liberty, Equality, Fraternity, p. 353, 2d edition. London, 1874.

AN ESSAY IN AID OF A GRAMMAR OF ASSENT
John H. Newman

SIMPLE ASSENT

The doctrine which I have been enunciating requires such careful explanation, that it is not wonderful that writers of great ability and name are to be
found who have put it aside for a doctrine of their own; but no doctrine on the
subject is without its difficulties, and certainly not theirs, though it carries
with it a show of common sense. The authors to whom I refer wish to
maintain that there are degrees of assent, and that, as the reasons for a
proposition are strong or weak, so is the assent. It follows from this that
absolute assent has no legitimate exercise, except as ratifying acts of intuition
or demonstration. What is thus brought home to us is indeed to be accepted
unconditionally; but as to reasonings in concrete matters, they are never
more than probabilities, and the probability in each conclusion which we
draw is the measure of our assent to that conclusion. Thus assent becomes a
sort of necessary shadow, following upon inference, which is the substance;
and is never without some alloy of doubt, because inference in the concrete
never reaches more than probability.

Such is what may be called the *à priori* method of regarding assent in its
relation to inference. It condemns an unconditional assent in concrete matters on what may be called the nature of the case. Assent cannot rise higher
than its source; inference in such matters is at best conditional, therefore
assent is conditional also.

Abstract argument is always dangerous, and this instance is no exception
to the rule; I prefer to go by facts. The theory to which I have referred cannot
be carried out in practice. It may be rightly said to prove too much; for it
debars us from unconditional assent in cases in which the common voice of
mankind, the advocates of this theory included, would protest against the
prohibition. There are many truths in concrete matter, which no one can
demonstrate, yet every one unconditionally accepts; and though of course
there are innumerable propositions to which it would be absurd to give an
absolute assent, still the absurdity lies in the circumstances of each particular
case, as it is taken by itself, not in their common violation of the pretentious
axiom that probable reasoning can never lead to certitude.

Locke's remarks on the subject are an illustration of what I have been
saying. This celebrated writer, after the manner of his school, speaks freely of

degrees of assent, and considers that the strength of assent given to each proposition varies with the strength of the inference on which the assent follows; yet he is obliged to make exceptions to his general principle,—exceptions, unintelligible on his abstract doctrine, but demanded by the logic of facts. The practice of mankind is too strong for the antecedent theorem, to which he is desirous to subject it.

First he says, in his chapter "On Probability," Most of the propositions we think, reason, discourse, nay, act upon, are such as we cannot have undoubted knowledge of their truth; yet some of them *border so near* upon certainty, that we *make* no doubt at all about them, but *assent* to them *as firmly,* and act according to that assent as resolutely, *as if they were infallibly demonstrated,* and that our knowledge of them was perfect and certain." Here he allows that inferences, which are only "near upon certainty," are so near, that we legitimately accept them with "no doubt at all," and "assent to them as firmly as if they were infallibly demonstrated." That is, he affirms and sanctions the very paradox to which I am committed myself.

Again; he says, in his chapter on "The Degrees of Assent," that "when any particular thing, consonant to the constant observation of ourselves and others in the like case, comes attested by the concurrent reports of all that mention it, we receive it as easily, and build as firmly upon it, as if it were certain knowledge, and we reason and act thereupon, *with as little doubt as if it were perfect demonstration.*" And he repeats, "These *probabilities* rise so near to certainty, that they *govern our thoughts as absolutely,* and influence all our actions as fully, as *the most evident demonstration;* and in what concerns us, we make little or no difference between them and certain knowledge. *Our belief thus grounded, rises to assurance.*" Here again, "probabilities" may be so strong as to "govern our thoughts as absolutely" as sheer demonstration, so strong that belief, grounded on them, "rises to assurance," that is, to certitude.

I have so high a respect both for the character and the ability of Locke, for his manly simplicity of mind and his outspoken candour, and there is so much in his remarks upon reasoning and proof in which I fully concur, that I feel no pleasure in considering him in the light of an opponent to views which I myself have ever cherished as true, with an obstinate devotion; and I would willingly think that in the passage which follows in his chapter on "Enthusiasm," he is aiming at superstitious extravagances which I should repudiate myself as much as he can do; but, if so, his words go beyond the occasion, and contradict what I have quoted from him above.

"He that would seriously set upon the search of truth, ought, in the first place, to prepare his mind with a love of it. For he that loves it not will not take much pains to get it, nor be much concerned when he misses it. There is nobody, in the commonwealth of learning, who does not profess himself a lover of truth,—and there is not a rational creature, that would not take it amiss, to be thought otherwise of. And yet, for all this, one may truly say, there are very few lovers of truth, for truth-sake, even amongst those who persuade themselves that they are so. How a man may know, whether he be so, in earnest, is worth inquiry; and I think, there is this one unerring mark of it, viz. *the not entertaining any proposition with greater assurance than the proofs it is built on will warrant.* Whoever goes beyond this measure of assent, it is plain, receives not truth in the love of it, loves not truth for truth-sake, but for some other by-end. For the evidence that any proposition is true *(except such as are self-evident)* lying only in the proofs a man has of it, whatsoever degrees of assent he affords it *beyond the degrees of that* evidence, it is plain *all that surplusage of assurance* is owing to some other affection, and not to the love of truth; it being as *impossible* that the love of truth should carry *my assent above the evidence* there is to me that it is true, as that the love of truth should make me assent to any proposition for the sake of that evidence which it has not that it is true; which is in effect to love it as a truth, because it is possible or probable that it may not be true."[1]

Here he says that it is not only illogical, but immoral to "carry our *assent above* the *evidence* that a proposition is true," to have "a surplusage of *assurance beyond* the degrees of that evidence." And he excepts from this rule only self-evident propositions. How then is it not consistent with right reason, with the love of truth for its own sake, to allow in his words quoted above, certain strong "probabilities" to "govern our thoughts as absolutely as the most evident demonstration"? how is there no "surplusage of assurance beyond the degrees of evidence" when in the case of those strong probabilities, we permit "our belief, thus grounded, to rise to assurance," as he pronounces we are rational in doing? Of course he had in view one set of instances, when he implied that demonstration was the condition of absolute assent, and another set when he said that it was no such condition; but he surely cannot be acquitted of slovenly thinking in thus treating a cardinal subject. A philosopher should so anticipate the application, and guard the enunciation of his principles, as to secure them against the risk of their being made to change places with each other, to defend what he is eager to denounce, and to condemn what he finds it necessary to sanction. However, whatever is to be thought of his *à priori* method and his logical consistency, his *animus*, I fear, must be understood as hostile to the doctrine which I am going to maintain. He takes a view of the human mind, in relation to inference and assent, which to me seems theoretical and unreal. Reasonings and convictions which I deem natural and legitimate, he apparently would call irrational, enthusiastic, perverse, and immoral; and that, as I think, because he consults his own ideal of how the mind ought to act, instead of interrogating human nature, as an existing thing, as it is found in the world. Instead of going by the testimony of psychological facts, and thereby determining our constitutive faculties and our proper condition, and being con-

---

[1] Reference is made to Locke's statements in "Essay on Development of Doctrine," ch. vii § 2.

tent with the mind as God has made it, he would form men as he thinks they ought to be formed, into something better and higher, and calls them irrational and indefensible, if (so to speak) they take to the water, instead of remaining under the narrow wings of his own arbitrary theory.

1. Now the first question which this theory leads me to consider is, whether there is such an act of the mind as assent at all. If there is, it is plain it ought to show itself unequivocally as such, as distinct from other acts. For if a professed act can only be viewed as the necessary and immediate repetition of another act, if assent is a sort of reproduction and double of an act of inference, if when inference determines that a proposition is somewhat, or not a little, or a good deal, or very like truth, assent as its natural and normal counterpart says that it *is* somewhat, or not a little, or a good deal, or very like truth, then I do not see what we mean by saying, or why we say at all, that there is any such act. It is simply superfluous, in a psychological point of view, and a curiosity for subtle minds, and the sooner it is got out of the way the better. When I assent, I am supposed, it seems, to do precisely what I do when I infer, or rather not quite so much, but something which is included in inferring; for, while the disposition of my mind towards a given proposition is identical in assent and in inference, I merely drop the thought of the premisses when I assent, though not of their influence on the proposition inferred. This then, and no more after all, is what nature prescribes, and this, and no more than this, is the conscientious use of our faculties, so to assent forsooth as to do nothing else than infer. Then, I say, if this be really the state of the case, if assent in no real way differs from inference, it is one and the same thing with it. It is another name for inference, and to speak of it at all does but mislead. Nor can it fairly be urged as a parallel case that an act of conscious recognition, though distinct from an act of knowledge, is after all only its repetition. On the contrary, such a recognition is a reflex act with its own object, viz. the act of knowledge itself. As well might it be said that the hearing of the notes of my voice is a repetition of the act of singing:—it gives no plausibility then to the anomaly I am combating.

I lay it down, then, as a principle that either assent is intrinsically distinct from inference, or the sooner we get rid of the word in philosophy the better. If it be only the echo of an inference, do not treat it as a substantive act; but, on the other hand, supposing it be not such an idle repetition, as I am sure it is not, supposing the word "assent" does hold a rightful place in language and in thought, if it does not admit of being confused with concluding and inferring, if the two words are used for two operations of the intellect which cannot change their character, if in matter of fact they are not always found together, if they do not vary with each other, if one is sometimes found without the other, if one is strong when the other is weak, if sometimes they seem even in conflict with each other, then, since we know perfectly well what an inference is, it comes upon us to consider what, as distinct from inference, an assent is, and we are, by the very fact of its being distinct, advanced one step towards that account of it which I think is the true one. The first step then towards deciding the point, will be to inquire what the experience of human life, as it is daily brought before us, teaches us of the relation to each other of inference and assent.

2. And in showing that assent is distinct from an act of inference, I have gone a long way towards showing in what it differs from it. If assent and inference are each of them the acceptance of a proposition, but the special characteristic of inference is that it is conditional, it is natural to suppose that assent is unconditional. Again, if assent is the acceptance of truth, and truth is the proper object of the intellect, and no one can hold conditionally what by the same act he holds to be true, here too is a reason for saying that assent is an adhesion without reserve or doubt to the proposition to which it is given. And again, it is to be presumed that the word has not two meanings: what it has at one time, it has at another. Inference is always inference; even if demonstrative, it is still conditional; it establishes an introvertible conclusion on the condition of incontrovertible premises. To the conclusion thus drawn, assent gives its absolute recognition. In the case of all demonstration, assent, when given, is unconditionally given. In one class of subjects, then, assent certainly is always unconditional; but if the word stands for an undoubting and unhesitating act of the mind once, why does it not denote the same always? what evidence is there that it ever means any thing else than that which the whole world will unite in witnessing that it means in certain cases? why are we not to interpret what is controverted by what is known? This is what is suggested on the first view of the question; but to continue:—

In demonstrative matters assent excludes the presence of doubt: now are instances producible, on the other hand, of its ever co-existing with doubt in cases of the concrete? As the above instances have shown, on very many questions we do not give an assent at all. What commonly happens is this, that, after hearing and entering into what may be said for a proposition, we pronounce neither for nor against it. We may accept the conclusion as a conclusion, dependent on premises, abstract, and tending to the concrete; but we do not follow up our inference of a proposition by giving an assent to it. That there are concrete propositions to which we give unconditional assents, I shall presently show; but I am now asking for instances of conditional, for instances in which we assent a little and not much. Usually, we do not assent at all. Every day, as it comes, brings with it opportunities for us to enlarge our circle of assents. We read the newspapers; we look through debates in Parliament, pleadings in the law courts, leading articles, letters of correspondents, reviews of books, criticisms in the fine arts, and we either form no opinion at all upon the subjects discussed, as lying out of our line, or at most we have only an opinion about them. At the utmost we say that we are inclined to believe this proposition or that, that we are not sure it is not true, that much may be said for it, that we have been much struck by it; but we never say that we give it a degree of assent. We might as well talk of degrees of truth as of degrees of assent.

Yet Locke heads one of his chapters with the title "Degrees of Assent;" and a writer, of this century, who claims our respect from the tone and drift of his work, thus expresses himself after Locke's manner: "Moral evidence," he says, "may produce a variety of degrees of assents, from suspicion to moral certainty. For, here, the degree of assent depends upon the degree in which the evidence on one side preponderates, or exceeds that on the other. And as this preponderancy may vary almost infinitely, so likewise may the degrees of assent. For a few of these degrees, though but for a few, names have been invented. Thus, when the evidence on one side preponderates a very little, there is ground for suspicion, or conjecture. Presumption, persuasion, belief, conclusion, conviction, moral certainty,—doubt, wavering, distrust, disbelief,—are words which imply an increase or decrease of this preponderancy. Some of these words also admit of épithets which denote a further increase or diminution of the assent."[1]

Can there be a better illustration than this passage supplies of what I have been insisting on above, viz. that, in teaching various degrees of assent, we tend to destroy assent, as an act of the mind, altogether? This author makes the degrees of assent "infinite," as the degrees of probability are infinite. His assents are really only inferences, and assent is a name without a meaning, the needless repetition of an inference. But in truth "suspicion, conjecture, presumption, persuasion, belief, conclusion, conviction, moral certainty," are not, "assents" at all; they are simply more or less strong inferences of a proposition; and "doubt, wavering, distrust, disbelief," are recognitions, more or less strong, of the probability of its contradictory.

There is only one sense in which we are allowed to call such acts or states of mind assents. They are opinions; and, as being such, they are, as I have already observed, when speaking of Opinion, assents to the plausibility, probability, doubtfulness, or untrustworthiness, of a proposition; that is, not variations of assent to an inference, but assents to a variation in inferences. When I assent to a doubtfulness, or to a probability, my assent, as such, is as complete as if I assented to a truth; it is not a certain degree of assent. And, in like manner, I may be certain of an uncertainty; that does not destroy the specific notion conveyed in the word "certain."

I do not know then when it is that we ever deliberately profess assent to a proposition without meaning to convey to others the impression that we accept it unreservedly, and that because it is true. Certainly, we familiarly use such phrases as a half-assent, as we also speak of half-truths; but a half-assent is not a kind of assent any more than a half-truth is a kind of truth. As the object is indivisible, so is the act. A half-truth is a proposition which in

---

[1] Gambier on Moral Evidence, p. 6.

one aspect is a truth, and in another is not; to give a half-assent is to feel drawn towards assent, or to assent one moment and not the next, or to be in the way to assent to it. It means that the proposition in question deserves a hearing, that it is probable or attractive, that it opens important views, that it is a key to perplexing difficulties, or the like.

3. Treating the subject then, not according to *à priori* fitness, but according to the facts of human nature, as they are found in the concrete action of life, I find numberless cases in which we do not assent at all, none in which assent is evidently conditional;—and many, as I shall now proceed to show, in which it is unconditional, and these in subject-matters which admit of nothing higher than probable reasoning. If human nature is to be its own witness, there is no medium between assenting and not assenting. Locke's theory of the duty of assenting more or less according to degrees of evidence, is invalidated by the testimony of high and low, young and old, ancient and modern, as continually given in their ordinary sayings and doings. Indeed, as I have shown, he does not strictly maintain it himself; yet, though he feels the claims of nature and fact to be too strong for him in certain cases, he gives no reason why he should violate his theory in these, and yet not in many more.

Now let us review some of those assents, which men give on evidence short of intuition and demonstration, yet which are as unconditional as if they had that highest evidence.

First of all, starting from intuition, of course we all believe, without any doubt, that we exist; that we have an individuality and identity all our own; that we think, feel and act, in the home of our own minds; that we have a present sense of good and evil, of a right and a wrong, of a true and a false, of a beautiful and a hideous, however we analyze our ideas of them. We have an absolute vision before us of what happened yesterday or last year, so as to be able without any chance of mistake to give evidence upon it in a court of justice, let the consequences be ever so serious. We are sure that of many things we are ignorant, that of many things we are in doubt, and that of many things we are not in doubt.

Nor is the assent which we give to facts limited to the range of self-consciousness. We are sure beyond all hazard of a mistake, that our own self is not the only being existing; that there is an external world; that it is a system with parts and a whole, a universe carried on by laws; and that the future is affected by the past. We accept and hold with an unqualified assent, that the earth, considered as a phenomenon, is a globe; that all its regions see the sun by turns; that there are vast tracts on it of land and water; that there are really existing cities on definite sites, which go by the names of London, Paris, Florence, and Madrid. We are sure that Paris or London, unless suddenly swallowed up by an earthquake or burned to the ground, is to-day just what it was yesterday, when we left it.

We laugh to scorn the idea that we had no parents, though we have no memory of our birth; that we shall never depart this life, though we can have no experience of the future; that we are able to live without food, though we have never tried; that a world of men did not live before our time, or that that world has had no history; that there has been no rise and fall of states, no great men, no wars, no revolutions, no art, no science, no literature, no religion.

We should be either indignant or amused at the report of our intimate friend being false to us; and we are able sometimes, without any hesitation, to accuse certain parties of hostility and injustice to us. We may have a deep consciousness, which we never can lose, that we on our part have been cruel to others, and that they have felt us to be so, or that we have been, and have been felt to be, ungenerous to those who love us. We may have an over-powering sense of our moral weakness, of the precariousness of our life, health, wealth, position, and good fortune. We may have a clear view of the weak points of our physical constitution, of what food or medicine is good for us, and what does us harm. We may be able to master, at least in part, the course of our past history; its turning-points, our hits, and our great mistakes. We may have a sense of the presence of a Supreme Being, which never has been dimmed by even a passing shadow, which has inhabited us ever since we can recollect any thing, and which we cannot imagine our losing. We may be able, for others have been able, so to realize the precepts and truths of Christianity, as deliberately to surrender our life, rather than transgress the one or to deny the other.

On all these truths we have an immediate and an unhesitating hold, nor do we think ourselves guilty of not loving truth for truth's sake, because we cannot reach them through a series of intuitive propositions. Assent on reasonings not demonstrative is too widely recognized an act to be irrational, unless man's nature is irrational, too familiar to the prudent and clear-minded to be an infirmity or an extravagance. None of us can think or act without the acceptance of truths, not intuitive, not demonstrated, yet sovereign. If our nature has any constitution, any laws, one of them is this absolute reception of propositions as true, which lie outside the narrow range of conclusions to which logic, formal or virtual, is tethered; nor has any philosophical theory the power to force on us a rule which will not work for a day.

When, then, philosophers lay down principles, on which it follows that our assent, except when given to objects of intuition or demonstration, is conditional, that the assent given to propositions by well-ordered minds necessarily varies with the proof producible for them, and that it does not and cannot remain one and the same while the proof is strengthened or weakened,—are they not to be considered as confusing together two things very distinct from each other, a mental act or state and a scientific rule, an interior assent and a set of logical formulas? When they speak of degrees of assent, surely they have no intention at all of defining the position of the mind itself relative to the adoption of a given conclusion, but they are recording their perception of the relation of that conclusion towards its premisses. They are contemplating how representative symbols work, not how the intellect is affected towards the thing which those symbols represent. In real truth they as little mean to assert the principle of measuring our assents by our logic, as they would fancy they could record the refreshment which we receive from the open air by the readings of the graduated scale of a thermometer. There is a connexion doubtless between a logical conclusion and an assent, as there is between the variation of the mercury and our sensations; but the mercury is not the cause of life and health, nor is verbal argumentation the principle of inward belief. If we feel hot or chilly, no one will convince us to the contrary by insisting that the glass is at 60°. It is the mind that reasons and assents, not a diagram on paper. I may have difficulty in the management of a proof, while I remain unshaken in my adherence to the conclusion. Supposing a boy cannot make his answer to some arithmetical or algebraical question tally with the book, need he at once distrust the book? Does his trust in it fall down a certain number of degrees, according to the force of his difficulty? On the contrary, he keeps to the principle, implicit but present to his mind, with which he took up the book, that the book is more likely to be right than he is; and this mere preponderance of probability is sufficient to make him faithful to his belief in its correctness, till its incorrectness is actually proved.

My own opinion is, that the class of writers of whom I have been speaking, have themselves as little misgiving about the truths which they pretend to weigh out and measure as their unsophisticated neighbours; but they think it a duty to remind us, that since the full etiquette of logical requirements has not been satisfied, we must believe those truths at our peril. They warn us, that an issue which can never come to pass, in matter of fact, is nevertheless in theory a possible supposition. They do not, for instance, intend for a moment to imply that there is even the shadow of a doubt that Great Britain is an island, but they think we ought to know, if we do not know, that there is no proof of the fact, in mode and figure, equal to the proof of a proposition of Euclid; and that in consequence they and we are all bound to suspend our judgment about such a fact, though it be in an infinitesimal degree, lest we should seem not to love truth for truth's sake. Having made their protest, they subside without scruple into that same absolute assurance of only partially-proved truths, which is natural to the illogical imagination of the multitude.

INFORMAL INFERENCE

It is plain that formal logical sequence is not in fact the method by which we are enabled to become certain of what is concrete; and it is equally plain, from what has been already suggested, what the real and necessary method is. It is the cumulation of probabilities, independent of each other, arising out of the nature and circumstances of the particular case which is under review; probabilities too fine to avail separately, too subtle and circuitous to be convertible into syllogisms, too numerous and various for such conversion, even were they convertible. As a man's portrait differs from a sketch of him, in having, not merely a continuous outline, but all its details filled in, and shades and colours laid on and harmonized together, such is the multiform and intricate process of ratiocination, necessary for our reaching him as a concrete fact, compared with the rude operation of syllogistic treatment.

Let us suppose I wish to convert an educated, thoughtful Protestant, and accordingly present for his acceptance a syllogism of the following kind:— "All Protestants are bound to join the Church; you are a Protestant: ergo." He answers, we will say, by denying both premises; and he does so by means of arguments, which branch out into other arguments, and those into others, and all of them severally requiring to be considered by him on their own merits, before the syllogism reaches him, and in consequence mounting up, taken all together, into an array of inferential exercises large and various beyond calculation. Moreover, he is bound to submit himself to this complicated process from the nature of the case; he would act rashly, if he did not; for he is a concrete individual unit, and being so, is under so many laws, and is the subject of so many predications all at once, that he cannot determine, offhand, his position and his duty by the law and the predication of one syllogism in particular. I mean he may fairly say, "Distinguo," to each of its premises: he says, "Protestants are bound to join the Church,—under circumstances," and "I am a Protestant—in a certain sense;" and therefore the syllogism, at first sight, does not touch him at all.

Before, then, he grants the major, he asks whether all Protestants really are bound to join the Church—are they bound in case they do not feel themselves bound; if they are satisfied that their present religion is a safe one; if they are sure it is true; if, on the other hand, they have grave doubts as to the doctrinal fidelity and purity of the Church; if they are convinced that the Church is corrupt; if their conscience instinctively rejects certain of its doctrines; if history convinces them that the Pope's power is not *jure divino*, but merely in the order of Providence? if, again, they are in a heathen country where priests are not? or where the only priest who is to be found exacts of them, as a condition of their reception, a profession, which the Creed of Pope Pius IV, says nothing about; for instance, that the Holy See is fallible even when it teaches, or that the Temporal Power is anti-Christian corruption? On one or other of such grounds he thinks he need not change his religion; but presently he asks himself, Can a Protestant be in such a state as to be really satisfied with his religion, as he has just now been professing? Can he possibly believe Protestantism came from above, as a whole? how much of it can he believe came from above? and, as to that portion which he feels did come from above, has it not all been derived to him from the Church, when traced to its source? Is not Protestantism in itself a negation? Did not the Church exist before it? and can he be sure, on the other hand, that any one of the Church's doctrines is not from above? Further, he finds he has to make up his mind what is a corruption, and what are the tests of it; what he means by a religion; whether it is obligatory to profess any religion in particular; what are the standards of truth and falsehood in religion; and what are the special claims of the Church.

And so, again, as to the minor premiss, perhaps he will answer, that he is not a Protestant; that he is a Catholic of the early undivided Church; that he is a Catholic, but not a Papist. Then he has to determine questions about division, schism, visible unity, what is essential, what is desirable; about provisional states as to the adjustment of the Church's claims with those of personal judgment and responsibility; as to the soul of the Church contrasted with the body; as to degrees of proof, and the degree necessary for his conversion; as to what is called his providential position, and the responsibility of change; as to the sincerity of his purpose to follow the Divine Will, whithersoever it may lead him; as to his intellectual capacity of investigating such questions at all.

None of these questions, as they come before him, admit of simple demonstration; but each carries with it a number of independent probable arguments, sufficient, when united, for a reasonable conclusion about itself. And first he determines that the questions are such as he personally, with such talents or attainments as he has, may fairly entertain; and then he goes on, after deliberation, to form a definite judgment upon them; and determines them, one way or another, in their bearing on the bald syllogism which was originally offered to his acceptance. And, we will say, he comes to the conclusion, that he ought to accept it as true in his case; that he is a Protestant in such a sense, of such a complexion, of such knowledge, under such circumstances, as to be called upon by duty to join the Church; that this is a conclusion of which he can be certain, and ought to be certain, and that he will be incurring grave responsibility, if he does not accept it as certain, and act upon the certainty of it. And to this conclusion he comes, as is plain, not by any possible verbal enumeration of all the considerations, minute but abundant, delicate but effective, which unite to bring him to it; but by a mental comprehension of the whole case, and a discernment of its upshot, sometimes after much deliberation, but, it may be, by a clear and rapid act of the intellect, always, however, by an unwritten summing-up, something like the summation of the terms *plus* and *minus* of an algebraical series.

This I conceive to be the real reasoning in concrete matters; and it has these characteristics:—First, it does not supersede the logical form of inference, but is one and the same with it; only it is no longer an abstraction, but carried out into the realities of life, its premises being instinct with the substance and the momentum of that mass of probabilities, which, acting upon each other in correction and confirmation, carry it home definitely to the individual case, which is its original scope.

Next, from what has been said it is plain, that such a process of reasoning is more or less implicit, and without the direct and full advertence of the mind exercising it. As by the use of our eyesight we recognize two brothers, yet without being able to express what it is by which we distinguish them; as at first sight we perhaps confuse them together, but on better knowledge, we see no likeness between them at all; as it requires an artist's eye to determine what lines and shades make a countenance look young or old, amiable, thoughtful, angry or conceited, the principle of discrimination being in each case real, but implicit;—so is the mind unequal to a complete analysis of the motives which carry it on to a particular conclusion, and is swayed and determined by a body of proof, which it recognizes only as a body, and not in its constituent parts.

And thirdly, it is plain, that, in this investigation of the method of concrete inference, we have not advanced one step towards depriving inference of its conditional character; for it is still as dependent on premisses, as it is in its elementary idea. On the contrary, we have rather added to the obscurity of the problem; for a syllogism is at least a demonstration, when the premisses are granted, but a cumulation of probabilities, over and above their implicit character, will vary both in their number and their separate estimated value, according to the particular intellect which is employed upon it. It follows that what to one intellect is a proof is not so to another, and that the certainty of a proposition, does properly consist in the certitude of the mind which contemplates it. And this of course may be said without prejudice to the objective truth or falsehood of propositions, since it does not follow that these propositions on the one hand are not true, and based on right reason, and those on the other not false, and based on false reason, because not all men discriminate them in the same way.

Having thus explained the view which I would take of reasoning in the concrete, viz. that, from the nature of the case, and from the constitution of the human mind, certitude is the result of arguments which, taken in the letter, and not in their full implicit sense, are but probabilities, I proceed to dwell on some instances and circumstances of a phenomenon which seems to me as undeniable as to many it may be perplexing.

That there are cases, in which evidence, not sufficient for a scientific proof, is nevertheless sufficient for assent and certitude, is the doctrine of Locke, as of most men. He tells us that belief, grounded on sufficient probabilities, "rises to assurance;" and as to the question of sufficiency, that where propositions "border near on certainty," then "we assent to them as firmly as if they were infallibly demonstrated." The only question is, what these propositions are: this he does not tell us, but he seems to think that they are few in number, and will be without any trouble recognized at once by commonsense; whereas, unless I am mistaken, they are to be found throughout the range of concrete matter, and that supralogical judgment, which is the warrant for our certitude about them, is not mere common-sense, but the true healthy action of our ratiocinative powers, an action more subtle and more comprehensive than the mere appreciation of a syllogistic argument. It is often called the "judicium prudentis viri," a standard of certitude which holds good in all concrete matter, not only in those cases of practice and duty, in which we are more familiar with it, but in questions of truth and falsehood generally, or in what are called "speculative" questions, and that, not indeed to the exclusion, but as the supplement of logic. Thus a proof, except in abstract demonstration, has always in it, more or less, an element of the personal, because "prudence" is not a constituent part of our nature, but a personal endowment.

And the language in common use, when concrete conclusions are in question, implies the presence of this personal element in the proof of them. We are considered to feel, rather than to see, its cogency; and we decide, not that the conclusion must be, but that it cannot be otherwise. We say that we do not see our way to doubt it, that it is impossible to doubt, that we are bound to believe it, that we should be idiots, if we did not believe. We never should say, in abstract science, that we could not escape the conclusion that 25 was a mean proportional between 5 and 125; or that a man had no right to say that a tangent to a circle at the extremity of the radius makes an acute angle with it. Yet, though our certitude of the fact is quite as clear, we should not think it unnatural to say that the insularity of Great Britain is as good as demonstrated, or that none but a fool expects never to die. Phrases indeed such as these are sometimes used to express a shade of doubt, but it is enough for my purpose if they are also used when doubt is altogether absent. What, then, they signify, is, what I have so much insisted on, that we have arrived at these conclusions—not *ex opere operato*, by a scientific necessity independent of ourselves,—but by the action of our own minds, by our own individual perception of the truth in question, under a sense of duty to those conclusions and with an intellectual conscientiousness.

This certitude and this evidence are often called moral; a word which I avoid, as having a very vague meaning; but using it here for once, I observe that moral evidence and moral certitude are all that we can attain, not only in the case of ethical and spiritual subjects, such as religion, but of terrestrial and cosmical questions also. So far, physical Astronomy and Revelation stand on the same footing. Vince, in his treatise on Astronomy, does but use the language of philosophical sobriety, when, after speaking of the proofs of the earth's rotatory motion, he says, "When these reasons, all upon different principles, are considered, they amount to a proof of the earth's rotation about its axis, which is as satisfactory to the mind as the most direct demonstration could be;" or, as he had said just before, "the mind rests equally satisfied, as if the matter was strictly proved."[1] That is, first there is no demonstration that the earth rotates; next there is a cluster of "reasons on *different* principles," that is, independent probabilities in cumulation; thirdly, these "*amount* to a proof," and "the mind" feels "*as if* the matter was strictly proved," that is, there is the equivalent of proof; lastly, "the mind rests *satisfied*," that is, it is certain on the point. And though evidence of the fact is now obtained which was not known fifty years ago, that evidence on the whole has not changed its character.

Compare with this avowal the language of Butler, when discussing the proof of Revelation. "Probable proofs," he says, "by being added, not only increase the evidence, but multiply it. The truth of our religion, like the truth of common matters, is to be judged by the whole evidence taken together . . . in like manner as, if in any common case numerous events acknowledged were to be alleged in proof of any other event disputed, the truth of the disputed event would be proved, not only if any one of the acknowledged ones did of itself clearly imply it, but though no one of them singly did so, if the whole of the acknowledged events taken together could not in reason be supposed to have happened, unless the disputed one were true."[2] Here, as in Astronomy, is the same absence of demonstration of the thesis, the same cumulating and converging indications of it, the same indirectness in the proof, as being *per impossibile*, the same recognition nevertheless that the conclusion is not only probable, but true. One other characteristic of the argumentative process is given, which is unnecessary in a subject-matter so clear and simple as astronomical science, viz. the moral state of the parties inquiring or disputing. They must be "as much in earnest about religion, as about their temporal affairs, capable of being convinced, on real evidence, that there is a God who governs the world, and feel themselves to be of a moral nature and accountable creatures."[3]

This being the state of the case, the question arises, whether, granting that the personality (so to speak) of the parties reasoning is an important element in proving propositions in concrete matter, any account can be given of the ratiocinative method in such proofs, over and above that analysis into syllogism which is possible in each of its steps in detail. I think there can; though I fear, lest to some minds it may appear far-fetched or fanciful; however, I will hazard this imputation. I consider, then, that the principle of concrete reasoning is parallel to the method of proof which is the foundation of modern mathematical science, as contained in the celebrated lemma with which Newton opens his *Principia*. We know that a regular polygon, in- scribed in a circle, its sides being continually diminished, tends to become that circle, as its limit; but it vanishes before it has coincided with the circle,

[1] Pp. 84, 85.
[2] "Analogy," pp. 329, 330, ed. 1836.
[3] Ibid., p. 278.

so that its tendency to be the circle, though ever nearer fulfilment, never in fact gets beyond a tendency. In like manner, the conclusion in a real or concrete question is foreseen and predicted rather than actually attained; foreseen in the number and direction of accumulated premisses, which all converge to it, and as the result of their combination, approach it more nearly than any assignable difference, yet do not touch it logically, (though only not touching it,) on account of the nature of its subject-matter, and the delicate and implicit character of at least part of the reasonings on which it depends. It is by the strength, variety, or multiplicity of premisses, which are only probable, not by invincible syllogisms,—by objections overcome, by adverse theories neutralized, by difficulties gradually clearing up, by exceptions proving the rule, by unlooked-for correlations found for received truths, by suspense and delay in the process issuing in triumphant re-actions,—by all these ways, and many others, it is that the practised and experienced mind is able to make a sure divination that a conclusion is inevitable, of which his lines of reasoning do not actually put him in posses-sion. This is what is meant by a proposition being "as good as proved," a conclusion as undeniable "as if it were proved," and by the reasons for it "amounting to a proof," for a proof is the limit of converging probabilities.

It may be added, that, whereas the logical form of this argument, is, as I have already observed, indirect, viz. that "the conclusion cannot be other-wise," and Butler says that an event is proved, if its antecedents "could not in reason be supposed to have happened *unless* it were true," and lawbooks tell us that the principle of circumstantial evidence is the *reductio ad absurdum,* so Newton too is forced to the same mode of proof for the establishment of his lemma, about prime and ultimate ratios. "If you deny that they become ultimately equal," he says, "let them be ultimately unequal;" and the con-sequence follows, "which is against the supposition."

Such being the character of the mental process in concrete reasoning, I should wish to adduce some good instances of it in illutration, instances in which the person reasoning confesses that he is reasoning on this very process, as I have been stating it; but these are difficult to find, from the very circumstance that the process from first to last is carried on as much without words as with them. However, I will set down three such.

1. First, an instance in physics. Wood, treating of the laws of motion, thus describes the line of reasoning by which the mind is certified of them. "They are not indeed self-evident, nor do they admit of accurate proof by experiment, on account of the effects of friction and the air's resistance, which cannot entirely be removed. They are, however, constantly and invar-iably suggested to our senses, and they agree with experiment, as far as experiment can go; and the more accurately the experiments are made, and the greater care we take to remove all those impediments which tend to render the conclusions erroneous, the more nearly do the experiments coincide with these laws.

"Their truth is also established upon a different ground: from these general principles innumerable particular conclusions have been deducted; sometimes the deductions are simple and immediate, sometimes they are made by tedious and intricate operations; yet they are all, without exception, consistent with each other and with experiment. It follows thereby, that the principles upon which the calculations are founded are true."[1]

The reasoning of this passage (in which the uniformity of the laws of nature is assumed) seems to me a good illustration of what must be considered the principle or form of an induction. The conclusion, which is its scope, is, by its own confession, not proved; but it ought to be proved, or is as good as proved, and a man would be irrational who did not take it to be virtually proved; first, because the imperfections in the proof arise out of its subject-matter and the nature of the case, so that it *is* proved *interpretativè;* and next, because in the same degree in which these faults in the subject-matter are overcome here or there, are the involved imperfections here or there of the proof remedied; and further, because, when the conclusion is assumed as an hypothesis, it throws light upon a multitude of collateral facts, accounting for them, and uniting them together in one whole. Consistency is not always the guarantee of truth; but there may be a consistency in a theory so variously tried and exemplified as to lead to belief in it, as reasonably as a witness in a court of law may, after a severe cross-examination, satisfy and assure judge, jury, and the whole court, of his simple veracity.

2. And from the courts of law shall my second illustration be taken.

A learned writer says, "In criminal prosecutions, the circumstantial evidence should be such, as to produce nearly the same degree of certainty as that which arises from direct testimony, and to exclude a rational probability of innocence."[2] By degrees of certainty he seems to mean, together with many other writers, degrees of proof, or approximations towards proof, and not certitude, as a state of mind; and he says that no one should be pronounced guilty on evidence which is not equivalent in weight to direct testimony. So far is clear; but what is meant by the expression "*rational* probability"? for there can be no probability but what is rational. I consider that the "exclusion of a rational probability" means "the exclusion of any argument in the man's favour which has a rational claim to be called probable," or rather, "the rational exclusion of any supposition that he is innocent;" and "rational" is used in contradistinction to argumentative, and means "resting on implicit reasons," such as we feel, indeed, but which for some cause or other, because they are too subtle or too circuitous, we cannot put into words so as to satisfy logic. It this is a correct account of his meaning, he says that the evidence against a criminal, in order to be decisive of his guilt, to the satisfaction of our conscience, must bear with it, along with the

---

[1]"Mechanics," p. 31.
[2]Phillipps' "Law of Evidence," vol. i. p. 456.

palpable arguments for that guilt, such a reasonableness, or body of implicit reasons for it in addition, as may exclude any probability, really such, that he is not guilty,—that is, it must be an evidence free from any thing obscure, suspicious, unnatural, or defective, such as (in the judgment of a prudent man) would hinder that summation and coalescence of the evidence into a proof, which I have compared to the running into a limit, in the case of mathematical ratios. Just as an algebraical series may be of a nature never to terminate or admit of valuation, as being the equivalent of an irrational quantity or surd, so there may be some grave imperfections in a body of reasons, explicit or implicit, which is directed to a proof, sufficient to interfere with its successful issue or resolution, and to balk us with an irrational, that is, an indeterminate, conclusion.

So much as to the principle of conclusions made upon evidence in criminal cases; now let us turn to an instance of its application in a particular instance. Some years ago there was a murder committed, which unusually agitated the popular mind, and the evidence against the culprit was necessarily circumstantial. At the trial the Judge, in addressing the Jury, instructed them on the kind of evidence necessary for a verdict of *guilty*. Of course he could not mean to say that they must convict a man, of whose guilt they were not certain, especially in a case in which two foreign countries, Germany and the American States, were attentively looking on. If the Jury had any doubt, that is, reasonable doubt, about the man's guilt, of course they would give him the benefit of that doubt. Nor could the certitude, which would be necessary for an adverse verdict, be merely that which is sometimes called a "practical certitude," that is, a certitude indeed, but a certitude that it was a "duty," "expedient," "safe," to bring in a verdict of guilty. Of course the Judge spoke of what is called a "speculative certitude," that is, a certitude of the fact that the man was guilty; the only question being, what evidence was sufficient for the proof, for the certitude of that fact. This is what the Judge meant; and these are among the remarks which, with this drift, he made upon the occasion:—

After observing that by circumstantial evidence he meant a case in which "the facts do not directly prove the actual crime, but lead to the conclusion that the prisoner committed that crime," he went on to disclaim the suggestion, made by counsel in the case, that the Jury could not pronounce a verdict of *guilty*, unless they were as much satisfied that the prisoner did the deed as if they had seen him commit it. "That is not the certainty," he said, which is required of you to discharge your duty to the prisoner, whose safety is in your hands." Then he stated what was the "degree of certainty," that is, of certainty or perfection of proof, which was necessary to the question, "involving as it did the life of the prisoner at the bar,"—it was such as that "with which," he said, "you decide upon and conclude your own most important transactions in life. Take the facts which are proved before you, separate those you believe from those which you do not believe, and all the conclusions that naturally and almost necessarily result from those facts, you may confide in as much as in the facts themselves. The case on the part of the prosecution is the *story* of the murder, told by the *different* witnesses, who *unfold the circumstances one after another*, according to their occurrence, together with the *gradual* discovery of some apparent connexion between the property that was lost, and the possession of it by the prisoner."

Now here I observe, that whereas the conclusion which is contemplated by the Judge, is what may be pronounced (on the whole, and considering all things, and judging reasonably) a proved or certain conclusion, that is, a conclusion of the truth of the allegation against the prisoner, or of the fact of his guilt, on the other hand, the *motiva* constituting this reasonable, rational proof, and this satisfactory certitude, needed not, according to him, to be stronger than those on which we prudently act on matters of important interest to ourselves, that is, probable reasons viewed in their convergence and combination. And whereas the certitude is viewed by the Judge as following on converging probabilities, which constitute a real, though only a reasonable, not an argumentative, proof, so it will be observed in this particular instance, that, in illustration of the general doctrine which I have laid down, the process is one of "line upon line, and letter upon letter," of various details accumulating and of deductions fitting in to each other; for, in the Judge's words, there was a story—and that not told right out and by one witness, but taken up and handed on from witness to witness—gradually unfolded, and tending to a proof, which of course might have been ten times stronger than it was, but was still a proof for all that, and sufficient for its conclusion,—just as we see that two straight lines are meeting, and are certain they will meet at a given distance, though we do not actually see the junction.

3. The third instance I will take is one of a literary character, the divination of the authorship of a certain anonymous publication, as suggested mainly by internal evidence, as I found it in a critique written some twenty years ago. In the extract which I make from it, we may observe the same steady march of a proof towards a conclusion, which is (as it were) out of sight;—a reckoning, or a reasonable judgment, that the conclusion really is proved, and a personal certitude upon that judgment, joined with a confession that a logical argument could not well be made out for it, and that the various details in which the proof consisted were in no small measure implicit and impalpable.

"Rumour speaks uniformly and clearly enough in attributing it to the pen of a particular individual. Nor, although a cursory reader might well skim the book without finding in it any thing to suggest, &c., . . . will it appear improbable to the more attentive student of its internal evidence; and the improbability will decrease more and more, in proportion as the *reader is capable* of judging, and appreciating the *delicate, and at first invisible touches*, which limit, to *those who understand them*, the individuals who can have written it to a very small number indeed. The utmost scepticism as to its authorship *(which we do not feel ourselves)* cannot remove it farther from him than to that of some one among his most intimate friends; so that, leaving others to discuss antecedent probabilities," &c.

Here is a writer who professes to have no doubt at all about the authorship of a book,—which at the same time he cannot prove by mere argumentation set down in words. The reasons of his conviction are too delicate, too intricate; nay, they are in part invisible; invisible, except to those who from circumstances have an intellectual perception of what does not appear to the many. They are personal to the individual. This again is an instance, distinctly set before us, of the particular mode in which the mind progresses in concrete matter, viz. from merely probable antecedents to the sufficient proof of a fact or a truth, and, after the proof, to an act of certitude about it.

I trust the foregoing remarks may not deserve the blame of a needless refinement. I have thought it incumbent on me to illustrate the intellectual process by which we pass from conditional inference to unconditional assent; and I have had only the alternative of lying under the imputation of a paradox or of a subtlety.

NATURAL INFERENCE

I commenced my remarks upon Inference by saying that reasoning ordinarily shows as a simple act, not as a process, as if there were no medium interposed between antecedent and consequent, and the transition from one to the other were of the nature of an instinct,—that is, the process is altogether unconscious and implicit. It is necessary, then, to take some notice of this natural or material Inference, as an existing phenomenon of mind; and that the more, because I shall thereby be illustrating and support-ing what I have been saying of the characteristics of inferential processes as carried on in concrete matter, and especially of their being the action of the mind itself, that is, by its ratiocinative or illative faculty, not a mere operation as in the rules of arithmetic.

I say, then, that our most natural mode of reasoning is, not from proposi-tions to propositions, but from things to things, from concrete to concrete, from wholes to wholes. Whether the consequents, at which we arrive from the antecedents with which we start, lead us to assent or only towards assent, those antecedents commonly are not recognized by us as subjects for analy-sis; nay, often are only indirectly recognized as antecedents at all. Not only is the inference with its process ignored, but the antecedent also. To the mind itself the reasoning is a simple divination or prediction; as it literally is in the instance of enthusiasts, who mistake their own thoughts for inspirations.

This is the mode in which we ordinarily reason, dealing with things directly, and as they stand, one by one, in the concrete, with an intrinsic and personal power, not a conscious adoption of an artificial instrument or expedient; and it is especially exemplified both in uneducated men, and in men of genius,—in those who know nothing of intellectual aids and rules, and in those who care nothing for them,—in those who are either without or above mental discipline. As true poetry is a spontaneous outpouring of thought, and therefore belongs to rude as well as to gifted minds, whereas no one becomes a poet merely by the canons of criticism, so this unscientific reasoning, being sometimes a natural, uncultivated faculty, sometimes approaching to a gift, sometimes an acquired habit and second nature, has a higher source than logical rule,—"nascitur, non fit." When it is characterized by precision, subtlety, promptitude, and truth, it is of course a gift and a rarity: in ordinary minds it is biassed and degraded by prejudice, passion, and self-interest; but still, after all, this divination comes by nature, and belongs to all of us in a measure, to women more than to men, hitting or missing, as the case may be, but with a success on the whole sufficient to show that there is a method in it, though it be implicit.

A peasant who is weather-wise may yet be simply unable to assign intelligible reasons why he thinks it will be fine tomorrow; and if he attempts to do so he may give reasons wide of the mark; but that will not weaken his own confidence in his prediction. His mind does not proceed step by step, but he feels all at once and together the force of various combined phenomena, though he is not conscious of them. Again, there are physicians who excel in the *diagnosis* of complaints; though it does not follow from this, that they could defend their decision in a particular case against a brother physician who disputed it. They are guided by natural acuteness and varied experience; they have their own idiosyncratic modes of observing, generalizing, and concluding; when questioned, they can but rest on their own authority, or appeal to the future event. In a popular novel,[1] a lawyer is introduced, who "would know, almost by instinct, whether an accused person was or was not guilty; and he had already perceived by instinct" that the heroine was guilty. "I've no doubt she's a clever woman," he said, and at once named an attorney practising at the Old Bailey. So, again, experts and detectives, when employed to investigate mysteries, in cases whether of the civil or criminal law, discern and follow out indications which promise solution with a sagacity incomprehensible to ordinary men. A parallel gift is the intuitive perception of character possessed by certain men, while others are as destitute of it, as others again are of an ear for music. What common measure is there between the judgments of those who have this intuition, and those who have not? What but the event can settle any differences of opinion which occurs in their estimation of a third person? These are instances of a natural capacity, or of nature improved by practice and habit,

[1][Anthony Trollope's] "Orley Farm."

enabling the mind to pass promptly from one set of facts to another, not only, I say, without conscious media, but without conscious antecedents.

Sometimes, I say, this illative faculty is nothing short of genius. Such seems to have been Newton's perception of truths mathematical and physical, though proof was absent. At least that is the impression left on my own mind by various stories which are told of him, one of which was stated in the public papers a few years ago. "Professor Sylvester," it was said, "has just discovered the proof of Sir Isaac Newton's rule for ascertaining the imaginary roots of equations. . . . This rule has been a Gordian-knot among algebraists for the last century and a half. The proof being wanting, authors became ashamed at length for advancing a proposition, the evidence for which rested on no other foundation than belief in Newton's sagacity."[1]

Such is the gift of the calculating boys who now and then make their appearance, who seem to have certain short-cuts to conclusions, which they cannot explain to themselves. Some are said to have been able to determine off-hand what numbers are prime,—numbers, I think, up to seven places.

In a very different subject-matter, Napoleon supplies us with an instance of a parallel genius in reasoning, by which he was enabled to look at things in his own province, and to interpret them truly, apparently without any ratiocinative media. "By long experience," says Alison, "joined to great natural quickness and precision of eye, he had acquired the power of judging, with extraordinary accuracy, both of the amount of the enemy's force opposed to him in the field, and of the probable result of the movements, even the most complicated, going forward in the opposite armies. . . . He looked around him for a little while with his telescope, and immediately formed a clear conception of the position, forces, and intention of the whole hostile array. In this way he could, with surprising accuracy, calculate in a few minutes, according to what he could see of their formation and the extent of the ground which they occupied, the numerical force of armies of 60,000 or 80,000 men; and if their troops were at all scattered, he knew at once how long it would require for them to concentrate, and how many hours must elapse before they could make their attack."[2]

It is difficult to avoid calling such clear presentiments by the name of instinct; and I think they may so be called, if by instinct be understood, not a natural sense, one and the same in all, and incapable of cultivation, but a perception of facts without assignable media of perceiving. There are those who can tell at once what is conducive or injurious to their welfare, who are their friends, who their enemies, what is to happen to them, and how they are to meet it. Presence of mind, fathoming of motives, talent for repartee, are instances of this gift. As to that divination of personal danger which is found in the young and innocent, we find a description of it in one of Scott's

[1]*Guardian*, June 28, 1865.
[2]"History," vol. x. pp. 286, 287.

romances, in which the heroine, "without being able to discover what was wrong either in the scenes of unusual luxury with which she was surrounded, or in the manner of her hostess," is said nevertheless to have felt "an instinctive apprehension that all was not right,—a feeling in the human mind," the author proceeds to say, "allied perhaps to that sense of danger, which animals exhibit, when placed in the vicinity of the natural enemies of their race, and which makes birds cower when the hawk is in the air, and beasts tremble when the tiger is abroad in the desert."[2]

A religious biography, lately published, affords us an instance of this spontaneous perception of truth in the province of revealed doctrine. "Her firm faith," says the Author of the Preface, "was so vivid in its character, that it was almost like an intuition of the entire prospect of revealed truth. Let an error against faith be concealed under expressions however abstruse, and her sure instinct found it out. I have tried this experiment repeatedly. She might not be able to separate the heresy by analysis, but she saw, and felt, and suffered from its presence."[1]

And so of the great fundamental truths of religion, natural and revealed, and as regards the mass of religious men: these truths, doubtless, may be proved and defended by an array of invincible logical arguments, but such is not commonly the method in which those same logical arguments make their way into our minds. The grounds, on which we hold the divine origin of the Church, and the previous truths which are taught us by nature—the being of a God, and the immortality of the soul—are felt by most men to be recondite and impalpable, in proportion to their depth and reality. As we cannot see ourselves, so we cannot well see intellectual motives which are so intimately ours, and which spring up from the very constitution of our minds; and while we refuse to admit the notion that religion has not irrefragable arguments in its behalf, still the attempts to argue, on the part of an individual *hic et nunc,* will sometimes only confuse his apprehension of sacred objects, and sub- tracts from his devotion quite as much as it adds to his knowledge.

This is found in the case of other perceptions besides that of faith. It is the case of nature against art: of course, if possible, nature and art should be combined, but sometimes they are incompatible. Thus, in the case of cal- culating boys, it is said, I know not with what truth, that to teach them the ordinary rules of arithmetic is to endanger or to destroy the extraordinary endowment. And men who have the gift of playing on an instrument by ear, are sometimes afraid to learn by rule, lest they should lose it.

There is an analogy, in this respect, between Ratiocination and Memory, though the latter may be exercised without antecedents or media, whereas the former requires them in its very idea. At the same time, association has so much to do with memory, that we may not unfairly consider memory, as

[1]"Life of Mother Margaret M. Hallahan," p. vii.
[2]"Peveril of the Peak.

well as reasoning, as depending on certain previous conditions. Writing, as I have already observed, is a *memoria technica*, or logic of memory. Now it will be found, I think, that, indispensable as is the use of letters, still, in fact, we weaken our memory in proportion as we habituate ourselves to commit all that we wish to remember to memorandums. Of course in proportion as our memory is weak or overburdened, and thereby treacherous, we cannot act otherwise; but in the case of men of strong memory, in any particular subject-matter, as in that of dates, all artificial expedients, from the "Thirty days has September," &c., to the more formidable formulas which are offered for their use, are as difficult and repulsive as the natural exercise of memory is healthy and easy to them; just as the clear-headed and practical reasoner, who sees conclusions at a glance, is uncomfortable under the drill of a logician, being oppressed and hampered, as David in Saul's armour, by what is intended to be a benefit.

I need not say more on this part of the subject. What is called reasoning is often only a peculiar and personal mode of abstraction, and so far, like memory, may be said to exist without antecedents. It is a power of looking at things in some particular aspect, and of determining their internal and external relations thereby. And according to the subtlety and versatility of their gift, are men able to read what comes before them justly, variously, and fruitfully. Hence, too, it is that in our intercourse with others, in business and family matters, in social and political transactions, a word or an act on the part of another is sometimes a sudden revelation; light breaks in upon us, and our whole judgment of a course of events, or of an undertaking, is changed. We determine correctly or otherwise, as it may be; but in either case it is by a sense proper to ourselves, for another may see the objects which we are thus using, and give them quite a different interpretation, inasmuch as he abstracts another set of general notions from those same phenomena which present themselves to us also.

What I have been saying of Ratiocination, may be said of Taste, and is confirmed by the obvious analogy between the two. Taste, skill, invention in the fine arts—and so, again, discretion or judgment in conduct—are exerted spontaneously, when once acquired, and could not give a clear account of themselves, or of their mode of proceeding. They do not go by rule, though to a certain point their exercise may be analyzed, and may take the shape of an art or method. But these parallels will come before us presently.

And now I come to a further peculiarity of this natural and spontaneous ratiocination. This faculty, as it is actually found in us, proceeding from concrete to concrete, is attached to a definite subject-matter, according to the individual. In spite of Aristotle, I will not allow that genuine reasoning is an instrumental art; and in spite of Dr. Johnson, I will assert that genius, as far as it is manifested in ratiocination, is not equal to all undertakings, but has its own peculiar subject-matter, and is circumscribed in its range. No one would for a moment expect that because Newton and Napoleon both had a genius for ratiocination, that, in consequence, Napoleon could have gener-alized the principle of gravitation, or Newton have seen how to concentrate a hundred thousand men at Austerlitz. The ratiocinative faculty, then, as found in individuals, is not a general instrument of knowledge, but has its province, or is what may be called departmental. It is not so much one faculty, as a collection of similar or analogous faculties under one name, there being really as many faculties as there are distinct subject-matters, though in the same person some of them may, if it so happen, be united,—nay, though some men have a sort of literary power in arguing in all subject matters, *de omni scibili*, a power extensive, but not deep or real.

This surely is the conclusion to which we are brought by our ordinary experience of men. It is almost proverbial that a hard-headed mathematician may have no head at all for what is called historical evidence. Successful experimentalists need not have talent for legal research or pleading. A shrewd man of business may be a bad arguer in philosophical questions. Able statesmen and politicians have been before now eccentric or superstitious in their religious views. It is notorious how ridiculous a clever man may make himself, who ventures to argue with professed theologians, critics, or geologists, though without positive defects in knowledge of his subject. Priestly, great in electricity and chemistry, was but a poor ecclesiastical historian. The Author of the Minute Philosopher is also the Author of the *Analyst*. Newton wrote not only his *Principia*, but his comments on the Apocalypse; Cromwell, whose actions savoured of the boldest logic, was a confused speaker. In these, and various similar instances, the defect lay, not so much in an ignorance of facts, as in an inability to handle those facts suitably; in feeble or perverse modes of abstraction, observation, com-parison, analysis, inference, which nothing could have obviated, but that which was wanting,—a specific talent, and a ready exercise of it.

I have already referred to the faculty of memory in illustration; it will serve me here also. We can form an abstract idea of memory, and call it one faculty, which has for its subject-matter all past facts of our personal experi-ence; but this is really only an illusion; for there is no such gift of universal memory. Of course, we all remember, in a way, as we reason, in all subject-matters; but I am speaking of remembering rightly, as I spoke of reasoning rightly. In real fact memory, as a talent, is not one indivisible faculty, but a power of retaining and recalling the past in this or that department of our experience, not in any whatever. Two memories, which are both specially retentive, may also be incommensurate. Some men can recite the canto of a poem, or good part of a speech, after once reading it, but have no head for dates. Others have great capacity for the vocabulary of languages, but re-collect nothing of the small occurrences of the day or year. Others never forget any statement which they have read, and can give volume and page, but have no memory for faces. I have known those who could, without effort, run through the succession of days on which Easter fell for years back; or could say where they were, or what they were doing, on a given day, in a given year; or could recollect accurately the Christian names of friends and strangers; or could enumerate in exact order the names on all the shops from Hyde Park Corner to the Bank; or had so mastered the University Calendar as to be able to bear an examination in the academical history of any M.A. taken at random. And I believe in most of these cases the talent, in its exceptional character, did not extend beyond several classes of subjects. There are a hundred memories, as there are a hundred virtues. Virtue is one indeed in the abstract; but, in fact, gentle and kind natures are not therefore heroic, and prudent and self-controlled minds need not be open-handed. At the utmost such virtue is one only *in posse;* as developed in the concrete, it takes the shape of species which in no sense imply each other.

So is it with Ratiocination; and as we should betake ourselves to Newton for physical, not for theological conclusions, and to Wellington for his military experience, not for statesmanship, so the maxim holds good generally, "Cuique in arte suà credendum est:" or, to use the grand words of Aristotle, "We are bound to give heed to the undemonstrated sayings and opinions of the experienced and aged, not less than to demonstrations; because, from their having the eye of experience, they behold the principles of things."[1] Instead of trusting logical science, we must trust persons, namely, those who by long acquaintance with their subject have a right to judge. And if we wish ourselves to share in their convictions and the grounds of them, we must follow their history, and learn as they have learned. We must take up their particular subject as they took it up, beginning at the beginning, give ourselves to it, depend on practice and experience more than on reasoning, and thus gain that mental insight into truth, whatever its subject-matter may be, which our masters have gained before us. By following this course, we may make ourselves of their number, and then we rightly lean upon ourselves, directing ourselves by our own moral or intellectual judgment, not by our skill in argumentation.

This doctrine, stated in substance as above, by the great philosopher of antiquity, is more fully expounded in a passage which he elsewhere quotes from Hesiod. "Best of all is he," says that poet, "who is wise by his own wit; next best he who is wise by the wit of others; but whoso is neither able to see, nor willing to hear, he is a good-for-nothing fellow." Judgment then in all concrete matters is the architectonic faculty; and what may be called the Illative Sense, or right judgment in ratiocination, is one branch of it.

THE NATURE OF THE ILLATIVE SENSE

It is the mind that reasons, and that controls its own reasonings, not any technical apparatus of words and propositions. This power of judging and

---

[1] Eth. Nicom. vi. 11, fin.

concluding, when in its perfection, I call the Illative Sense, and I shall best illustrate it by referring to parallel faculties, which we commonly recognize without difficulty.

For instance, how does the mind fulfil its function of supreme direction and control, in matters of duty, social intercourse, and taste? In all of these separate actions of the intellect, the individual is supreme, and responsible to himself, nay, under circumstances, may be justified in opposing himself to the judgment of the whole world; though he uses rules to his great advantage, as far as they go, and is in consequence bound to use them. As regards moral duty, the subject is fully considered in the well-known treatises of Aristotle.[1] He calls the faculty which guides the mind in matters of conduct, by the name of *phronesis,* or judgment. This is the directing, controlling, and determining principle in such matters, personal and social. What it is to be virtuous, how we are to gain the just idea and standard of virtue, how we are to approximate in practice to our own standard, what is right and wrong in a particular case, for the answers in fulness and accuracy to these and similar questions, the philosopher refers us to no code of laws, to no moral treatise, because no science of life, applicable to the case of an individual, has been or can be written. Such is Aristotle's doctrine, and it is undoubtedly true. An ethical system may supply laws, general rules, guiding principles, a number of examples, suggestions, landmarks, limitations, cautions, distinctions, solutions of critical or anxious difficulties; but who is to apply them to a particular case? whither can we go, except to the living intellect, our own, or another's? What is written is too vague, too negative for our need. It bids us avoid extremes; but it cannot ascertain for us, according to our personal need, the golden mean. The authoritative oracle, which is to decide our path, is something more searching and manifold than such jejune generalizations as treatises can give, which are most distinct and clear when we least need them. It is seated in the mind of the individual, who is thus his own law, his own teacher, and his own judge in those special cases of duty which are personal to him. It comes of an acquired habit, though it has its first origin in nature itself, and it is formed and matured by practice and experience; and it manifests itself, not in any breadth of view, any philosophical comprehension of the mutual relations of duty towards duty, or any consistency in its teachings, but it is a capacity sufficient for the occasion, deciding what ought to be done here and now, by this given person, under these given circumstances. It decides nothing hypothetical, it does not determine what a man should do ten years hence, or what another should do at this time. It may indeed happen to decide ten years hence as it does now, and to decide a

---

[1]Though Aristotle, in his Nicomachean Ethics, speaks of φρόνησι) as the virtue of the δοξαστικὸν generally, and as being concerned generally with contingent matter (vi. 4), or what I have called the concrete, and of its function being, as regards that matter, ἀποφάναι (*ibid.* 3), he does not treat of it in that work in its general relation to truth and the affirmation of truth, but only as it bears upon τά πρακτά.

second case now as it now decides a first; still its present act is for the present, not for the distant or the future.

State or public law is inflexible, but this mental rule is not only minute and particular, but has an elasticity, which, in its application to individual cases, is, as I have said, not studious to maintain the appearance of consistency. In old times the mason's rule which was in use at Lesbos was, according to Aristotle, not of wood or iron, but of lead, so as to allow of its adjustment to the uneven surface of the stones brought together for the work. By such the philosopher illustrates the nature of equity in contrast with law, and such is that *phronesis,* from which the science of morals forms its rules, and receives its complement.

In this respect of course the law of truth differs from the law of duty, that duties change, but truths never; but, though truth is ever one and the same, and the assent of certitude is immutable, still the reasonings which carry us on to truth and certitude are many and distinct, and vary with the inquirer; and it is not with assent, but with the controlling principle in inferences that I am comparing *phronesis.* It is with this drift that I observe that the rule of conduct for one man is not always the rule for another, though the rule is always one and the same in the abstract, and in its principle and scope. To learn his own duty in his own case, each individual must have recourse to his own rule; and if his rule is not sufficiently developed in his intellect for his need, then he goes to some other living, present authority, to supply it for him, not to the dead letter of a treatise or a code. A living, present authority, himself or another, is his immediate guide in matters of a personal, social, or political character. In buying and selling, in contracts, in his treatment of others, in giving and receiving, in thinking, speaking, doing, and working, in toil, in danger, in his recreations and pleasures, every one of his acts, to be praiseworthy, must be in accordance with this practical sense. Thus it is, and not by science, that he perfects the virtues of justice, self-command, magnanimity, generosity, gentleness, and all others. *Phronesis* is the regulating principle of every one of them.

These last words lead me to a further remark. I doubt whether it is correct, strictly speaking, to consider this *phronesis* as a general faculty, directing and perfecting all the virtues at once. So understood, it is little better than an abstract term, including under it a circle of analogous faculties, severally proper to the separate virtues. Properly speaking, there are as many kinds of *phronesis* as there are virtues; for the judgment, good sense, or tact which is conspicuous in a man's conduct in one subject-matter, is not necessarily traceable in another. As in the parallel cases of memory and reasoning, he may be great in one aspect of his character, and little-minded in another. He may be exemplary in his family, yet commit a fraud on the revenue; he may be just and cruel, brave and sensual, imprudent and patient. And if this be true of the moral virtues, it holds good still more fully when we compare what is called his private character with his public. A good man may make a bad king; profligates have been great statesmen, or magnanimous political leaders.

So, too, I may go on to speak of the various callings and professions which give scope to the exercise of great talents, for these talents also are matured, not by mere rule, but by personal skill and sagacity. They are as diverse as pleading and cross-examining, conducting a debate in Parliament, swaying a public meeting, and commanding an army; and here, too, I observe that, though the directing principle in each case is called by the same name,—sagacity, skill, tact, or prudence,—still there is no one ruling faculty leading to eminence in all these various lines of action in common, but men will excel in one of them, without any talent for the rest.

The parallel may be continued in the case of the Fine Arts, in which, though true and scientific rules may be given, no one would therefore deny that Phidias or Rafael had a far more subtle standard of taste and a more versatile power of embodying it in his works, than any which he could communicate to others in even a series of treatises. And here again genius is indissolubly united to one definite subject-matter; a poet is not therefore a painter, or an architect a musical composer.

And so, again, as regards the useful arts and pesonal accomplishments, we use the same word "skill," but proficiency in engineering or in shipbuilding, or again in engraving, or again in singing, in playing instruments, in acting, or in gymnastic exercises, is as simply one with its particular subject-matter, as the human soul with its particular body, and is, in its own department, a sort of instinct or inspiration, not an obedience to external rules of criticism or of science.

It is natural, then, to ask the question, why ratiocination should be an exception to a general law which attaches to the intellectual exercises of the mind; why it is held to be commensurate with logical science; and why logic is made an instrumental art sufficient for determining every sort of truth, while no one would dream of making any one formula, however generalized, a working rule at once for poetry, the art of medicine, and political warfare?

This is what I have to remark concerning the Illative Sense, and in explanation of its nature and claims; and on the whole, I have spoken of it in four respects—as viewed in itself, in its subject-matter, in the process it uses, and in its function and scope.

First, viewed in its exercise, it is one and the same in all concrete matters, though employed in them in different measures. We do not reason in one way in chemistry or law, in another in morals or religion; but in reasoning on any subject whatever, which is concrete, we proceed, as far indeed as we can, by the logic of language, but we are obliged to supplement it by the more subtle and elastic logic of thought; for forms by themselves prove nothing.

Secondly, it is in fact attached to definite subject-matters, so that a given individual may possess it in one department of thought, for instance, history, and not in another, for instance, philosophy.

Thirdly, in coming to its conclusion, it proceeds, always in the same way, by a method of reasoning, which as I have observed above, is the elementary principle of that mathematical calculus of modern times, which has so wonderfully extended the limits of abstract science.

Fourthly, in no class of concrete reasonings, whether in experimental science, historical research, or theology, is there any ultimate test of truth and error in our inferences besides the trustworthiness of the Illative Sense that gives them its sanction; just as there is no sufficient test of poetical excellence, heroic action, or gentlemanlike conduct, other than the particular mental sense, be it genius, taste, sense of propriety, or the moral sense, to which those subject-matters are severally committed. Our duty in each of these is to strengthen and perfect the special faculty which is its living rule, and in every case as it comes to do our best. And such also is our duty and our necessity, as regards the Illative Sense.

BELIEF AND EVIDENCE
Leslie Stephen

Dr. Newman, in his "Grammar of Assent," quotes a passage from Locke, and proceeds to show cause against the doctrine which it enunciates. Locke says that there is "one unerring mark of" the love of truth for truth's sake,—namely, "the not entertaining any proposition with greater assurance than the proofs it is built on will warrant." Locke goes on to argue that if a man believes more strongly in a proposition than the evidence warrants, all the "surplusage of assurance" must be due to some other affection than the love of truth. Dr. Newman's criticism of Locke's doctrine brings out the cardinal point of the theory expounded in the "Grammar of Assent." This circumstance gives additional interest to Locke's statement, and illustrates its bearing upon some modern controversies. I do not propose, however, to discuss what may be called the personal question between Locke and Newman, to inquire whether Locke has stated his own view with complete accuracy, or been rightly understood or adequately answered by Dr. Newman. I will briefly examine the substantial merits of the question, simply observing that I agree with the view supported by Locke and impugned by Dr. Newman.

The theorem which I have thus to support is, that our belief in any proposition should be proportioned to the evidence upon which it rests. By this, it must of course be understood that each individual should proportion his belief to the evidence which is accessible to himself. I am bound, for example, to believe that the sun contains certain materials, because their existence in it is now proved by spectrum analysis. A generation ago, I should have been bound to have no opinion, because there was no evidence upon the subject. Is is now reasonable to believe in the Copernican, as it was once reasonable to believe in the Ptolemaic system. A love of truth must, that is, often lead to error, because we are without the evidence which alone can establish the truth. But if we acted upon Locke's principle, and modified our views as the evidence demanded a change, the race would continually approximate towards a larger body of definitively established truths.

I.

I ought to believe a proposition which is proved to be true. That, I presume, may be taken for granted. It would, indeed, be a superfluous truism, but for the fact that there are other affections besides the love of truth which constantly lead to at least the unconscious breach of the rule. The rule is not the less stringent if the proposition proved is expressible in this form: "The chances that a certain proposition is true are so-and-so." Chance, in this phrase, implies a certain mixture of knowledge and ignorance. I know that one side of a dice must turn up; I know that there are six sides which on an average turn up equally often; I do not in the least know which of the sides will turn up next time. The formula, "it is 5 to 1 against the next throw being an ace," is a compendious mode of asserting these propositions. If, then, I deny the chances to be 5 to 1, I virtually deny a proposition which is proved to be true. I assert that I have knowledge when I have it not, or deny the established truth that the six sides turn up equally often. In either case, I tell a lie, or disbelieve a proposition which I know to be true. That is, I lie to others or to myself; and lying is immoral.

A large proportion of the beliefs to which we refer in daily life are of this type. I know that there are a thousand men in a given place, and I know, say, that one of them is blind. When I meet a man in the given place, my belief that he can see ought to be represented accurately by the formula,—It is 999 to one that he can see. Otherwise I believe what I know to be false,—viz. that the numbers of seeing and blind men are different from what they are, or that I have some knowledge in the particular case when, *ex hypothesi*, I have it not.

The burden of proof must therefore lie upon any one who asserts that my degree of belief should vary from the standard thus laid down. For I should clearly have to ask him the question,—If my belief ought to vary from the degree thus prescribed, in what way, and according to what laws, ought it to vary? And what do you mean by "ought?" If by "ought" you mean that such a variation is morally right, although not producing conformity of belief to facts, you maintain the paradox that it is morally right to believe a falsehood. If (as seems more likely) you mean that the variation is right, because it will secure greater conformity of belief to facts, you are then vitually asserting that there is an extra-logical faculty for arriving at the truth. Now, as I should be inclined to describe reason as the faculty or faculties by which we arrive at the truth, this would, in my sense of the words, be a contradiction in terms. But at any rate, the question is entirely shifted. We are really invited to inquire not whether we ought to believe a proved proposition, but what are the faculties by which propositions are proved. Is there, for example, some super-sensuous faculty which presents us with intuitive truths, differing in kind from the faculties by which we discover the truths of mathematics or of the natural sciences? That is an interesting question but obviously irrelevant to Locke's theorem. If I have such a faculty, of course I am bound to use it; if not, not. In the first case, there will be another method of proof, but we must still demand proof.

II.

I will now ask what are the objections to which the doctrine is liable.

In the first place, there is the general ground of scepticism in regard to all empirical truths. If we admit the validity of the distinction between necessary and contingent truths, it may be urged that there is an impassable gulf between the propositions susceptible of demonstrative evidence and those capable only of proofs resting upon experience. Thus the belief that 2 + 2 = 4 is said to be a necessary truth. The belief that all men die is an empirical truth. Yet we appear to believe the two propositions with equal intensity. Are we justified in such belief, and if not, are we forced to admit that, as a matter of fact, the certitude outruns the evidence in the latter case, and therefore that we have a case of Locke's "surplusage" of belief? This, I may remark in passing, is part of Dr. Newman's contention, and may, therefore, deserve notice.

The belief in such an empirical truth as the mortality of all men implies, in the first place, a belief in what is called the uniformity of Nature. How that proposition is to be logically established, or whether it can be logically established at all, is a question needless to be discussed. In any case, the belief is assumed in every step of every argument about matters of fact. To deny it is to fall into absolute scepticism, for it is to cut out the very nerve of proof in every proposition drawn from experience. It is virtually admitted even in Dr. Newman's or Paley's argument for miracles. They defend miracles by denying them to be miraculous. The intervention of powerful invisible beings is as much a part of that regular stated order which Butler properly identifies with Nature as the action of electricity. It is rare with Paley, comparatively common with Dr. Newman but not properly abnormal. If Elias was taken to heaven in a chariot of fire, and so escaped death, we may also count upon a chariot of fire, whenever precisely similar circumstances occur—unless, indeed, God is identified with the arbitrary; or in other words, the non-existent. We cannot stir a step in any kind of reasoning about facts without implying the universal postulate. To reason in such matters is to assume the uniformity of Nature.

Granting this uniformity, indeed, we may still say that no statement about facts is necessarily true. My perceptions are admittedly fallible. I may have made a mistake in any particular observation, and therefore in every particular observation. I may be under a permanent hallucination; the world, or any world, may be a dream, and the ultimate realities hidden from me or from every one. The objection, indeed, applies to necessary, as well as to contingent truths in all fruitful applications. Two and two make four, but I may always be mistaken in my counting. I may be seeing double. The supposed two things may be really one or three. If I add up a larger sum, the liability to error increases at every step. The process may be potentially infallible, each particular step may be self-evident, but I cannot be certain, when the whole chain of reasoning is not actually present to my mind, that an error may not have intruded somewhere. Such arguments tell against all belief equally, except against that which expresses the immediate testimony of consciousness, and therefore are either nugatory or tend to universal scepticism.

It is, however, clear without following out such refinements, that we can in fact attain to a high degree of certainty in matters of fact. The process (which, I should add, is fully admitted by Dr. Newman) rests upon the convergence of innumerable probabilities. Admit the fundamental postulate of uniformity, and the evidence in behalf of particular facts becomes *indefinitely* strong. We believe, for example, in human mortality, not only because A, B, and C have died, where A, B, and C stand for uncounted millions, but because the experiment of living has been tried under such an enormous variety of conditions, that the probability of death being the expression of some law implied in the constitution of all living beings, and not the result of an accidental condition, becomes indefinitely great. The physiologist may confirm our belief by explaining the vital processes, but can hardly render it more peremptory and intense.

Now, where is the "surplusage" of belief in this case? If it were only proved, say, that nine men in ten, or 999 in 1,000 died, it would surely be wrong to say absolutely that all men die. I venture to say that all men die, because to my mind the bare theoretical possibility of error in such a theorem is measured by a fraction so infinitesimal that my mind is unable to conceive it. It is like a fraction of which the numerator should represent a standard yard, and the denominator a line from here to the most distant fixed stars. We are justified in rejecting such possibilities, as the mathematician is justified in rejecting those infinitesimals which, as he says, are smaller than any assignable quantity. Once admit that there is any probability,—that is, any admixture of real knowledge in such cases, and this conclusion follows. You must be a complete sceptic, or you must admit the possibility of an *indefinite approximation to certainty*. I call the Atlantic pure salt water; I call it so not the less if you empty into it a tea-cupful of milk or the thousandth part of a tea-cupful. You may say that in the former case it is a thousand times purer than in the latter, and it actually is so, if purity is measured by the proportion between the whole and the intrusive element. But in both cases it is *practically pure*. The error cannot affect any conceivable proposition upon the subject. Impartial truth approaches to absolute and necessary truth as the curve approaches its asymptote. It will go on getting nearer to all eternity, but after a finite distance it is so near that no human eyes, however aided, can discover the difference. If it be necessary to modify Locke's proposition at all in virtue of such criticism, I should add to the proposition that we ought to believe what is proved, the proposition that as the mind's eye is not one of Weller's extra-double-million-magnifying microscopes, we must be content to overlook the existence of doubts so infinitesimal as to be imperceptible. All language must be approximate, as all knowledge includes a certain element of inaccuracy. In speculative discussions we may say that such doubts exist, in the business of life they must be left out of account. I say that Mont Blanc is 15,760 feet high, without meaning that microscopic examination would not add some fraction of an inch to the account.

Secondly, it may be admitted that in conduct we have constantly to make assumptions resting upon much smaller evidence, and that such assumptions tend to pass into beliefs. I assume on evidence, far from demonstrative, and of course not comparable to the evidence which establishes general empirical truths, that I shall live for an hour, that this house will not fall to-night, that a given man is guilty of murder. In such cases (which are innumerable) I so far dismiss from my mind probabilities which are quite susceptible of being appreciated, that I refuse to allow them to influence my conduct. I know for a fact that I may be killed in any given railway journey; I know that my conviction of the guilt of Palmer rested upon fallible evidence; the chance of the contrary truth may be, perhaps, one millionth or one billionth. But I act as if it were absolutely non-existent; I take my ticket without an atom of fear, and hang Palmer without remorse. Moreover, such action undoubtedly tends to convince me of the truth of the assumption on which it proceeds. It requires a man of unusual candour, for example, to listen to any evidence which will upset his conviction of a supposed murderer's guilt. Ought I, therefore, not to act, lest acting should induce error?

In all cases but one the answer is given unhesitatingly. You must act, or life would come to a stop. You must resist the tendency which action has to convince you of the truth of the implied belief, because that tendency is illogical. "All men," says Young, "think all men mortal but themselves,"— that is, the interests of life tend to blind us to the constant possibility and the ultimate certainty of death. The moral is, that we should act as if we were to live the average time; but impress forcibly upon our minds that this is an assumption for practical purposes, not a dogma to be entertained as a certainty. The single exception is in the case of religious truth. We are told to act as if the truth of a religion were demonstrated. That is a sound, practical piece of advice, if its truth is, in fact, probable. We are told, further, that by so acting we shall come to believe. That, again, is true; but according to all analogy, it indicates not an end to be sought, but a danger to be avoided. *We ought carefully to impress upon our minds the possibility that we may be wrong, or else we shall be in danger of peremptorily rejecting evidence which ought to be admitted.* We hang a criminal, but we ought to be ready to accept evidence of his innocence; and should, therefore, carefully remember that we are acting on presumption, not on proof. We act as if there were a Hell, but till its existence be actually demonstrated, we should keep our minds open to the admitted possibility that it may be a delusion, otherwise we transgress Locke's canon, and admit some other passion than the love of truth to guide our conclusions.

Thirdly, there is another confusion which perplexes the discussion. *Amongst the evidences of a belief, we must reckon the beliefs of our neighbours. This is, in fact, the chief, or even the sole evidence for many beliefs.* When Protestants attacked the authority of the Church, they often overlooked or implicitly denied this obvious truth. They spoke as though every cobbler were to judge for himself of the evidence as to the authenticity and authority of the Bible, and so far to place himself on a par with Bentley or Scaliger. It requires little argument to show the futility of such an assumption. By far the greater part of all our beliefs rests upon authority in the sense of evidence. Thus, I believe England to be an island. Why? Not because I have been round it myself, but simply on evidence, and especially upon this consideration, that it is impossible to account for the existence of the belief on any other hypothesis than the hypothesis of its truth. It could not have grown up and be so deeply interwoven with innumerable practical assumptions, unless it were true. I believe in the Newtonian doctrine for a similar reason. Not simply because honest men tell me it is true, but because of the convergence of opinion of all qualified experts: because of the intimate connection of this belief with the whole body of scientific beliefs; and because proofs are given every day that the assumption of its truth leads to accurate conclusions. The measure of my certainty is the improbability that a false belief could have grown up under such conditions. Beliefs of this kind may often have stronger grounds than any belief resting on personal inference. I believe that there are 365 days in a year, not because I have counted them, but because the computation has been verified millions of times, and any mistake must have been detected.

It is more important to observe that the existence of a belief taken *simpliciter* is not a proof, nor always a presumption of its accuracy. It may be the very contrary. Since error exists, and lasts for centuries amongst many millions, the fact that a belief is widely spread is not sufficient. It is easy to imagine cases in which an increase of such evidence should diminish our belief. A man is declared by a presumably competent witness to have a bad character. That is, so far, a reason for believing his character to be bad. But now a dozen more witnesses come forward, who have no means of personal knowledge, and who are equally convinced of his wickedness. That is a presumption that the belief in his badness did not, even in the case of the competent observer, rest upon personal observation, but upon preconceived prejudice. If it should turn out that all the witnesses share some common ground of dislike, that they represent some hostile creed or interest, their hostilities may be explainable. It becomes evident, that is, that the belief is illogical; it is an expression of antipathy, not based upon evidence of facts. The belief being one of the relevant phenomena to be explained, I observe that its existence in cases where no evidence is obtainable diminishes the value in the case where evidence might be attainable. It demonstrates that another explanation of the belief is possible besides the explanation that it is true.

I see a remarkable chasm in a mountainous country,—and a native tells me a story, from which it has gained the name of "Lover's Leap." I believe him, for there is no improbability in the fact. But when I find the same or an analogous story connected with similar chasms in every mountainous region, I see that the probability of the story being created by the imaginative faculty is far greater than the probability of a similar series of incidents having occurred in every country. The same remark applies to innumerable stories of the same kind, and proves that the wide diffusion of a belief may be a sound reason for doubting its validity.

It follow, then, that the beliefs which have to be taken into account in determining our own should be weighed as well as counted. That intellectual contagion which leads us to accept the beliefs current around us without examination represents, again, a dangerous, not a logical process. It explains the cause of belief, and may thereby show the cause to be unreasonable. The more belief rests upon such illogical influences, the less its authority is regarded as testimony.

Thus, I should say that the evidence to which, by Locke's rule, our belief must be proportionate, should include the evidence derived from the beliefs of others, but with certain distinctions. In all causes whatever, the belief of other men is a relevant phenomenon. We have to account for its existence. But we must further ask whether the easiest mode of accounting for it is the assumption that it is a true belief. We may, perhaps, for this purpose, arrange beliefs in three classes.

First, there are many beliefs, *e.g.*, the belief of Englishmen that England is an island, which the believers are forced to verify constantly. They are compelled to test the accuracy of the belief daily, and in the most stringent way. If it were false, they could not help finding it out. In such cases the existence of a belief possesses an evidential authority which may be indistinguishable from the authority of demonstration.

Secondly, we have beliefs which admit of, but do not require verification. Such is the belief of Englishmen that part of the shore of Smith's Sound is an island. Some Englishmen may have tested the truth of the belief, but the verification is not so absolutely forced upon them. Such, again, are many beliefs of a sanitary kind. In every country people believe that temperance is good for health, but they also hold with equal confidence beliefs which are questionable or altogether unsound. An Italian believes that it is dangerous to go out at sunset, and his belief probably rests upon experience; but perhaps he also believes that the danger of malaria may be repelled by magic or by a relic, and in this case his belief is generated by fancy, instead of experience. From the bare fact of the existence of the belief we cannot be sure whether it has or has not been tested. It affords, therefore, a presumption of varying force, but no conclusive evidence of its truth. Many such beliefs rest upon experience; others are dictated by fancy, that is, arbitrary or illogical associations of ideas. They survive, although actual experiment would have demonstrated their fallacy, and we must therefore regard the testimony as ambiguous.

Finally, we have a number of beliefs, including all superstitions, which do not admit of verification at all, or at most of a sham verification. A savage believes in the powers of a rainmaker; that is a belief capable of verification, but which he has not, in fact, verified; a familiarity with other superstitions of a similar character enables us at once to set it down in a class of erroneous beliefs. This is a case in which the very prevalence of the belief shows that it cannot be true, for we see that it or its analogues flourish altogether independently of any verifiable observation. Or they are, perhaps, deductions from another set of beliefs, which are manifestly the work of the imaginative, not of the observing faculty. They record men's dreams, not their actual experiences. As they have been generated independently of experience, they survive without requiring its confirmation, and thus, except as they may include some little nucleus of observation, they have no claim whatever upon our belief. Belief has a tendency to generate belief, but that tendency is only logical where the original belief is known to be a verifiable and a verified belief; in other cases it represents a tendency contrary to logic, and, therefore, to be resisted by lovers of truth.

III.

A remark or two may be added as to the application of these principles. The obvious and undeniable fact that we find men of equal ability holding diametrically opposite principles, shows that certitude is no test of objective truth. *Does it follow that nobody ought to be certain, and that we should endeavour to preserve our minds in a position of neutral equilibrium, or that we ought arbitrarily to select one certitude, and put doubt peremptorily out of our minds? Neither conclusion is satisfactory, either from a moral or a logical point of view.*

Morally speaking, our plain duty is candour; that is, we are bound to entertain freely all relevant evidence, including, of course, the evidence of the beliefs entertained by others, and especially by qualified experts. But that process must often lead minds, differing in capacity and acquired knowledge to different conclusions. The most candid Tyrolese peasant will be a Catholic; the most candid Scotch peasant a Calvinist; and the most candid philosopher will be something else. Candour does not secure the individual from error, though it secures the progress of the race towards an ever closer approximation to truth. There is much truth probably in the worst religions, and the errors may be gradually eliminated. The moral duty which results is the duty of toleration and modesty. The fact that we are all fallible clearly involves the duty of looking without irritation upon those with whom we disagree and of speaking modestly ourselves. Dr. Newman says that a witness who has erroneously sworn to the identity of a prisoner, may, nevertheless, be equally confident when the right man is produced. Yet I should fancy that his first error would suggest the propriety of caution to himself, and would certainly cause bystanders to diminish their confidence in his word.

The fact, however, that I am fallible cannot make me doubt my own opinions. If I have acted rightly, I have already taken my fallibility into account when forming them. Knowing that I am often illogical and inaccurate, I have made allowance for my weakness before I reached a conclusion. When the conclusion is formed, I do not destroy its force by remembering once more that I am fallible. The general fact of my liability to error, the certainty that my opinions are somewhat wrong or, at least, inadequate, is an excellent reason for not pressing them dogmatically upon others, but not a reason for doubting doctrines reached with due caution and regard to my own weakness.

I, for example, may be peremptorily certain of the falsity of the Catholic theology. I do not mean certain that it includes no truth, or is not an approximation to the truth suitable to a certain stage of mental development. I merely mean that I reject whatever part of it comes into conflict with modern scientific beliefs, resting, as it seems to me, not only upon reasons which I have tested or devised, but upon an incomparably greater weight of rational authority. The fact that many men of greater ability than my own accept the system need not give me pause. Taken by itself, and supposing that evidence is to be counted, not weighed, it would be a relevant fact. If all that I know of a given belief were the fact that ten men of a certain capacity believed it and nine of equal capacity disbelieved it, the fact would afford a certain small presumption of its truth. But when I go further, the presumption may disappear or be supplanted by a contrary conviction. If, for example, the belief of the ten is avowedly founded on an illogical process, and always vanishes under the free application of logic, it goes for nothing. It proves at most the existence of an instinct, not a reasoned belief. And if, again, the principle of arbitrary authority be admitted, if nine of the men believe simply because one believes, and that one has given no proofs of his knowledge, the effective evidence is simply the evidence of the one. The spread of a belief by blind contagion is a fact which so far deprives the phenomenon of any logical significance. The evidence of the multitude of believers is reduced to the evidence of the few who have accepted their creed on reasonable grounds. The value of the evidence varies inversely with the acceptance of the principle of authority.

The fact that a creed has prevailed widely and for long periods has, indeed, a certain value. It implies a kind of verifying process. It shows that the belief cannot include errors so great as to be incompatible with the standard of civilisation actually obtained; an argument, however, which applies to the whole body of genuine beliefs current in a case, and not to the ostensible creed or any special part of it, which may be, more or less, neutralised by the remainder. It shows further that the belief enables men to find a sufficient expression for their personal and social emotions during the period of its vitality. It has a poetical if not a scientific value. To analyse the relations of the two would be a task of extreme complexity. This only may be assumed briefly, that the charm of a given creed for the imagination and the emotions affords a presumption that it contains much truth; for a system which entirely misrepresented the relations between men and the world, could hardly enable them to express their deepest feelings. The logical error would be represented by emotional discord. On the other hand, the tendency of men to put their emotions in place of their feelings, to believe what is pleasant rather than what is true, shows the necessity of rigidly verifying every creed, especially if it is the product of a time when erroneous conceptions of the universe were notoriously prevalent. Inversely, the disappearance of any creed in a progressive society, its failure to provide for emotional utterance or to satisfy intellectual demands, is a strong presumption that it contained an erroneous element. When the demand for verification is met, not by urging and stimulating the fullest possible application of every means of investigation, but by making belief prior to investigation a moral duty, the significance of such advice, however dexterously wrapped up, is sufficiently obvious. The fact that men who believe in a creed come to find it satisfactory, is not of much importance in a religious, though it might be in a scientific inquiry. To assume the truth of a doctrine and then to act upon it is often the only way of testing it. It is an excellent way, if it is certain—as it is certain in many scientific inquiries—that action based on an erroneous belief will make the error manifest. But no such result can be expected in many religious beliefs, inasmuch as in any hypothesis, false beliefs satisfy those who act upon them as well as true. Believe and act on the belief that paper is not inflammable, and you will soon find out your mistake. Believe and act on the belief that hell can be avoided by obeying the prescriptions of a priest, and you will never discover your mistake in this world. The impossibility of a verification is illogically evaded by converting assumption into a dogmatic belief, and preaching it as a duty. The defect of proof is supplied by deliberately inculcating unreasonable intensity of belief, and declaring that assent ought to outrun evidence. Such beliefs may be satisfactory to those who hold them, but can be no evidence to outsiders.

ON THE RELATION OF EVIDENCE TO CONVICTION
Richard H. Hutton

I understand Mr. Leslie Stephen's paper read before this Society to maintain that conviction should always be proportioned to evidence. Now I desire to give reasons for thinking that 'evidence" is only *one* legitimate ground for conviction, and that the sanest and soberest minds would suffer in sanity and sobriety if they endeavoured to clear their minds of all conviction not founded on evidence, and of all degrees of conviction not proportioned to the amount of evidence.

I mean by 'evidence' for a conviction, any consideration which, consciously grasped, tends to incline a fair judgment in the direction of that conviction; and I mean by conviction, that absolute inability to doubt a conclusion, that 'conquest' of the judgment by a particular belief, which may be due either to evidence, or to erroneous prejudice and prepossession, or to other causes, such, for example, as that "pre-established harmony' between the nature of man and the external universe which, whether you ascribe it to intellectual, or moral, or spiritual instincts, or to 'natural selection,' or to other causes, is, I believe, as potent a source of conviction, and of the kind of conviction that leads to wise action, as evidence itself.

Now I do not understand Mr. Leslie Stephen to think that the position of the lower animals would be improved by their ceasing to assume the truth, if we may so speak, of anything answering in them to conviction, for which they have no evidence. I do not suppose that he would wish the pointer-puppies, for instance, on their first initiation into sport, to expostulate with themselves on the gross superstition which inclined them, on the perception of a particular odour, to point in the direction from which the source of the odour proceeded. Yet that "untaught ability" (as Mr. Bain defines 'instinct') to indicate a particular locality on nothing that could be called evidence, since they can have no experience teaching them to connect the subjective feeling of smell with the inference as to direction which they draw, and help others to draw, from it, is probably accompanied in the dog by something as near to conviction that there is something in the direction indicated, which it is his function to point out, as a dog is capable of approaching to conviction at all. It is perfectly manifest, I suppose, that a sceptical chicken (if we could imagine one) which, feeling a strong inclination to chip the shell at the proper time for hatching, were to repel that inclination as entirely destitute of good evidence, would, like some human philosophers in like plight, perish of inanition, in the world to which its scepticism had needlessly confined it. Mr. Leslie Stephen, if I understand his paper aright, wishes to confine this duty of reducing our convictions, so far as may be possible, to the measure and proportions of the evidence we can find for them, to men alone; but in the case of mature men at least, I understand him to think it a universal duty, and that he is supported in that opinion by many of the ablest and most accomplished members of our Society. True, Mr. Stephen admits some qualifications to this duty. He admits, I think, that you are often right in acting on evidence which you have once had before you, have held to be satisfactory, and have forgotten, but the drift of which you distinctly re-member; and you may act on the evidence which others have examined, and which you have never examined yourself at all, so long as you take as much pains as is in your power to convince yourself that they are the best-informed and most candid judges to be found. But in all these cases, you should diminish your confidence just in proportion to the danger that the evidence you once thought sufficient might now, if re-examined by new lights, seem to you insufficient; or that the authority you now deem the best might turn out to be far from the best, or even though the best, very insufficient for intellectual guidance. These qualifications are obviously just, and I mention them only to show in how extremely doubtful a condition of judgment we ought on this theory always to be on almost all truths.

For consider, first, that all attestation depends upon memory, and that without an *unevidenced* belief in the infallibility of at least a good many acts of memory, most evidence itself would become worthless. Dr. Ward has worked this out before our Society in a paper of great force contributed now many years ago. Hardly one man in a thousand has before his mind's eye at the moment the mathematical evidence for the truth of the multiplication-table. For the ordinary purposes of life, my confidence that $6 \times 9 = 54$, is my confidence in the infallibility of my own memory that so it is. Of course, a minute's reflection will show me that six nines are more by four units than five tens; but I have not usually time for so much reflection, and if I had, I should not be a bit surer of it after working out the demonstration than I was before. But if I do not misunderstand the drift of Mr. Stephen's paper, I have no right to this belief in the infallibility of my own memory, and ought to be decidedly more certain after I receive the full evidence, than I was before on the mere strength of that flash of the mind which assured me that I was remembering rightly. So when, after a fruitless search for a familiar word or name, I light upon it, and say with absolute certainty,—That's it,—a cer-tainty for which I can produce no evidence outside the positive asseveration of my own memory,—I ought, if I understand Mr. Stephen aright, to take myself to task for my unevidenced confidence, and deduct something even from my general self-confidence on account of this grossly unreasonable certainty. And as, of course, all mere testimony depends on such acts of memory, one of the chief evidences of our human predisposition to insanity, ought to be the general confidence of ordinary memories.

Still more, of course, in instances of exceptional calculating-power, like Zerah Colburn's, who found the cube root of 268,336,165, almost instantaneously,—and indeed, did many calculations much more wonderful,—but who, "when interrogated as to the method by which he obtained these results," "constantly declared that he did not know *how* the answers came into his mind," the lad's belief in his own estimates was—at all events, till they had been repeatedly verified by the usual calculations—on Mr. Stephen's theory of belief, a pure superstition. Yet his case must have been very unlike that of most other remarkable arithmeticians if he were not quite as certain of his results before any one had taken the trouble to test his accuracy, as he was after long experience proved him to be an accurate calculator. Clearly, in the sense in which I have been using the word, Colburn had no evidence at first that his process was calculation at all, and in common reason ought, if Mr. Stephen be right, to have acquired only very slowly indeed a certain provisional belief in his own *aperçus of the answers to arithmetical questions*.

Now, what I maintain, in opposition to Mr. Stephen, is, that in all spheres of human life, beginning with memory and ascending to the highest departments of human duty and feeling, there are trustworthy as well as untrustworthy sources of conviction which are not founded on "evidence," though many of them are more or less verifiable by evidence, and that no greater calamity could happen to human beings than to discard all such sources of conviction, even though, as of course would be the case, in rejecting the trustworthy they would reject also a great many thoroughly untrustworthy convictions at the same time.

Take, first, the case of moral conviction. Does any one suppose for a moment that a child ought to have 'evidence' in the sense in which I have used the word (i.e., a clear grasp of considerations tending to incline a fair judgment in the direction of that conviction) of the evil of impure thoughts, before yielding to the conviction that they are evil? On the contrary, I maintain that the less a child (or a man) weighs arguments against yielding to impure thoughts, the sounder his conviction on the subject will be, and the better he will be. Explain it how you will,—whether from the Darwinian point of view of the storage of past experience till it takes the form of a new instinct, an explanation which does not, I think, cover all the facts, or from the intuitional point of view, or any other,—nothing is more certain than that a human being who begins life on a moral platform in which he assumes, as fixed data, from the earliest dawn of conscience, principles which formulate the best lessons of the unhappy and happy experience of others, has a vast moral advantage over his fellow-creatures, the extent of which it is hard to exaggerate. But what I want to point out is that such a child and man receive without evidence at all, as part of the data of life, convictions which Mr. Stephen tells us should never be firmer than the amount of evidence which goes to support them. Perhaps he will say that the evidence exists, though not in the breast of the individual who uses it, for such primary moral truths as the evil of impurity of thought. Well, but if the evidence does not exist in his breast, for him it does not exist at all. He has taken it on trust. He has not inquired. He believes, from the earliest dawn of conscience, that the injunction 'Resist impure thoughts' carried its own authority with it. He wanted no reason. Indeed he would not listen to reason. Reason on such a subject was itself a disloyalty to an authority higher than reason. And just as in relation to mathematical perceptions, though all men have unreasoned axioms from which they start, some men, like Zerah Colburn, have much higher and more complex unreasoned insights than others, so in moral issues, while all of us have unreasoned axioms to start from, some start from so high a platform of complex moral truth as to become the teachers and leaders of their race.

Again, on aesthetic subjects, I cannot conceive any one saying that conviction should be strictly proportioned to evidence. The poet or artist is so by virtue of seeing, without evidence, and by virtue of the glance of his own higher faculty, what it takes ordinary men much labour, even with such help, to discern. Can we imagine a "conviction founded on evidence" that the higher flights of imaginative genius will take the human spirit by storm! When Shakespeare makes Cleopatra say over the corpse of Antony what probably no woman in real grief ever did or would say, that "there is nothing left remarkable beneath the visiting moon," doubtless he had the strongest conviction that it would go right home to the imagination of men, and somehow paint for them that scene of real passion and despair as nothing which woman's lips ever uttered could have painted it. And when Wordsworth said to the girl who had climbed Helvellyn:—

> "Potent was the spell that bound thee,
>   Not unwilling to obey,
> For blue Æther's arms flung around thee
>   Stilled the paintings of dismay,"

he had, I am quite sure, the deepest conviction that that very bold metaphor went to the heart of the feeling poured into the soul by the blue air on a mountain-top, and would recall that feeling to thousands of minds from which it had half vanished. But assuredly neither of these convictions either were or could have been founded on evidence at all. They were founded on the aperçu of an inborn faculty. And though, of course, convictions of this kind are of no importance in relation to the formation of character or opinion, they illustrate none the less on that account how much all convictions, in the case of a being of complex nature like man, depend on that fine adjustment of his nature to the external universe which summarises, as it were, in brief, those infinite acccumulations of the 'evidence' of past events, on which alone, if you conceive the same structure built up through conscious intellectual processes, the same results could be arrived at.

Now, of course I do not mean to deny,—on the contrary, strongly to assert,—that very many of our customary starting-points in life are false and vicious unreasoned assumptions, as well as true and salutary unreasoned assumptions, and that so far as the former can be refuted by evidence, they ought to be. But even in relation to the false convictions which go on no evidence, but which are often caught up in the network of some imperious affection, I think it will be found to be true that it is quite as often not by intellectual evidence, but rather by the displacing influence of some larger and wider affection, that they are undermined and removed. Take the false view that unbelievers in Christianity are usually bad men,—in which so many grow up. Is that prejudice oftenest displaced by an array of evidence to prove the proposition false, or by some sudden glimpse of the self-denial and refined sadness of a sceptic in whose countenance you read, as in a book, that

"The intellectual power through words and things
    Goes sounding on its dim and perilous way,"

—a countenance on which you find stamped the self-denial needed to weigh and ponder and compare and suffer, and from the study of which, in a word, you jump, by the most illegitimate reasoning process imaginable, to an assumption widely divergent from that from which you have hithertho started in thought?

My own belief—and one founded, I think, on large evidence—is, that in almost every sphere of human nature, we start from unevidenced convictions which are as much part of the very moral stock-in-trade and capital of such a race as ours. as the pecuniary savings of one generation are of the pecuniary capital of the next; that it would be the greatest possible calamity if there were suddenly such a shrinkage in human conviction as would conform the strength of all our convictions to the evidence which was or ever had been in the possession of those who hold them; that amongst these convictions are of course many false ones, as well as many true ones, and that evidence is very useful in unsettling the false ones, though by no means the only, hardly, perhaps, the most potent, force at our service for that work; and that there is at all events a great amount of fair presumption against the attempt to weaken the foundations of human society by requiring men to hold their ultimate moral convictions in exact proportion to evidence alone, if for no other reason, still for this, that the effect of ages of belief surely ought to be to generate belief indefinitely stronger than any evidence the individual can command.

The only reply I can conceive to this argument is that 'evidence' does not cease to be evidence when it has been ingrained by centuries of experience into the very form and structure of human life. But then that reply assumes that the individual should not hold his opinion in proportion to the evidence which he himself has weighed, but in proportion to something indefinitely stronger,—the impulse which has come down to him to believe in full what his fathers only learned inch by inch to believe. And next, it is far from likely that the theory of hereditary accumulation of tendency, represents anything like the whole explanation of ultimate human beliefs, though it probably represents a part of it. Indeed, when once you have admitted that it is quite legitimate to believe with a strength in proportion to no evidence that is or ever has been in your own possession, you have no means at all of saying how much of that certainty of belief really belongs to the evidence which your ancestors had previously accumulated, and how much may be due merely to new faculty, or new intuition, or new inspiration, or to that new inpouring of spiritual life into our race which, whatever its origin,—and I hold it of course, to be divine,—does at all events flow in periodic tides, so far as human judgment is competent to pronounce.

PHILOSOPHY OF THE THEISTIC CONTROVERSY
William George Ward

Throughout our present series of essays we have explained that, whereas our affirmative argument for Theism will be such, we hope, as to hold its own against all gainsayers, the opponents, nevertheless, whom we directly assail are those only of one particular school. We do not directly encounter Hegelians and Pantheists, but only Phenomenists and Agnostics. This statement must, of course, be understood with obvious qualifications: we cannot, *e.g.*, establish the existence of a Personal God, without replying to whatever objections are raised by the Pantheist. But we shall not directly criticize the spirit and teaching of any Antitheistic school, except only that which proceeds on the lines of Phenomenism and which opposes Theism in the name of Inductive Philosophy. No other Antitheistic School has large influence in England; nor again, as we shall point out in the sequel, is any other so fundamentally and obtrusively opposed to religion in regard to the very meaning and due conduct of life. When we began our series we dealt with Mr. Stuart Mill as representing this school, for he was its acknowledged leader and most typical specimen. Since his death, however, not only his philosophical reputation has declined in quite an extraordinary degree; but, which is partly, no doubt, the cause of that declension, his posthumous "Essays on Religion" have exhibited one or two most remarkable instances of hesitation in carrying out his principles to their full and legitimate issue. On the present occasion, therefore, and hereafter, we shall treat him as one only out of many, and refer to those only of his utterances which are common to him with all Phenomenists.

The purpose of our present essay, we may say briefly, is to exhibit in their mutual relation these two antagonistic doctrines of Theism and Phenomenistic Antitheism. We hope first to summarize and emphasize what we have said on former occasions concerning the intellectual inanity, or rather self-contradictoriness, of Antitheistic Phenomenism in the shape which it now assumes. We hope next to consider what are the reasons of that profound antipathy to Theism which is so conspicuous in the adherents of Phenomenism; for this is, of course, an absolutely necessary inquiry if we are to fight against its adherents with any hope of success. We hope, lastly, to exhibit a catalogue of those arguments for Theism which we shall successively enforce in future essays; to indicate their general character; and to exhibit their ground of conclusiveness. We begin, then, with the first of these three themes.

It was a remarkable characteristic of Mr. Stuart Mill that he invariably treated his opponents not with courtesy only, but with kindliness and generosity. Dr. Bain, also, we must say, is uniformly courteous and respectful in his language. But such habits are far from universal among living members of the school. Thus Professor Huxley—as quoted in the *Tablet* of Aug. 20, 1881—says of those who believe that God created the universe, that "they have not reached that state of emergence from ignorance in which the necessity of a discipline to enable them to be judges has, as yet, dawned on the mind." Here is bounce and swagger with a vengeance: no Christian, then, possesses even the rudiments of due mental discipline. Without calling into question the Professor's possession of due mental discipline, we shall, nevertheless, contend that the philosophical system which he maintains is so feeble and self-contradictory as to be destitute of all claim on the slightest intellectual respect.

We here speak of Phenomenists, be it observed, as Philosophers, not as scientists. We heartily admit that innumerable truths of great importance have been established by inductive science; and that no men have laboured more ably and more successfully in the vineyard of inductive science than these our opponents. So far we have, of course, no quarrel with them whatever, and would only point out that many others have wrought with equal success in the same field who have been firm believers in Religious Doctrine. But Professor Huxley and his sympathizers are not content with holding that the processes of inductive science are reasonable and legitimate; they take an all-important step farther. According to them, the fact that inductive processes are legitimate suffices to establish a certain philosophical tenet which we call Phenomenism. And they then set forth a further premiss, with which we entirely concur—viz. that, if this tenet be true, man has no means of knowing God's Existence. We entirely admit, then, that Phenomenism is Antitheistic; but we maintain that, as held by them, it is most manifestly false and self-contradictory.

What, then, is Phenomenism? Nothing can be more easily understood by any one who will use his mind, than the distinction between this tenet and its contradictory, Intuitionism. The Phenomenist, as such, professes to build his intellectual fabric exclusively on "experienced facts;" to accept nothing except some experienced fact as a first premiss in argument, as a truth immediately known. It is by so comporting himself that he thinks he sympathizes with the true spirit of inductive science; and guards against the evil habit so common among other philosophers, the erecting gratuitously into the rank of objective truths what are merely impressions of the speculator's own mind.* On the other hand, the Intuitionist alleges that there are

---

* "The notion that truths external to the mind may be known by intuition independently of observation and experience, is, I am persuaded, for these times the great intellectual support of false doctrines and bad intentions. By the aid of this theory every inveterate belief and every intense feeling, of which the origin is not remembered, is enabled to dispense with the

various truths, immediately evident and admissible therefore as primary premises, which are in no sense "experienced facts." These he calls "truths of intuition." Accordingly we have, on former occasions, defined an "intuition" to be "an intellectual avouchment, reliably declaring as immediately certain some truth other than the mere existence and characteristics of such avouchment." The Intuitionist considers accordingly that these "truths of intuition" are no less immediately certain, no less trustworthy as primary sources of knowledge, than are experienced facts themselves.

We said just now that Phenomenism, as held by the contemporary school of Antitheistic Phenomenists, is most manifestly false and self-contradictory. What we meant was, that if Phenomenists were true to their characteristic tenet—if they honestly and consistently held to their principle, that experienced facts are the exclusive basis of real knowledge—they would commit philosophical suicide; they would contradict those affirmations, to which they have committed themselves most confidently and unanimously. This is to be our first ground of attack.

They consider that the strongest and most irresistible proof of the Phenomenistic tenet is to be found in the marvels wrought by inductive science. "Inductive science," they say, "has achieved its incredible successes precisely by its stern rejection of all first premises except experienced facts." Now, Dr. Bain ("Deductive Logic," p. 273) points out what is very obvious, viz. that "the guarantee, the ultimate* major premiss of all induction," is "nature's uniformity." And we are now going to argue that this first premiss of all induction, the premiss, without which no experienced fact can have the slightest scientific value—that this premiss is itself quite incapable of being proved on the exclusive basis of experienced facts. But, if this our thesis be established, it follows that "the stern rejection of all first premises except experienced facts" not only is not the characteristic of inductive science, but on the contrary would be the absolute destruction of that science. We proceed at once to develop this argument.

What do Dr. Bain and his sympathizers understand by the phrase "nature's uniformity"? They mean (1) that no phenomenon ever takes place without a corresponding phenomenal antecedent; and (2) that any given phenomenal antecedent is invariably and unconditionally followed by the same phenomenal consequent. It is their own emphatic statement that the

---

obligation of justifying itself by reason, and is erected into its own all-sufficient justification. There never was such an instrument devised for consecrating all deep-seated prejudices."— Stuart Mill's "Autobiography," pp. 225, 226.

"The difference between these two schools of Philosophy—that of Intuition and of Experience and Association—lies at the foundation of all the greatest differences of practical opinion in our age of progress."—*Ib*. *p. 273*.

Certain persons "addict themselves with intolerant zeal to those forms of philosophy in which intuition usurps the place of evidence, and internal feeling is made the test of objective truth."—"Essays on Religion," p. 72.

* Should not this word rather be "primary"?

uniformity of nature, understood in this precise sense, is absolutely essential as a foundation for inductive science. Suppose it were possible, *e.g.*, that I should compose a substance to-day of certain materials, and find it by experience to be combustible; while I might compose another to-morrow of the very same materials, united in the very same way, in the very same proportions, and by experience find the composition *in*combustible. If such a case were possible, argues the Phenomenist, the whole foundation of inductive science would be taken from under my feet.* Belief, then, in the uniformity of nature is admitted by Phenomenists themselves to be an absolutely essential condition, for the prosecution of inductive science.

The first question, then, we ask them is, by what right they *assume* this fact of nature's uniformity? How can they prove, unless they admit intuitive premisses, that phenomena throughout the universe do proceed with that undeviating regularity which their science requires? Mr. Stuart Mill, in controversy with ourselves, professed to give such a proof as we challenged; but his argument was so flimsy, that we had difficulty in believing him really to have given his mind to the subject. Dr. Bain, on the contrary, frankly admits that no such argument is forthcoming; and that the fact of nature's uniformity must be taken for granted without any proof whatever. (See his "Deductive Logic," p. 273.) "We can give no reason or evidence," he says, "for this uniformity." For our own part, however, we are disposed to admit that the *present* uniformity of phenomenal sequence may be inferred from experienced facts—not indeed with certainty, but with very considerable probability. Inductive science proceeds on this basis; and in these modern centuries its fecundity has been marvellous indeed. This supposition is certainly improbable in a very high degree, that investigations, proceeding on a thoroughly false basis, can have issued in so vast a multitude of entirely unexpected, yet experimentally verified, conclusions. The incredibly rapid progress, then, of inductive science has endued with a rapidly increasing

---

*We do not ourselves admit that the uniformity of nature is by any means so complete as Phenomenists consider. Their statement, indeed, as it stands, is directly anti-religious; it denies the existence of Freewill and of miracles, and it virtually denies also the efficacy of prayer, whether offered for temporal blessings, or for strength against temptation, or for progress in virtue. We set forth at sufficient length what we here mean, in our essay on "Science, Prayer, Freewill, and Miracles." In that essay—while we protest vigorously against any such sweeping proposition concerning the extent of nature's uniformity as Phenomenists love to set forth—we entirely admit, nevertheless, and maintain, that there does exist a certain very extensive uniformity throughout the phenomenal world. We consider, indeed, that both Freewill and Miracles constitute a very large exception to that uniformity; and we consider also that God is ever premoving and stimulating the natural action of natural forces in the direction marked out by His Providence. But a very large area of uniformity still remains, and one, we maintain, which amply suffices as a basis of solid induction.

In our present essay, our argument does not require that we dwell at greater length on this particular divergence between Phenomenists and ourselves: and we shall accept, therefore, for argument's sake and without further protest, their understanding of the term "nature's uniformity."

degree of probability the fundamental principle on which that science rests—viz. the uniformity of phenomenal sequence. We should, indeed, confidently maintain that even such an argument as we have here given possesses no real validity, except by the help of this or that implicit intuition, which men unconsciously and irresistibly assume as genuine. This, however, is a question on which we shall not now insist, because we wish here to content ourselves with the broadest and most palpable considerations. We will willingly admit, therefore, for argument's sake, that the modern progress of inductive science has enabled the Phenomenist, consistently with his own principles, to regard the *present* uniformity of nature as sufficiently established.

But now it is manifest on the surface that these grounds of probability, whatever their value, apply exclusively to what may be called *the scientific epoch*. Go back three thousand years, not to speak of an indefinitely more recent period, there was no assemblage of facts, discovered by careful processes of induction; nor any persistent exploration of nature. Phenomenists declare that they will accept no conclusion unless it be rigidly deduced from experienced facts. What facts in the world are there to which they can point as premises for the conclusion that uniform phenomenal sequence existed three thousand years ago? If *experienced facts* were all the premises on which the argument could reasonably proceed, there is hardly so much as a preponderance of probability for the conclusion that nature's uniformity existed then as it exists now. Assuredly, the notion of there being any approximation to *certainty* on the matter is absolutely childish. Yet Phenomenists, in their whole argumentation concerning creation, evolution, and similar themes, invariably assume, as a matter of course, that the laws of nature proceeded during thousands, not to say millions, of years ago, with the same regularity and uniformity with which they proceed now. Was there ever poorer and more paltry child's play than this? Let it be carefully observed that we are not here attempting any inquiry whatever, direct or indirect, how far *intuitive* premises may be producible, which shall suffice for establishing the past uniformity of nature: we are but criticizing these repudiators of intuition, these devotees of experienced facts. And it is really too absurd when one finds them ridiculing with lofty contempt the dogma, *e.g.*, of creation, and resting their criticism on no stronger basis than their extravagant assumption—extravagant, that is, on *their* principles—concerning the laws of nature in time past. In fact, their argument is exactly like what is uncomplimentarily called a lady's reason: "It is because it is." "We hold firmly that creation never took place." "Why?" "Because the laws of nature always existed." "On what ground do you hold that these laws existed." "Because otherwise it might be necessary to admit the dogma of creation."

And if, on Phenomenistic principles, there is such very slender probability for the statement that nature proceeded uniformly throughout time past, what shall we say of the statement that nature will proceed uniformly in time *future?* Yet, as Dr. Bain himself observes, "all our interest is concentrated on what is yet to be: the present and past are of no value, except only as a clue to the events that are to come" ("Deductive Logic," p. 273). The processes of induction lose their whole practical use, unless there be assurance that the laws of nature will be hereafter the same which they now are. But to say, as the Phenomenist must consistently say, that *experienced facts* can afford assurance for this, is simply a contradiction in terms. Experienced facts belong to the past or present. And it is self-contradictory to say that any inference can be drawn from them in regard to the *future*, except by help of some premiss alleged to be intuitive; as, *e.g.*, "the future will resemble the past;" or, as Dr. Bain more accurately words it, "What has uniformly been in the past will be in the future." "This assumption," Dr. Bain proceeds ("Deductive Logic," p. 274), "is an ample justification of the inductive operation: without it we can do nothing; with it we can do everything. Our only error is in proposing to give any reason or justification of it; to treat it otherwise than as *begged* at the very outset." Is Saul, then, also among the prophets? Is Dr. Bain at last an Intuitionist? For as to this "assumption" of which he speaks, what is it at last but precisely what we have called an alleged "truth of intuition"? Manifestly, if inductive science cannot reasonably be constructed except on the basis of this "assumption," it cannot reasonably be constructed at all on the exclusive basis of experienced facts.

Here, therefore, we will revert to what we just now said. The stern rejection, we said, of all first premisses except experienced facts, not only is not a characteristic of inductive science, but would be the destruction of that science. Take Dr. Bain's thesis that "the future will resemble the past." It would, of course, be an unspeakable absurdity to say that this is an experienced fact. But neither can any experienced facts be alleged which in any combination will suffice by themselves logically to *prove* this thesis, or even to make it ever so faintly probable. A science, then, which should be based exclusively on experienced facts would not throw one glimmering of light on the future. It might show that, *at this moment,* such or such a medicine is a remedy for such a disease; such or such a chemical combination issues in such or such a result; such or such an arch bears such or such a weight, etc. But it would throw absolutely no light whatever on the question whether such statements will be even proximately correct, a day or an hour beyond this moment. Dr. Bain points out very truly that such a science would be absolutely valueless. What we are ourselves saying is that, at all events, it would be fundamentally different from what is now called "inductive science." That which is now called "inductive science" would be utterly overthrown and subverted, if its votaries rejected all first premisses except experienced facts.

We have argued that, if no first premisses were admissible except experienced facts, two grave consequences would inevitably ensue. Firstly, man could have neither certain nor even probable information concerning nature's uniformity in times long past; nor, secondly, could he form so much as any reasonable conjecture of the kind concerning even the most immediate future. Here, however, a further question will most reasonably be asked. Let intuitive premises be admitted no less than phenomenal—in other words, let true, and not false, philosophical principles be assumed—what will *then* be ascertained as sound doctrine in regard to man's extent of knowledge concerning past and future phenomenal uniformity? We merely indicate this question to show that we have not forgotten its reasonableness. Plainly it is quite irrelevant to our own argument; and we really do not happen to be acquainted with any writer who, to our mind, fairly confronts it. Its consideration is one of the various philosophical lacunæ—much more numerous, we think, than might have been expected—which arrest the course of a straightforward student, and dissatisfy him with existent philosophical treatises.

So much, then, on that one foundation of inductive science—of the science which Phenomenists specially claim as their own—the doctrine of phenomenal uniformity. But all this is really as nothing compared with the further objection to Phenomenism, which we have pressed on many former occasions, and to which we have never received a reply even superficially plausible. Every man, throughout every minute of his waking life, is eliciting one or other of those intuitive acts which are called acts of *memory*. If he accept these acts as testifying objective truth, he is *ipso facto* an Intuitionist and no Phenomenist. If he do not so accept them, his knowledge is below that of the very brutes, being strictly confined to his consciousness of the present moment.* Let us explain our meaning in this statement.

The Phenomenist purports to build his whole philosophical structure on "experienced facts;" and he must mean, of course, facts which he *knows* to have been experienced. We ask him how he can possibly know that there is any given fact in the whole world which has been experienced by any one whomsoever. Most certainly he does not know more as to what *others* have experienced than of what he has experienced *himself*. We ask him, then, straightforwardly, how can you possibly know, concerning any given mental phenomenon in the whole world, that you have once experienced it? You reply that you have the clearest and most articulate memory thereof. Well, we do not doubt at all that you have that present *impression* which you call a most clear and articulate memory. But how do you know—how can you legitimately even guess—that your present impression corresponds with a past fact? See what a tremendous proposition this is which you, who call yourself a cautious man of science, unscrupulously take for granted. You have

---

*We have here often made an explanation, which it may be better to make again. Those avouchments of memory, to which we refer in the text, are those only which concern a man's *quite recent* experience—the memory of a minute or a few minutes back. A man's memory of what took place a long time ago is often far from infallible.

been so wonderfully endowed—such is your prodigious assertion—that in every successive case your clear and articulate present *impression* and *belief* of something as past corresponds with a past mental *fact*. That this should happen even once is surely, on Phenomenistic principles, a very remarkable coincidence; but you assume, as a matter of course—without so much as any attempt at proof—that this marvellous fact occurs some thousand times in every hour of your waking life. What is the true *rationale* of your proceeding? There is but one answer which can possibly be given. You are acting like a reasonable man, *i.e.* like an Intuitionist. You accept your intuitive act of memory as an infallible voucher for your firm conviction, that certain experiences have befallen you in time past which are entirely external to your present consciousness.

Had space permitted, we might with advantage have recapitulated a much larger portion of our earlier controversies against Phenomenism; but we must proceed, without further delay, to point our moral. Mr. Stuart Mill complains that the opposite school alleges certain tenets as self-evident; "erects them into their own absolutely sufficient vouchers and justifications; and uses them for the purpose of consecrating all deep-seated prejudices." Now, a truth which is "its own absolutely sufficient voucher and justification," is precisely what we call a truth of intuition; and we have admitted throughout that, without the assumption of intuitive premisses, Theism cannot be argumentatively established. But, as we have now been arguing, Theism is not the *only* important doctrine so circumstanced. On the contrary, there is absolutely no doctrine, existent or conceivable, which *can* be established without the help of intuitive premisses; nay, if men do not avail themselves of such premisses, their knowledge will be below that of the very brutes. Whatever else, therefore, may or may not be true, the Phenomenist's position, at all events, is a suicidal absurdity.

Of course, an Antitheist, having become an Intuitionist, may most reasonably raise a further question. He may maintain that, whereas the intuitions alleged by him are genuine, those alleged by his opponents are spurious. In our future essays we shall have to join issue on this indictment, as regards each successive tenet, which we shall allege as intuitive. We may as well, however, point out at once that our opponent will here have an uncommonly difficult part to play. "It is an undoubtedly valid intuition," he will have to say, "which declares that the uniformity of nature dates back, say, six thousand years. It is an undoubtedly valid intuition which declares that the said uniformity will continue in the future for quite an indefinite period. It is an undoubtedly valid intuition which declares in each successive case that my feelings of five minutes ago were what my memory now declares them to have been. But it is no valid intuition which declares that $2 + 5$ necessarily equals $3 + 4$; or that to slander my neighbour is necessarily wrong." Here is surely a startling and paradoxical position, if ever such there were. Still, all this is external to our immediate theme. What we are now urging is this. The proposition maintained by Mr. Mill and his school that there are *no* genuine intuitions, no truths external to present experience, "which are their own sufficient vouchers and justifications"—this proposition, at all events, is out of court. It is a proposition clamorously repudiated by the common sense and clear insight of mankind: it expresses a theory which may now fairly be relegated to the limbo of exploded philosophical absurdities.

INCOHERENCE OF EMPIRICAL PHILOSOPHY.
Henry Sidgwick

By Empirical Philosophy, I do not mean particularly the philosophy of J. S. Mill, or of Professor Bain, or of any other individual thinker; I mean a broader and simpler view of the world of knowledge, which these writers have in common, but which they share with many others who had not worked out their views in detail. I mean, in fact, the philosophy which students of Natural Science generally have, or tend to have; and also other persons who cannot be called students of Natural Science, but whose minds are impressed and dominated by the triumphant march of modern physical investigation. And in order that my point of view in criticising may be understood, I should like to add that I count myself among these latter persons. I have a general, unanalysed conviction, independent of close reasoning of any kind, that the continually extending conquests of the human intellect over the material world constitute at the present time the most important fact for one who wishes to philosophise,—that is, to think rightly about the universe, or about knowledge in general. Any philosophy that is not thoroughly competent to deal with this fact has thereby a presumption against it that it is behind its age. Just as at the outset of modern philosophy in the age of Descartes (as well as earlier still, in the age of Plato), Mathematics naturally presented itself as the type of solid and definite knowledge, so, it seems to me, the type is now furnished by the sciences that rest on experience; to which mathematics—in the natural *primá facie* view—stands in the subordinate relation of an instrument.

I am therefore as much disposed as any one can be to go to experience for a test of truth, and to accept the conditions that experience imposes as guarantees of credibility. Only I find myself unable, even with the aid of the eminent thinkers above mentioned, to work out a coherent system of philosophy on this basis. Hence the title and scope of my paper.

I will first state briefly the cardinal positions of Empirical Philosophy, as I conceive it.

I. That the ideas, concepts, &c., which are the materials of knowledge, come from experience; *i.e.*, from presentation to the mind of the realities which the ideas represent.

I give this doctrine first, because of the important place which it seems to have held in the view of the founder of English Empiricism, Locke; and which it has consequently occupied in most expositions of the philosophy since his time. I shall not, however, discuss its validity in the present paper; because however interesting it may be from a purely psychological point of view, it does not appear to me to have any fundamental philosophical importance.

For, in the first place, we may fully grant that all ideas are derived from experience; and yet hold that universal and immutable relations among these ideas admit of being intuitively known by abstract reflection, and that it is the apprehension of such relations that constitutes knowledge, in the highest sense of the term. In fact, this is just Locke's view, as all readers of the Fourth Book of his "Essay" are aware,—though it is commonly overlooked in the references popularly made to "Locke and Bacon" as co-originators of the Philosophy of Experience. For such a view, though "empirical" as regards the materials out of which knowledge is constructed, is essentially "intuitional" or "a priori" as regards the mode of constructing them into knowledge; and this latter is the point philosophically most important.

But secondly, even as regards the materials of knowledge, it does not appear that the ascertainment of the origin of ideas can have any decisive effect; on account of the great changes which ideas frequently undergo, in the course of their use as instruments of scientific reasoning. We may find instances of such change in the nomenclature and terminology of almost any science. To begin with mathematics: I have no doubt myself that the ideas of "straight line," "circle," "square" are derived from experience; that is, from seeing and moving among things that appeared straight, round, and square. But it is now admitted by all schools, that in the degree of refinement in which these notions are now used in mathematical reasonings, it is impossible to produce any objects of experience which perfectly exemplify them. In physical sciences, however, this change of meaning is often more marked. Take the notion "Force." This seems indubitably derived from experience of muscular exercise, and hence its original significance must have included, at least, some vague representation of the movements of muscles, or of the limbs moved by muscles, and also some of the specific feeling of muscular effort. But by "Force," as used in physical reasonings, we mean merely a cause which we conceive obscurely through its relation to its effect, motion; which motion, again, may be merely possible, not actual. Hence, whatever be the conditions within which our knowledge of forces is confined, it does not appear that the origin or original content of the notion can have much to do with these conditions. Similarly in chemistry, the ideas of "acid" and "salt" must have originally represented merely the flavours experienced by tasting the things so called; but now we regard such flavours as mere accidents of the relation of the things we call "acids" and "salts" to our palate, and not even universally inseparable accidents. In psychology, again, the difference between the original character of the ideas by means of which we think about mental processes, and the character they ultimately acquire when our reasoning has become scientifically precise, is still more striking.

For almost all our terms originally represented physical, not psychical, facts; and the physical significance often clings to the idea in such a way as to confuse our psychological reasonings, unless we take pains to get rid of it; while at the same time, thinkers of all schools would agree that we *have* to get rid of it. Thus, "impression" meant the physical fact of stamping or pressing, "apprehension" meant "grasping with the hand," "intention" and "emotion" suggested physical "straining" and "stirring up." But we all put these physical meanings out of our view, when we are trying to think clearly and precisely about physical phenomena; however interesting it may be to note them when we are studying the history of thought. Hence, I conclude that the settlement of the time-honoured question of the "origin of our ideas"—so far as it admits of being settled by received scientific methods—will not really determine anything, either as regards the *materials* of knowledge, or as regards the mode of constructing knowledge out of them.

I pass on, then, to consider the second fundamental doctrine of Empiricism.

II. That all kinds of knowledge, all true judgments or propositions, are founded on experience: not necessarily, I understand, upon sensible experience—that would be Sensationalism, rather than Empiricism—but upon experience of some kind: that is, upon immediate cognitions of some individual facts. By the phrase "founded on experience" must be meant that all true judgments are either such immediate cognitions, or capable of being proved by these. This must be meant, as otherwise the proposition does not characterize Empiricism with sufficient distinctness. For modern transcendentalism claims, in a certain sense, to be "founded on experience;" it claims that the universal truths which it regards as the principles of knowledge are implied in particular experiences, though they do not require to be proved by them. Again, some theological creeds which we commonly regard as superstitions are, in a manner, "founded" on specific religious experiences; but we consider them superstitious, because they include propositions which we do not think capable of being proved by such experiences.

Now, friends and foes alike regard it as a negative characteristic of popular Empirical Philosophy that it aims at clearing away transcendentalism and superstition, metaphysical chimaeras and theological dreams, what is falsely taken for knowledge by the credulity of the speculative and the credulity of the sentimental.

Let us examine, then, how the proposition so defined is to be established as a cardinal doctrine of philosophy.

Now here we must first ask what it is that philosophy offers or attempts to do for us in respect of knowledge. Obviously, it does not only tell us that certain propositions are true, certain things known; it aims at establishing a general theory of what *can* be known, at giving us a general criterion, by which we may distinguish real from apparent knowledge. Now, such a general criterion, as established by empirical philosophy, must obviously be empirical, otherwise the philosophy would be inconsistent with itself: that is, it must be founded on experience, on particular cognitions that this, that, and the other thing not merely appear to be, but really *are* known. Now, how are these particular knowledges respecting knowledge to be obtained? They must either be proved or assumed: and it does not much matter which we say, because if we say that they are proved, this proof can only be given by assuming similar particulars, since it would obviously be inconsistent with the criterion to be established if we allowed any part of its proof to rest on universal propositions as an ultimate basis.

What, then, are these particulars which Empirical Philosophy must assume at the outset of its procedure, and which, therefore, cannot require to be guaranteed by the criterion which this procedure is supposed ultimately to establish? Popular Empiricism seems to me to give at different times two different answers to this question; and by shifting about from the one to the other, and sometimes mixing the two, its argument, I think, gains in plausibility what it loses in clearness.

1. Sometimes the answer is, explicitly or implicitly, that we start with what is generally admitted to be solid knowledge,—that is, not the disputed and controverted matter which is found to some extent in all departments of study, and of which Metaphysics and Theology entirely consist; but the undoubted facts of history, natural and civil, and the generalisations of positive science. Such knowledge, we see, is commonly supposed to be based upon experience, and hence the examination of it naturally leads us to the empirical criterion. Mathematics, no doubt, constitutes a *primâ facie* exception to the generalisation that "all solid knowledge is based on particular experiences," since mathematicians commonly hold that their conclusions are attained by *a priori* reasoning from universal truths intuitively known. But let us suppose that this exception can be explained away, in Mill's or some other manner; and let us grant that being "founded on experience" is a characteristic which we find, on examination, to belong to all beliefs which are commonly admitted as constituting solid knowledge. It must still be clear that Empiricism cannot give the presence of this characteristic, as a reason for philosophically taking this generally admitted knowledge to be really and certainly what it seems; otherwise it would argue in a manifest circle, as it would start with assuming those beliefs to be knowledge which possess a certain characteristic, and then infer that this characteristic is the true criterion of sound knowledge. Hence it must give some other reasons for accepting these beliefs, and this reason can only be that they *are* generally admitted to be knowledge; that is, it must start with accepting the criterion of General Consent; the acceptance of which, we may observe, is commonly thought to be a distinctive mark of an antagonistic school,—that of "Intuitive" or "Common Sense" philosophy. This, however, is not in itself an objection,—*fas est et ab hoste doceri*. It is more important to note that if Empiricism accepts this criterion at the outset of its procedure, it cannot

shake it off, as it seems inclined to do, at the end. For even if we find that all that is commonly admitted to be knowledge has also the characteristic of being founded on experience, this can give us no ground for ultimately regarding Experience, rather than General Consent, as the true criterion of knowledge. Hence this line of reasoning cannot justify us in rejecting any beliefs that may be equally guaranteed by general consent, even when they are not founded on experience; it cannot, therefore, establish the Empirical theory of "what we *can* know."

This seems so plain, that I need not enter into further difficulties involved in the acceptance of the criterion of General Consent,—as that the consent of the majority to science and history is ignorantly given, or not really given at all; while if we mean "consent of experts," we have to decide arbitrarily who are experts; that the consent of one age differs from that of another, and that in past ages the criterion would have certified many doctrines that we now reject as erroneous and superstitious, &c.—especially since these considerations have been forcibly urged by more than one empirical philosopher. Suppose, then, that we give up the criterion of General Consent, so far as our philosophical procedure is concerned. Only, mind that we must give it up in earnest, and must not afterwards, in philosophising, introduce propositions because "no sensible man," or "no one with the slightest knowledge of physical science," doubts them. We must pass, then, to consider the second answer that Empiricists give to our question,—What particulars of knowledge have we to start with, in order to establish the Empiricist theory of knowledge?

2. The answer that Mill and others generally give to the question, when formally put is, that they start, as philosophers, with what is immediately known, without inference of any kind, and establish all other truths by canons of inference based upon experience.

The question then arises,—How are we to know philosophically what *is* immediately known? Are we to take the general agreement of mankind as evidence of this? That would bring us round again to all the difficulties already discussed. Are we to accept each man's own view of what he immediately knows? This certainly seems in accordance with empirical principles, as all experience must be primarily the experience of individual minds. But if we take, unsifted and uncriticised, what any human being is satisfied that he or she immediately knows, we open the door to all sorts of malobservation in material matters, and to all sorts of superstition in spiritual matters,—as superstitious beliefs commonly rest, in a great measure, upon what certain persons believe themselves to have seen, heard, or otherwise personally experienced. And in fact, no empiricist adopts this alternative; there is no point upon which empirical philosophers are more agreed than on the incapacity of ordinary persons to distinguish their immediate from their mediate knowledge. Shall we, then, say that we take each man's experience so far as it commends itself to other men? But if we mean "other men generally," this is only our old criterion of General Consent, in a negative instead of a positive aspect. Why should any man's experience be submitted to the judgment of men in general. It seems plausible to talk of one man's experience being confirmed by that of others. But I do not see what right we have to assume that one man's immediate cognitions *ought* to coincide with the immediate cognition of others; still less, why they ought to coincide with their inferences.

In short, it seems clear that if Empiricists do not trust common men's judgment as to their own immediate knowledge, they can hardly put them forward as trustworthy judges of the immediate knowledge of others. Thus the only course remaining seems to be that we should accept the experience of individuals after it has passed the scrutiny of experts.

But thus we are forced to face the question,—Who are experts in discriminating different kinds of knowledge? I ask this rather anxiously, because I see a serious danger threatening us; that, namely, of having to admit among experts the Transcendental or Intuitional Metaphysicians, who say that they immediately know universal truths. If we once admit them, I do not see how we can hope to establish the cardinal doctrine of Empiricism. Yet how can we exclude them, except by assuming the empirical philosophers to be the only real experts? which will hardly do in an argument that aims at proving the empirical philosophy to be true.

Well, I do not wish to take my stand on this difficulty. I have no love for the transcendental metaphysicians; and perhaps there may be some way of excluding them which I do not at present see. Let them be excluded; and let us only recognize, as experts in discriminating immediate knowledge, persons who will not allow anything to be immediately known except particular facts. Still, serious difficulties remain; because even these experts disagree profoundly among themselves. I am not now referring to any minor divergences, but to the fundamental disagreement between two lines of empirical thought which—if I may coin a word for clearness' sake—I will call respectively *materialistic* and *mentalistic*. When a Materialistic Empiricist affirms that physical science is based upon experience he means that it is based on immediate knowledge of particular portions of something solid and extended, definitely shaped and sized, moving about in space of three dimensions. Whether he regards this matter as also coloured, resonant and odorous, is a more doubtful question; but probably he would say that colour, sound, and odour are effects on the mind—or perhaps on the brain?—of the molecular movements of material particles. I cannot profess to make his views on this point even apparently consistent, if he is a thorough-going materialist, without making him say what seems extravagantly absurd; but it is enough for our present purposes that he at any rate believes himself to know immediately—through touch, if in no other way—matter with the qualities first mentioned.

The Mentalistic Empiricist, on the other hand, maintains that nothing can be immediately known except mental facts, consciousness or feeling of some kind; and that if we are right in assuming a non-mental cause of these mental facts—which he is generally inclined to doubt—we must at any rate regard this cause as unknown in every respect except its mere existence, and this last as only known by inference.

These two views seem to me mutually exclusive. It is true that there are some persons of comprehensive intellect, like Mr. Herbert Spencer, who appear to combine the two; but the simpler sort of empirical philosophers, who take either one view or the other, but not both together, are, I think, clearly a majority. And we may observe that the main line of English empirical philosophy, from Locke downwards, is definitely Mentalistic.

How, then, is Empiricism to deal with this disagreement?—for it cannot be denied to be rather serious. The more thoughtful Materialists, like Dr. Maudsley, do not exactly say that there are no mental facts which we may contemplate introspectively. But they hold that no scientific results have ever been reached by such contemplation; and they say very truly that physical science has always progressed by taking the materialistic point of view, and that there is no admitted progressive science of psychology, proceeding by the introspective method, which can be set beside the physical sciences. Hence, they boldly infer that there never will be such a science; and in fact, they are inclined to lump the Mentalists along with Transcendentalists and others, under the common notion of Metaphysicians (used as a term of abuse), and to charge them all together with using the Subjective Method, condemned as fruitless by experience. The Mentalists do not quite reply in the same strain; indeed, they have rather a tenderness for the Materialists, whose aid, as against Transcendentalism and Superstition, is not to be despised. But they say that the Materialists are inexpert in psychological analysis, and that what they call "matter" is really, when analyzed, a complex mental fact, of which some elements are immediately known and others added by unconscious inference.

Well, let us suppose this controversy somehow settled. Let us grant, as the supposition most favourable to Empiricism, that we immediately know the external world, so far as it is necessary to know it for the purpose of constructing physical science. But now who are the "we" who have this knowledge? Each one of us can only have experience of a very small portion of this world; and if we abstract what is known through memory, and therefore mediately, the portion becomes small indeed. In order to get to what "we" conceive "ourselves" to know as "matter of fact" respecting the world, as extended in space and time—to such merely historical knowledge as we commonly regard not as "resting" on experience, but as constituting the experience on which science rests—we must accept the general trust-worthiness of memory, and the general trustworthiness of testimony under proper limitations and conditions. I do not for a moment say that we have no right to make these assumptions; I only do not see how we can prove that we have such a right, from what we immediately know. Empiricists sometimes reply that these and similar assumptions are continually "verified" by experience. But what does "verified" exactly mean? If it means "proved true," I defy any one to construct the proof, or even to advance a step in it, without assuming one or more of the propositions that are to be verified. What is really meant, I conceive, by "verification" in this case is that these assumptions are accompanied by anticipations of feelings or perceptions which are continually found to resemble or agree with the more vivid feelings or perceptions which constitute the main stream of experience. Now, granting that such resemblance or agreement may be immediately known, I yet cannot see that anything is gained towards the establishment of the cardinal doctrine of Empiricism. For there is a similar agreement between actual experience and the anticipations accompanying all the general propositions—mathematical, logical, or physical—which philosophers of a different school affirm themselves to know immediately; so that this "verification" can hardly justify one set of assumptions, as against the other.

Similar difficulties occur when we examine how Empirical Philosophy passes from particular facts to general laws of nature; and especially to the "law of causation," which Mill and others use deductively for the philosophical establishment of other laws. But I could not dwell on these difficulties, without saying over again what has been more than once better said by others; and perhaps the above points may suffice for an evening's debate. After all that I have said, a man of sense will doubtless conclude that he will go on trusting experience and the empirical sciences. Here I shall quite agree with him. We cannot get along without the empirical sciences. But we might perhaps make a shift to dispense with Empirical Philosophy.

CERTITUDE IN RELIGIOUS ASSENT*
William George Ward

F. Newman deserves the warm gratitude of his co-religionists, were it only as being the first to fix Catholic attention on what is certainly the one chief stronghold of philosophical objectors against the Church; and he deserves still more gratitude for the singular power of argument and felicity of illustration which he has brought to his task. There are undoubtedly various incidental statements in his volume with which we are far from agreeing; but it is not our intention to say much of them on the present occasion. The series of able articles from the pen of F. Harper, now appearing in the *Month*, will doubtless in due course be collected in a separate publication; and their appearance in that state will give us the opportunity of expressing our own humble opinion on the points at issue. But we are at all events thoroughly in accordance with what we regard as F. Newman's central position; and to this part of his work we shall confine ourselves in what we are now going to say.

What, then, is that "chief stronghold of philosophical objectors against the Church," on which F. Newman has been the first to fix Catholic attention? This—that since the strength of assent, given to any proposition, should invariably be proportioned to the amount of evidence on which that proposition rests, no man loves truth for its own sake who does not labour, in every single matter of thought, to effect this equation between his strength of proof and his firmness of conviction. See, *e.g.*, F. Newman, pp. 155, 156; p. 167; p. 169, etc. Let us begin, then, with pointing out the powerful argument which an anti-Catholic could at once build up, if this foundation were conceded him.

"Catholics are taught to regard it as a sacred duty that they shall hold, most firmly and without a shadow of doubt, the truth of certain marvels which are alleged to have taken place nineteen centuries ago. As to examining the *evidence* for those truths, the great mass of Catholics are of course philosophically uncultured and simply incompetent to such a task. But even were they competent thereto, they are prevented from attempting it. Except a select few of them, they are all forbidden to read or knowingly to hear one syllable of argument on the other side. Under such circumstances, *proof* for

An Essay in Aid of a Grammar of Assent. By JOHN HENRY NEWMAN, D.D., of the Oratory. London: Burns, Oates, & Co.

their creed they can have none; any more than a *judge* can have proof who has only heard witnesses on one side, and them not cross-examined. So far from proportioning their assent to the evidence on which their doctrine rests, the assent claimed from them in the very highest, while the evidence afforded them is less than the least.

"But take even any one of the select few who are permitted to study both sides of the question. He will tell you quite frankly that his belief was as firm before his examination as it is now; nay, and that he regards it as a sin, which unrepented would involve him in eternal misery, if he allowed himself so much as one deliberate doubt on the truth of Catholicity. I place before him some serious difficulty, which tells against the most central facts of his religion: he had never heard of the difficulty before, and he is not now at all sure that he will be able to answer it. I should have expected, were it not for my knowledge of Catholics, that the confidence of his conviction would be *diminished* by this circumstance; for, plainly, an unanswered difficulty is no slight abatement from the body of proof on which his creed reposes. But he says unblushingly that if he were to study for ten years without seeing how to meet the point I have suggested, his belief in his Church, whose claim of authority he recognizes as divinely authorized, would be in no respect or degree affected by the circumstance.

"Nor is it for themselves alone, but for all mankind, that Catholics prescribe this rebellion against reason. They maintain that every human being, to whom their Gospel is preached, is under an obligation of accepting with firmest faith the whole mass of Catholic facts—the miraculous Conception. Resurrection. Ascension, etc.; while it is simply undeniable that 999 out of every 1000 are absolutely incapable of appreciating ever so distantly the evidence on which these facts are alleged to repose.

"Nor, to do them justice, do they show the slightest disposition to conceal or veil their maxims. The Vatican Council itself has openly anathematized all those who shall allege that Catholics may lawfully suspend their judgment on the truth of Catholicity, until they have obtained for themselves scientific proof of its truth.[1]

"I have no general prejudice against Catholics; on the contrary, I think many of them possess some first-rate qualities. But while their avowed intellectual maxims are those above recited, I must regard them as external to the pale of intellectual civilization. I have no more ground on which I can argue with a Catholic than I have ground on which I can argue with a savage."

We shall have repeatedly, in our present essay, to comment on the principle set forth and applied to this objection; and it will be much more

---

[1] Si quis dixerit parem esse conditionem fidelium, etc., ita ut Catholiei justam causam habere possint fidem, quam sub Ecclesiæ magisterio jam susceperunt, assensu suspenso in dubium vocandi donee demonstrationem scientitieam credibilitatis et veritatis fidei suæ absolverint, anathema sit."—"Dei Filius," c. 3, canon 6.

convenient, therefore, at once to give it a name. Perhaps we may be permitted to call it the principle of "equationism;" the principle which alleges that there is an obligation on every one who loves truth, of setting himself expressly to the task of effecting an "equation" between the strength of his convictions and the amount of proof on which they respectively rest. And to those Catholics who regard with suspicion the general tendency of F. Newman's volume, we would entreat them to consider how the objection of equationists, as above stated, can be otherwise met than by the substantial adoption of his doctrine. However, we have no kind of right to constitute ourselves his interpreters. Our purpose in the present essay is only to solve the above objection in our own way, making abundant use for that purpose of the invaluable materials which he has supplied. And we shall understand the doctrine of these equationists, not as one of their number might explain it when cross-questioned, but in the sense it must bear if it is to warrant the anti-Catholic objections just now recited.

We cannot proceed, however, one step in our task till we have made some explanation of our terminology. F. Newman uses the word "certitude" in a sense different from that usually given by Catholic philosophers. They divide certitude into two elements: as signifying, firstly, the reasonable absence of all doubt; and, secondly, a certain *degree* of positive adhesion to the truth embraced. F. Newman includes in the term only the *former* of the two elements; and in saying, therefore, that certitude has no *degrees* as regards the absence of doubt, he entirely concurs with them in their doctrine.[2] We shall ourselves, so far, use the word "certitude" in F. Newman's sense. In p. 204, however, he draws a distinction between what he calls "material" and "formal" certitude; which we do not find useful for our own purpose, and which we shall therefore not adopt.[3] We shall speak of "certitude" existing in my mind as to any truth, whenever I undoubtingly assent to that truth on grounds which legitimately generate such undoubtingness; on grounds, we mean, which *conclusively establish* the truth in question. Undoubting assent itself we shall call "absolute assent;" whether it do or do not rest on fully adequate grounds. By "absolute assent," in other words, we understand an assent which is not only *unaccompanied* by doubt, but which is so firm as to *expel* doubt; to be *incompatible* with the presence of doubt. And we shall say that an absolute assent, resting on *in*adequate grounds, possess "*putative* certitude" only.

---

[2] Take Liberatore, for instance. "Quòd una [certitudo] alteri præstet, facile suadetur: si non attendas ad partem negativam, nimirum *exclusionem dubii*, quæ indivisibilis omnino est et *gradus non habet;* sed attendas ad partem positivam, nimirum intensitatem adhæsionis, etc."—"Logica," n. 11. Dmowski, again. "Omnis naturalis certitudo formaliter spectata est æqualis." Vol. i. p. 32.

[3] There is one part of F. Newman's view on which he himself lays very great stress, but which we have not yet been able to apprehend. It is his speaking of "assent" as in its nature "unconditional," and independent of the inferential act which may have led to it.

Here, however, before going further, we must interpose an explanation which has no bearing indeed on our argument, but which is necessary for the prevention of possible misunderstanding. No "certitude," in the sense we have given the word, can be *greater* than another; but it may be very much more *irresistible* than another. Wherever grounds for certitude exist, doubt is unreasonable; but in one case, very far more than another, it is *possible*. Suppose I have gone through Euclid I., prop. 47, and satisfied myself that the whole argument is cogent. I am as *certain* of that proposition as I am of the axiom that things equal to the same are equal to each other; but plainly it is far more *possible*, though not more *reasonable*, to doubt the former than the latter verity.

This, then, being laid down, we give two answers to the equationist doctrine: our answers, we believe, being substantially the same with F. Newman's. Firstly, there are no *degrees* of certitude; and consequently, when complete certitude is once obtained, additional *proofs* can add nothing to the certitude itself as regards all absence of doubt. For instance: to speak quite within bounds, by the time I was twenty-five years old, I possessed abundantly sufficient ground for complete certitude that there are such cities in the world as Paris and Vienna. Since that date my *proofs* for this conclusion have much more than doubled; but it is simply ludicrous to say that I should now be more than twice as certain of the fact as I was then. I was completely certain of it then; and I cannot be *more* than completely certain of it now.

Take another case. My father is a man of singularly spotless integrity; and I have lived continually with him, from my infancy down to the prime of life in which I now am. It is very long since I acquired a complete certitude of such being his character. Five years ago a heavy charge was brought against his morals; and he frankly told me that he was wholly unable for the moment to explain those suspicions which pressed against him so heavily. Indubitably there was at that time one argument of weight on the adverse side; and equationists must in consistency maintain, that my only reasonable course was to diminish *pro tanto* my confidence in his character. But though they are bound *in consistency* to maintain it, we do not dream that they *will* maintain it. On the contrary, the common voice of mankind declares that, had I so acted, I should have done what is no less intellectually unreasonable than morally detestable. It is intellectually unreasonable; because if I possess certitude of any truth, I thereby *also* possess certitude that apparent objections against it are worthless.

This latter illustration leads us to a second remark, which is of vital moment in the present discussion. It is in the highest degree noteworthy, how many of men's strongest, most important, and most reasonable convictions rest on *implicit* premises. Nay, many truly momentous conclusions depend on premises which are not only implicit, but in their present shape are no more than confused memories of the past. My conviction that Paris and Vienna exist, my conviction that my father is a man of spotless integrity, are both cases in point. To insist that in either of these cases I shall expressly labour to equate the strength of my conviction with the degree of its evidence, would be to take the surest means of rendering it utterly *dis-proportioned* thereto. In either case premiss has for years succeeded premiss, each leaving its legitimate impression on my mind and then forgotten. How is it possible that I can labour to equate my conviction with its evidence, when that evidence, in its original and adequate shape, is wholly inaccessible, having left behind it but a vague record on my memory? In like manner, every acute and intelligent person, who has lived an active life among men, possesses, stored within him, all sorts of miscellaneous convictions on the fit way of dealing with mankind, the result of his past experience. These are, indeed, among his most valuable possessions, so far as this world is concerned; and yet it would be the merest child's play if he professed to remember the individual experiences which have gradually built them up. It is rather a hopeless task certainly for the thinker to aim at proportioning his conviction to its premisses, when these premisses, in their original and adequate shape, are no longer present to his mind.[4]

Equationists, however, may hope to meet the *first* of our two objections by asking leave to amend their plea. They will no longer, perhaps, speak of proportioning the *degree* of conviction to the *degree* of evidence; but will urge that every one should sedulously take heed that he holds no proposition with absolute assent for which he does not possess evidence abundantly sufficient. And their doctrine certainly deserves much more respectful consideration in its new shape than it deserved in its old.

We conclude, then, that, putting aside one or two exceptional instances on which there is no need to insist, it would *cateris paribus* be a *great advantage,* if no one yielded more unreserved assent to any proposition than is warranted by the evidence he possesses.[5] But this is a most different proposition from saying, that all men should expressly *aim* at obtaining for themselves this advantage. Take an obvious illustration. It would be a great advantage *cœteris paribus,* putting aside one or two exceptional instances, if all men enjoyed excellent bodily health; but it does not at all follow from this that men would act wisely in *pursuing* this object through every detail of their life. Such a course would lead to two evils: for, firstly, this minute care would so occupy their attention as indefinitely to weaken their energy in

---

[4] We cannot, however, concur with F. Newman, if we rightly understand him (p. 160), that such a conviction is now "self-sustained in our minds." On the contrary, we would submit that those confused memories of the past which now exist, are its reasonable and amply sufficient basis.

[5] If our readers are surprised that we should admit *any* "exceptional instances," we will mention, as one of their number, the assent given by a child of ten years old to his parent's trustworthiness. Would it really be universally an advantage, that this assent should not be more unreserved than his premisses warrant?

more important directions; and, secondly, the constant *endeavour* for bodily
health would be injurious to bodily health. Now let us apply this illustration:
and we will begin with far the less important reason of the two.

Firstly, then, we say, if all men were thus to busy themselves with
pruning down their putative certitudes, they would disastrously diminish
their energy in other more important directions. Let us take one case out of a
thousand. No one will deny that *philanthropists* have done great service to
mankind; yet how far stronger are their beliefs than their premises warrant!
Each one holds implicitly an undoubting conviction that his own particular
hobby is the one most important element of human happiness. Now, we ask
which of the two following alternatives is more for the welfare of mankind?
On the one hand, that he should proceed steadily in his admirable and
disinterested efforts for benefiting his fellow-men? Or, on the other hand,
that he should largely divert his energy from this noble course, to the far less
congenial employment of lowering down his view on the importance of what
he is about to the exact level warranted by evidence? Again, take a much
graver case. I am fifteen years old; and I have a father, not of comparatively
spotless excellence as in a former illustration, but of mixed character; by no
means predominantly wicked, yet with serious faults. And for one reason or
another it is very important for me to have a true implicit *impression* of that
character. Would it on that account be desirable that I should apply myself
directly to the study? labour to obtain all requisite candour? contend la-
boriously against my tendency, prompted by affection, to undervalue his
defects?

But now, secondly, and much more importantly, however desirable it
may be that putative certitudes should be pruned down, it continually
happens that the worst possible means of *effecting* this object will be for the
thinker himself to aim directly at its accomplishment. In the immense
majority of cases men are absolutely incapable of any such effort. Take the
whole class of labourers, farmers, tradesmen; or take a large number of
hunting country gentlemen. They hold with absolute assent a large number
of convictions: many resting on fully sufficient grounds, many on grounds
more or less inadequate, many on no grounds at all. Various influences may
be brought to bear on these men by a more cultured mind, with the result of
considerably diminishing this intellectual evil; but it is more like a bad joke
than a grave suggestion, to advise that they shall be summoned to pass under
review their various beliefs, and reject those which are insufficiently supported. The grave philosopher, who should urge this, could not get them to
understand so much as what he means. And even if he could, they would be
no more competent to the task than the said philosopher would himself be
competent to the task of riding across country after the hounds. Each man
has his speciality.

Then even as regards one of the most cultivated mind. Is it true that he
has always the power of confronting his conclusion with the ground on which

it rests, in order to estimate its reasonableness? Why, in many cases, as we have already pointed out, those grounds are no longer accessible in their original shape, having left behind them but a vague record on the memory. But further, even when his premisses are actually before him, they very often defy his power of analysis. F. Newman has illustrated this with exquisite felicity.

> As by the use of our eyesight we recognize two brothers, yet without being able to express what it is by which we distinguish them, as at first sight we perhaps confuse them together, but on better knowledge, we see no likeness between them at all; as it requires an artist's eye to determine what lines and shades make a countenance look young or old, amiable, thoughtful, angry, or conceited, the principle of discrimination being in each case real, but implicit—so is the mind unequal to a complete analysis of the motives which carry it on to a particular con- clusion, and is swayed and determined by a body of proof, *which it recognizes only as a body, and not in its constituent parts* (p. 285).

Take, as one instance, the case of medicine to which F. Newman refers at p. 325. A third-rate practitioner is one who forms his conclusions *the- oretically:* who derives universal propositions from his acquaintance with treatises, and deals no otherwise with each particular case than by classing it under one or other of these universal propositions. The physican of *genius,* while availing himself to the utmost of past experience as recorded in treatises, at the same time studies each several case on its own merits and forms a conclusion based on the whole phenomena before him. Is that conclusion to be accounted *unreasonable,* until he is able to produce those phenomena one by one before his conscious observation? Then, all the most important cures have been wrought by unreasonable men; and the patient, if a "lover of truth," would rather have been left to die "secundum artem." Turn, indeed, where you will externally to the region of pure mathematics, the same fact will meet your observation. The careful student of history, *e.g.,* will pronounce, with absolute confidence, that such or such a nation would be so or so affected by such or such a circumstance; that such or such a change has been wrought in that nation's character since such or such a period. Is he able to exhibit in detail, for his own satisfaction, the precise premisses which have led him to these conclusions? No one will think so. F. Newman again points to a different field of illustration. He gives extracts (p. 321) from a work with which we are not otherwise acquainted, on "the authorship of a certain anonymous publication as suggested mainly by inter- nal evidence." We preserve F. Newman's italics. "Rumour," says this au- thor—

> Speaks uniformly and clearly enough in attributing it to the pen of a particular individual. Nor, although a cursory reader might well skim the

book without finding in it anything to suggest, etc., . . . will it appear improbable to the more attentive student of its internal evidence; and the improbability will decrease more and more, in proportion as the *reader is capable* of judging and appreciating the *delicate, and at first incisible touches*, which limit, to *those who understand them*, the individuals who can have written it to a very small number indeed. The utmost scepticism as to its authorship, *which we do not feel ourselves*, cannot remove it farther from him than to that of some one among his most intimate friends; so that, leaving others to discuss antecedent probabilities, etc. (p. 321).

On this passage F. Newman thus comments:—

Here is a writer who professes to have no doubt at all about the authorship of a book, which at the same time he cannot prove by mere argumentation set down in words. The reasons of his conviction are too delicate, too intricate; nay, they are in part invisible, except to those who from circumstances have an intellectual perception of what does not appear to the many. They are personal to the individual. This again is an instance, distinctly set before us, of the particular mode in which the mind progresses in concrete matter, viz. from merely probable antecedents to the sufficient proof of a fact or a truth, and, after a proof, to an act of certitude. (*Ib.*)

Criticism of this kind affords a large field for illustrating the proposition with which we are engaged. There are many passages, *e.g.*, of which a good scholar would pronounce with most absolute certitude that they were not written by Cicero or by Tacitus, as the case may be. Yet how hopeless his attempt of exhibiting, for his own inspection, the various premisses which make this conclusion legitimate![6]

Now, we do not for a moment deny that even the most philosphically cultured men often enough yield absolute assent to some propositions on insufficient evidence; nor again do we deny that they may with great advantage put themselves through some course of intellectual discipline, with the view of diminishing this evil. Some of their conclusions, doubtless—though we believe that these are with most men comparatively few—have been entirely arrived at by *explicit* reasoning; *i.e.* by *argument:* and, it will certainly be very useful to confront these from time to time with the arguments on which they rest. Then, as to those far more numerous assents which rest mainly or partly on implicit premisses, it is often very important that a philosphically cultured lover of truth shall impartially examine every *argument,* whether favourable or adverse to them, with which he can become acquainted. And there is another remedy against prejudice which is also available to such minds: viz. that they labour to analyze their various

---

[6] On this part of our theme, see our essay on "Explicit and Implicit Thought."

opinions, compare them with each other, and compare them also with all cognizable phenomena. But after allowing all this, it still remains true, with the highly educated man no less than with the most uncultured, that the number of convictions is very considerable, for which he has no evidence capable of being placed distinctly before his mind. And it is also true, that there are not a few among the number which he intimately feels to rest on evidence super-superabundantly sufficient, nay in some cases simply irresistible; and which he could not eradicate without rending his whole moral and intellectual nature.

ON CERTITUDE IN RELIGIOUS ASSENT

A Letter to the Author of an Article in the 'Dublin Review' for April 1871.

James Fitzjames Stephen

Sir:—In a remote part of the world I read the following notice in a number of the *Spectator* published in April last:

> This is an extremely good number of the *Dublin*. The first article, aimed at the doctrine that 'certainty,' however legitimate, may generally in ordinary human affairs be exactly proportioned to evidence—may be pared down in proportion as old evidence fails, and made to mount higher in proportion as new evidence accrues—is evidently by the editor, and extremely able. We cannot, of course, go with it in the application which Dr. Ward makes to the faith of Catholics; but its philosophical principle, that certainty, whether legitimate or not, is a state of mind not liable to vary by the subtraction or addition of new items of evidence—i.e. neither is, nor generally ought to be, proportionate to the number of valid arguments by which it may be defended, or in inverse proportion to the number of valid arguments by which it may be assailed, is established beyond all refutation.

As I happen to hold an opinion diametrically opposed to that which you are here said to have 'established beyond all refutation,' I procured and read your article. It interested me so much that I decided to take this mode of giving you my thoughts on the subject. Whether or not I have the advantage of addressing Dr. Ward (as the writer in the *Spectator* suggests), I cannot, of course, say; but if it is so, I am very fortunate in having to do with so able an opponent.

Your article begins by stating the views you ascribe to a class of persons for whom you invent the name of 'equationists.' Having refuted them, or I should say us, to your own satisfaction, you go on to say that we 'may hope to meet the first of your objections' 'by asking leave to amend' our 'plea.' You then are good enough to make the amendment, and to observe that 'their doctrine certainly deserves much more respectful consideration in its new shape than it deserved in its old, and then you proceed to demolish the amended plea.

Permit me to observe that to draw your antagonist's pleadings, to pick holes in them, to amend his pleas, to compliment him on comparative good sense, and finally to refute him, is a little like playing a game at chess, with your right hand against your left, allowing your left hand to make a bad move, and advising it to be more cautious for the future. If the plea of the 'equationists' required amendment, you drew it, and not they, and your compliment about respectful consideration is in reality a reproof to yourself for beginning your argument by misstating your antagonist's case. It is surely a good rule in controversy to begin by deciding clearly what it is that you propose to encounter. It would have been better if, instead of inventing imaginary pleas and imaginary amended pleas, for men for whom you have found it necessary to coin a completely new and not, I think, a very felicitous nickname, you had referred to the views of some adequate exponent of the doctrine to which you object, and had refuted those views as stated by him. This is the course which Dr. Newman took in the *Grammar of Assent,* to which you so frequently refer. He addressed himself (with what success I do not now enquire) to the refutation of Locke's doctrine on the matter in question, and was thus freed from the necessity of adopting the curious procedure to which you have resorted.

This is a matter of no great importance, but it serves as an introduction to what follows. As you want an antagonist, will you kindly accept me as one for fault of a better? I will state my views in my own way, showing incidentally how the arguments advanced in your article apply to them; and if you think it worth while, you will be able to show me where and why I am wrong.

I. In what follows I use the following words in the following senses, unless the contrary appears from the context:

(*a*) BELIEF.—All states of mind described by such words as conviction, persuasion, opinion, faith, and the like.

(*b*) ASSENT.—When one person signifies to another the fact that he believes a given proposition, he is said to assent to that proposition.

(*c*) EVIDENCE.—All arguments in support of the truth of propositions drawn from matters of fact, and all matters of fact from which any such arguments are drawn.

II. Belief may be absolute or qualified.

Absolute belief is belief unaccompanied by present doubt. It is consistent with a present consciousness of the possibility of future doubt.

Qualified belief is belief accompanied by present doubt as to the truth of the matter believed.

All belief is susceptible of degrees of stability.

III. Belief may be produced in many ways, and amongst others by evidence; but there is no assignable connection between belief and the truth of the matter believed, except in so far as the belief, however produced, is supported by evidence.

IV. If belief is supported by evidence, the probability of its truth depends upon the degree in which the evidence by which it is supported satisfies, or approaches to the satisfaction of, the recognised canons of induction and deduction.

V. Whether belief is supported by evidence or not, there is no assignable connection between its truth and the degree of assurance or stability with which it is held.

I proceed to explain more fully the purport and effect of these propositions; which I will take in their order.

First, as to the sense in which the different words are used. The definition of the word 'belief' is intended, amongst other things, to express the opinion that all language which relates to mental operations is of necessity vague and metaphorical. We are obliged to use many words about them which differ from each other only by indefinable shades of meaning, and we gain nothing, and lose a great deal, by attempting to invest them with a precision which is really unattainable. Thus a 'persuasion' may perhaps be an opinion adopted without repugnance; a 'conviction' probably originally meant an opinion which a man struggled against, but was compelled to adopt with regret; 'faith' rather implies some degree of personal confidence in and affection for a person on whose authority a proposition is believed; 'opinion' and 'belief' are much more nearly neutral, but 'opinion' has, so to speak, an intellectual, and 'belief' more or less of a moral, complexion. These words, however, and many others, do not denote different things, but rather the same thing looked at from different points of view, namely, the habit of thinking that certain words are true. If I could find a more colourless word than belief to express this idea, I would use it.

The definition of the word 'assent,' as distinguished from belief, is intended to guard against an ambiguity which continually recurs in Dr. Newman's *Grammar of Assent*, and upon the neglect of which a great part of his argument appears to me to be founded. 'Assent' is sometimes used as equivalent to belief, but its more proper use, I think, is the acceptance by one of two persons of a statement or offer made by another. When the word is used as equivalent to belief, the idea conveyed surely is, that the proposition to be assented to is suggested to the person assenting by some one else, the person assenting being called upon to say yes or no, just as he might have a contract offered to him which he must either take or leave. Taking the word 'assent' in this sense, it is no doubt perfectly true that assent must be absolute and unqualified. A qualified acceptance of a contract is no acceptance at all. It is a new offer, itself requiring acceptance; and in the same sense it may be denied that a qualified assent to a proposition is an assent to it. It seems to me, however, that when we speak of absolute or unqualified assent, or indeed of assent at all, we refer rather to the way in which a man agrees with somebody else to treat a proposition, than to the way in which he regards it in his own mind. If, for instance, two men discuss a subject, and the one affirms and the other assents to a particular proposition, the discussion must proceed throughout on the supposition that that proposition is true.

I think, however, that Dr. Newman's view as to the absolute character of assent is a matter of no importance, for he does not say that this absolute assent is irrevocable; and whether we are to speak of an absolute assent revocable when the evidence on which it was founded is altered, or of an assent which admits of degrees, is a question about the use of language. The allegation that when I have once assented to the proposition 'A is true,' I can never revoke it, is no doubt of immense importance, but I should think that no one ever made it. If it is admitted that for an absolute assent to the proposition 'A is true,' I may, as I see cause, substitute an absolute assent to the propositions 'A is probably true,' 'A is probably true,' 'It is altogether doubtful whether A is or is not true,' 'A is probably false,' 'A is false,' I do not see that it much matters whether you do or do not call assent absolute. It seems to me very much the same thing whether you say that the degrees of assent depend on the amount of the evidence; or that assent is always absolute, but that the nature of the proposition to which it is given depends upon the evidence. Does it matter whether a man is absolutely certain that A B's guilt is highly probable, or whether he gives a degree of assent not quite reaching to certainty, to the proposition that A B is guilty?

The sense in which I use the word 'evidence' requires three remarks. First, I use it in that wide popular sense in which it is used, for instance, in the title of Paley's *Evidences*.

Secondly, I restrict the word to arguments founded upon facts and to the facts upon which the arguments are founded; and by facts I understand things which have an independent existence, of which existence we are assured by some means of perception on which mankind usually rely. That which we see, hear, or touch, is a fact; the internal feelings, to which we give the names of love, hope, fear, will, and the like are facts; and when we assert the existence of anything to be a fact, what we mean is that we or some other sentient being does, or if favourably situated for the purpose, would perceive it.

Thirdly, I do not confine the word 'evidence' to sound arguments. I comprehend in it all arguments drawn from facts and all the facts from which they are drawn. The conditions under which evidence is a test of truth are referred to in proposition No. IV.

My second proposition consists of several parts, which I will explain successively.

'Belief may be absolute or qualified.' This distinction I need not dwell upon, as you would admit it.

'Absolute belief is belief unaccompanied by present doubt.' This again requires no explanation, but the succeeding clause does. 'It is consistent with a present consciousness of the possibility of future doubt.' Almost every incident of our daily life is an illustration of this. Every man absolutely believes a great number of propositions, which, if he thinks of the subject at all, he would admit himself to be ready to doubt if circumstances altered, or if facts now unknown to him came to his knowledge. His confidence in what he believes is in fact measured accurately by his confidence in the nonexistence of such present or future facts. This applies equally to cases to which we attain the very highest and the very lowest importance. An illustration from each end of the scale will set this in a clear light. A man believes absolutely in his wife's virtue. No shadow of a doubt on the subject has ever crossed his mind even in imagination, yet every man would admit that if he had before him ocular demonstration of the contrary he would believe it, or that if he were to see love letters written by his wife to another man he would be forced to doubt. His absolute belief in his wife is a belief that he never has had, has not now, and never will at any future time have, reasonable grounds for changing it. If it were a mere determination never to change it, even in the event of his having reasonable grounds for doing so, he would be an object of contempt, and his wife would feel that the belief in question was not belief in her virtue, but obstinate attachment to his own fancies.

To pass to the other end of the scale, a man reads in the newspaper a list of the births, deaths, and marriages of people who are strangers to him. He absolutely believes the assertions made to be true; that is, he feels no doubt whatever on the subject, because he knows that such announcements are usually true, and does not care to enquire into matters with which he has no concern. Next day he reads in the same paper a contradiction as to one of the deaths announced. He absolutely believes that, and surely under the circumstances his conduct is perfectly rational.

I may here introduce an incidental remark upon your argument on what you consider the more rational form of what you call 'equationism.' As stated by you, that doctrine is as follows: 'Everyone should take heed that he hold no proposition with absolute assent for which he does not possess evidence abundantly sufficient,' and you yourself concede that with certain exceptions, it 'would be a great advantage if no one yielded more unreserved assent to any proposition than is warranted by the evidence he possesses.' Surely you leave out of account a further equation which you might have noticed, namely, an equation between the trouble of an enquiry, and the value of the result. The faintest rumour is evidence amply sufficient for the absolute belief of an indifferent proposition which a man is ready at a moment's notice, if need be, to exchange for absolute disbelief or for any other state of mind which the evidence may warrant. Did any author of reputation ever maintain the proposition, that all persons ought expressly to aim at holding no proposition with absolute assent for which they do not possess evidence abundantly sufficient, whatever may be the nature of the proposition to which such assent is given, and whatever may be the qualifications of the persons concerned for undertaking the enquiry? This is what you regard as the most reasonable form of 'equationism,' and this is the view against which your arguments and illustrations are directed.

The next member of my second proposition is, 'Qualified belief is belief accompanied by present doubt as to the truth of the matter believed.'

This might be worded thus: 'Many states of mind commonly called belief are consistent with some degree of conscious doubt.'

This may, perhaps, require more illustration than the rest of the proposition of which it forms part. Ordinary people when they appear as witnesses in a Court of Justice almost invariably indicate the presence of some degree of doubt in their minds by the use of the word 'believe,' 'Is that the man?' 'It is,' is the expression of absolute belief. 'I believe it is,' is the expression of qualified belief. 'Do you swear positively or only to the best of your belief?' is a question which I suppose was never misunderstood, or supposed to mean anything else than, 'Are you quite sure, or do you feel some little doubt coexisting with a general feeling of belief?' Everyone who has had much to do with Courts of Justice must have been struck with the number of forms of expression by which witnesses, whom it was impossible to suspect of any speculative tendencies, would seek to express the idea that whilst they themselves believed in the existence of some fact, they were conscious of defects in the grounds of their belief, which produced some degree of misgiving as to its truth.

Perhaps an even better illustration may be found in the use of the words 'belief' and 'faith' in reference to religion. 'Lord, I believe, help Thou mine unbelief,' is surely the language of a person who, when he uttered these words, had immediate personal experience of the fact that belief and doubt may coexist, or at all events, succeed each other in such rapid alternation that it is impossible to say that they do not coexist. Look, again, at the contrast, between faith and sight, seeing in 'a glass darkly,' and 'seeing face to face.' Expressed in modern language, what more is meant by such phrases than this? In this life we can never have demonstrative certainty of a future state, but only a passionate anticipation of it, based upon grounds which do not warrant certainty, but when we are actually in it we shall positively know it. Theodore Parker (if I am not mistaken, for I cannot verify my reference) observed in some of his writings that when he actually found himself in the next world he should not be a bit surer of its existence than he was when he wrote; and that if the dead were to rise and appear to him, he should ask them why they gave themselves so much trouble, as he wanted no additional evidence on the point. I never heard of anyone out of America who was so completely satisfied upon these subjects. I think it is impossible to suppose that such was the case with St. Paul. Did not Johnson reply to Boswell's remark, that we have ample evidence of a future state, 'Sir, I want more'?

As a third and last illustration, take the direction which judges always give to juries in criminal cases, that they ought to be sure, 'beyond all reasonable doubt,' of the prisoner's guilt before they convict him. The turn of the phrase, and the way in which it is continually applied, show the compatibility of a certain sort of certainty with a certain sort of doubt. Without going into the subject at length, I think you will find upon examination that the following is the true account of the matter. When for any practical purpose we have determined to assume the truth of a particular hypothesis, notwithstanding the possibility that it may be false, we habitually think of it as true, and turn our minds away from the possibility that it may be false. We thus both believe and doubt; but regarding the belief as on the whole prudent, we put the doubt out of sight, and as the matter takes its place among past events the doubts fade and the belief remains. The mind of man is not so constituted that it can long retain the attitude of thinking that the odds in favour of a certain event having happened, are, say, ninety-nine to one. After acting upon the supposition that the event occurred, the conviction that it did occur rapidly comes to be the abiding one in our minds, though the possibility that it may not have occurred is still recognised and may under particular circumstances assume renewed force. At all events, the case is one in which belief and doubt coexist, and though verdicts given in trials are perhaps the most pointed illustration of belief of this kind, it is, I think, a class in which nearly all the decisions on which people base their practical conduct in the common affairs of life might be included.

The next member of the second proposition is, 'All belief is susceptible of degrees of stability.'

This is one answer to your argument against what you falsely suppose to be the less rational form of what you call 'equationism.'

You argue thus: Equationists say that 'there is an obligation on everyone who loves truth of setting himself expressly to the task of effecting an equation between the strength of his convictions and the amount of proof on which they rest.'

To this you object, 'There are no *degrees* of certitude, and consequently when complete certitude is once obtained additional *proofs* can add nothing to the certitude itself as regards all absence of doubt,' and you enforce this objection by two illustrations; which slightly compressed are as follows:

Illustration 1. I was as sure of the existence of Paris many years ago, and before I actually visited it, as I am now, when I have visited it, yet the strength of my proof of its existence has increased.

Illustration 2. By many years' experience I know my father to be a very good man, and I continue to think so, although some years ago 'a heavy charge was brought against his morals, and he privately told me that he was wholly unable for the moment to explain those suspicions which pressed against him so heavily.'

The 'equationist' is forced by this argument, and these illustrations, to 'ask leave to amend his plea.'

The answer to this argument is twofold. The second answer I shall give in considering the last member of the proposition under consideration.

The first answer is, that even absolute belief, and, *à fortiori*, qualified belief, admits of degrees of stability, just as equilibrium does. The true way of testing the strength of convictions is not by referring to the earnestness with which particular people hold them, as to which I shall have more to say hereafter, but by testing the difficulty of removing them from the mind of a man amenable to reason. You believe a fact on the evidence of two witnesses. One is proved to be a notorious liar. You still believe the fact; but the strength of your conviction, that is the difficulty of removing it, is diminished, and if the other witness were also proved to be a liar, your conviction would cease. A sheet of lead covering ten square yards, and six inches thick, is in a state of equilibrium, so is a spoon balanced on the edge of a glass; but the degree of stability, which, if you like, you may call the strength of the equilibrium, differs enormously in the two cases. To take your own illustrations can you seriously deny that it would be more difficult to persuade a man of the non-existence of a city which he had actually seen than to persuade him of the non-existence of a city of which he had only heard or read? Or that a degree of evidence is easily conceivable which might convince the most affectionate son that his father was a hypocrite and a liar? Or that each successive instance in which an unexplained charge was brought against the father's character would be a step in the process? A wall continues to stand long after the first cannon-ball has struck it, but the final breach is the accumulated effect of all the balls that are fired, the first no less than the last: and it is the same with convictions; they continue to exist long after those who hold them are aware of arguments or evidence against their truth; but at last, by degrees, or suddenly, as the case may be, they give way and cease to exist. Surely this proves that their strength may be gradually diminished.

My next proposition is, that belief may be produced in various ways, and amongst others by evidence; but there is no assignable connection between belief and the truth of the matter believed, except in so far as the belief, however produced, is supported by evidence.

That belief may be produced by evidence, no one will deny. That it may be produced by other means, is a proposition of which the full importance has not been observed. There is hardly any cause which in particular cases may not give rise to belief. People believe what they hope, what they fear, what gives them pleasure, what gives them pain, what they have always been taught to believe, what they have always been warned against believing, quite irrespectively of the evidence; and the energy and fervour of the beliefs which originate in these various passions is, to say the least, as great as if the belief had been produced by evidence. I should say it was generally greater.

If any illustration of this is needed, look at the case of religious belief. In a majority of cases, so great that no numerical proportion could express it, religious belief is produced, not by evidence, but by some other cause, the commonest of which is probably a combination of custom and education with moral sympathy. You meet with this in all creeds. It is true not merely of every form of Christianity, but of Mahometanism, Buddhism, Hindooism, and Fetishism. Perhaps it is to be seen more clearly than anywhere else in the newest forms of intuitional Theism or Deism. The fact, however, is so notorious, and illustrations of it are so abundant, that I need not insist upon the truth of what I say.

So far I think we might go in company. I am not quite sure whether you would deny my next proposition or not: 'There is no assignable connection between belief and the truth of the matter believed, except in so far as the belief, however produced, is supported by evidence.'

The proposition, you will observe, avoids saying that true beliefs must always be produced by good evidence. Belief, as I have already observed, may be produced in numberless ways, and, however it is produced, it may happen to be true. For instance, A dreams of B's death and thereupon believes B to be dead. B actually is dead. Here is a case of true belief produced by bad evidence, but capable of being supported by good evidence. The good evidence was not the cause of the belief, but it is the only rational warrant for its continuance. If B could still be seen alive and well and occupied in his usual pursuits, A's belief would either be given up or would be very likely to consign A to a madhouse.

It is not easy to prove the negative, that there is no assignable connection between belief and the truth of the matter believed, 'except in so far as belief is supported by evidence;' but I will offer a few observations in support of it. In the first place, no one denies the proposition, that there is an assignable connection between belief and the evidence by which it is supported; you, at all events, do not, as I shall show immediately. In what cases, then, if any, is there an assignable connection between the belief and the truth of a proposition not supported by evidence at all?

Your article does not suggest any answer to this question, though, as I shall presently show, it suggests something which might be mistaken for one, connected with what you describe as belief on implicit processes. Beliefs which are always true, and yet are supported by no facts and no arguments founded on facts, are difficult even to imagine. I hardly know, indeed, what meaning you can assign to the word 'true,' except that of a proposition which corresponds with facts, and the word 'evidence,' in the sense in which I now use it, means the facts and arguments which show the correspondence between the two. This is almost identical with the proposition, that there is no assignable connection between belief and truth, except through the medium of evidence, because evidence is what connects belief with truth.

Again, belief, however irrational, is always caused by some facts or other—by evidence in some form, if the very weakest possible hint is allowed to be good evidence. If a man believes a thing because he has dreamed of it, or because he has an unaccountable impression that it has happened or is about to happen, or because something has happened which he regards as an omen, or because he believes it to have been supernaturally revealed either to himself or to some one else; the dream, presentiment, omen, or supposed revelation is the evidence on the strength of which he believes. Now suppose a man does believe a particular thing on some such ground; suppose, for instance, he believes that a friend is dead because he has dreamed of his death, would it be relevant and appropriate to point out to him that he had often dreamed the same thing before when his friend was not dead, that he had often had such dreams after reading stories which affected him, one of which he had read the day before his dream, that if his friend had died he would probably have since heard of it independently, which was not the case, and so on? The admission that such arguments might be used is an admission that belief, to be true, ought to be supported by good evidence. A denial that such arguments might be used would remove the person who made it beyond the pale of discussion.

Perhaps, however, I am doing you an injustice by labouring this point, for your article concludes by setting forth the evidence on which men ought to believe in God and the Church. If you admit that these beliefs rest upon evidence, I do not suppose you would say that there are any which do not. Indeed, even self-evident truths do so. 'Two and two make four,' 'Two straight lines cannot enclose a space,' 'I am,' are all assertions of a state of facts which we perceive as often as we open our eyes, or are conscious of our own existence.

I will conclude what I have to say on this proposition by noticing a topic to which you give great prominence in your article—I mean the subject of what you call 'Implicit Processes.' You refer to a previous article in the *Dublin Review*, which I have not had the advantage of seeing, called, 'Explicit and Implicit Thought.' You say that a man of 'the most cultivated mind has not always the power of confronting his conclusion with the grounds on which it rests, in order to estimate its reasonableness. In many cases those grounds are no longer accessible in their original shape, having left behind them but a vague record on the memory.' You contrast a 'third-rate practitioner who forms his conclusions theoretically' with a 'physician of genius,' who 'forms a conclusion based on the whole phenomena before him,' and you ask, 'Is that conclusion to be accounted unreasonable until he is able to produce those phenomena one by one before his conscious obser-vation?' You triumphantly add, 'Then all the most important cures have been wrought by unreasonable men.' A little before you remark, 'Every acute and intelligent person who has lived an active life among men possesses, stored within, all sorts of miscellaneous convictions on the fit way of dealing with mankind, the result of his past experience. These are, indeed, his most valuable possessions as far as this world is concerned; and yet it would be the merest child's play if he professed to remember the individual experiences which have gradually built them up.'

You use these arguments to refute a proposition which I do not maintain, namely, 'The there is an obligation on everyone who loves truth of setting himself expressly to the task of effecting an "equation" between the strength of his convictions and the amount of proof on which they respectively rest.' If you can find anyone who maintains that proposition, I think he would have little difficulty in showing that you have not refuted it. As, however, I do not maintain it, I will point out how your remarks are related to the propositions which I do maintain. They do not, in any way, touch them. They merely direct attention to the fact that a particular kind of evidence deserves great weight in particular cases. All that you say, may be reduced to this form. When a person of much experience and observation draws an inference from a number of facts which he observes, but cannot describe in words or classify so as to exhibit their logical relation to each other, his opinion is entitled to weight, even after he has forgotten the facts on which it was originally based, or when he is incompetent to state them. Who ever denied this? Who ever doubted that if an experienced physician on looking carefully at a person who wished to insure his life recommended a board not to insure him, they would do well to act upon that advice although the physician might not be able to analyse the grounds on which he gave it? You might give still stronger illustrations than you do. Take the power which a savage possesses of finding his way through an apparently pathless forest, and the instinctive likings and dislikings which children and dogs are said to exhibit for particular persons.

The question is not whether such evidence as this is of weight, but whence its weight is derived? Is it to be believed because it is inarticulate, or if and in so far as it is observed to lead to the truth? Surely the present answer is the right one. In the case of the physician and the insurance office the confidence of the board would depend upon their general opinion of the physician's skill. They would have observed that he was usually right in such matters, and would accordingly presume that he was right in the particular case in question. So with the savages. The reason why such confidence is accorded to them, is that they are found in fact to be able to reach the places to which they profess to act as guides. You trust a bloodhound, not because he cannot explain himself, but because experience shows that he can track down his prey. You trust a sailor, a weather-wise peasant, a child's instinctive aversion, not because they cannot give their reasons, but if and in so far as experience shows that the inarticulate processes through which they go land them in true conclusions. What is more common than for people to be very inarticulate and very positive, and yet to be entirely wrong?

Perhaps the strongest general illustration that can be given of the fallibility of implicit processes of thought, is falling in love. Here you have the most passionate belief proceeding upon implicit processes, which no one could present to himself or others in their logical relation, but the truth of the belief bears no sort of proportion to its fervour. In some cases mutual passionate admiration is justified by the perfect adaptation of two persons to each other. In some cases the result is the bitterest of all deceptions, and every conceivable shade of difference intervenes between these extremes.

There is a sort of romance and mystery about these implicit mental processes which disposes people to attach too much weight to them; but surely you will admit that the weight which a reasonable man ought to attach to them would depend on the degree in which they are verified by experience. However stupid and inarticulate a man might be, even if he were to all appearance an absolute idiot, I should not believe him when he told me it was going to rain, unless I had observed on former occasions that his prophecies came true.

It is curious that you and Dr. Newman should be disposed to attach so much weight, as you apparently do, to this sort of evidence. It would be possible to turn it to a purpose which you hardly seem to suspect. You write as if all the implicit evidence (to adopt your own phraseology) were favourable to the religious view of things. Do not you neglect a good deal of evidence of the same kind which looks in the other direction? Look at the past history and present condition of thought upon religious subjects. Can it be said that the implicit processes of the minds of men in general, the deliberate semi-conscious judgment of mankind, pronounced not formally, but gradually, and embodied rather in acts and habits of mind than in express words, has affirmed what you regard as religious truth? Archbishop Manning once said, that 'politics and science had in these latter days fallen away from the faith.' Your constant complaint against the generation in which you live is its unbelief, its apostasy from the faith which you hold. The commonest theme of preachers of all persuasions is, that men's lives are not in harmony with what they profess to believe, a proof, surely, and the strongest of which the nature of the case admits, that they do not really believe what they profess to believe. Now, what is all this but a judgment proceeding upon an implicit process of thought, that religion as you understand it is not true? You must take this fact into account when you dwell upon the importance of these implicit forms of thought, unless, indeed, you are prepared to lay down this canon—the implicit processes of thought by which I and my friends arrive at our creed, ought to be trusted.

My fourth proposition is as follows: If belief is supported by evidence, the probability of its truth depends upon the degree in which the evidence by which it is supported satisfies the recognised canons of inductive and deductive proof.

I have shown in my third proposition that the truth of beliefs not supported by evidence is a mere matter of chance. If, for instance, you believe that a Mr. Smith lives in a certain house in London, you may be right; but it is a mere chance whether you are or not, unless you can appeal to some fact or other as the cause of your belief, and to some argument to show a connection between the fact and the belief caused by it. The present proposition goes a step further, and specifies the sort of connection which you must show between the evidence and the belief founded upon it in order that the belief might be proved to be true. The kind of connection which you must establish is that which Mr. Mill describes in that part of his work on Logic which explains the process of induction and deduction. A passage in your article admits the validity of these processes.

A man, you say, is convinced by the expression of a 'certain relative's face that he is out of sorts with him.' You give his reasons, which are as follow: 'There is an enormous number of past instances in which the symptoms have coexisted with ill-humour' (your friend, by the way, must be rather ill-tempered); 'there is no single case in which they have existed *without* it; they all admit of being referred to ill-humour as effects to their cause; they are so heterogeneous that any other cause except ill-humour which shall account for them all is quite incredible; while it is no less incredible that they coexist fortuitously, &c., &c., &c. Why, in all probability the very Newtonian theory of gravitation does not rest on firmer and more irrefragable grounds.' You could not make a clearer admission that, in the main at least, you agree in Mr. Mill's analysis of the process of proof as to matters of fact, and that you consider that the inductive and deductive processes described by him are safe guides to truth. The passage quoted is a summary of the greater part of what he says about the method of agreement, the method of difference, and the like; and it would appear from the last sentences of the extract that you regard the application of such methods as constituting demonstration of your friend's ill-humour or of the system of the universe, as the case may be. This is a pretty wide range to take, but I entirely agree with you. I fully admit that the process by which you arrive at the truth in the two cases is identical in principle; and I go farther. I say it is the only one by which propositions as to matters of fact can ever be proved to be true at all, and that except in so far as assertions about facts are proved or are capable of being proved by it, they cannot be shown to be true. This requires full illustration.

I see a book on my table, and I believe there is a book on my table. Why? Because the presence of permanent and consistent sensation consolidated by reason (whatever that may be) into the form of a proposition is inconsistent with the absence of the fact which that proposition affirms. Whether or not the fact, and the sensations so consolidated, are not one and the same thing, is a question which I leave you, if so minded, to discuss with Bishop Berkeley. This is an instance of the application of Mr. Mill's method of difference. Book and perception of a book go together. No book and no perception go together, but there is a perception of a book: therefore, there is a book.

A says to B, 'I dined yesterday with C.' Hereupon A believes the fact stated. What is the process through which he arrives at that belief? Drawn out in form, it would be as follows. B tells me that he dined yesterday with C. Why did he say so? Either (1) because it was true, or (2) because he thought it was true, though it was not, or (3) because he wished to deceive me. Now it is impossible that he could be mistaken, and I cannot imagine from what I know of him that he wished to deceive me. Therefore, it is true. Here again we have the method of difference. The argument is from the effect (B's assertion) to the cause (the truth of assertion); and the process of transition from the one to the other consists in enumerating the causes which could have produced the effect, and showing that each of them, except the one inferred from the effect, is inconsistent with known facts, viz. the knowledge and the integrity of the man who makes the statement. You will find that the same principle applies to every sort of fact which can form the subject of investigation for every purpose, historical, judicial, or scientific. Take the standing riddles of history. Did Sir Philip Francis write Junius? Did Mary murder Darnley? Is Socrates according to Plato or Socrates according to Xenophon most like the real man? Who wrote Homer? Take contemporary events. Did Prince Bismark deceive Louis Napoleon, or did Louis Napoleon try to conspire with Prince Bismark? Take judicial proceedings: Is the person who describes himself as Roger Tichborne a real baronet or an impostor? Did Miss Saurin or Miss Storr tell the truth about their squabbles in the nunnery? Take scientific enquiries. Does the sun move round the earth, or the earth round the sun? Is there a force of gravitation, and does it vary inversely as the square of the distance, or how otherwise? What is the true theory of dew? Is what we see of the sun a gaseous envelope with a comparatively dark kernel, or is it a blazing mass, parts of which are at times comparatively dark? In all of these and an infinite number of other enquiries the method which we employ is fundamentally the same, though of course it leads to infinitely various results.

In many cases we cannot reach certainty because there are possibilities which we are unable for want of evidence to exclude, or if you prefer that mode of expression, the certainty at which we arrive is in most cases hypothetical, as thus—Unless A and B and C are either telling a lie or are mistaken, each of which hypotheses is improbable, D owes a debt to E. Unless there are facts about the murder of Julius Cæsar with which we are unacquainted, he was murdered in the Senate House at Rome in the manner usually described. The solution of every question about facts, however, which can be conceived, is reducible to this shape—the facts are so and so. The possible manners of accounting for them are such and such, and of these so many must be rejected as inconsistent with such and such facts. If all but one are rejected, the truth of that one is proved. If more than one inference is not rejected, all the unrejected inferences are probable in a greater or less degree according to the commonness of their occurrence in the ordinary course of nature or human affairs.

Suppose, for instance, the question is whether the heavenly bodies are or are not inhabited by beings like ourselves, how can we proceed? In the first place we know that human life cannot be sustained at all except under certain conditions, such as the presence of atmosphere and water. Further, we know that there are no atmosphere and no water on that side of the moon which is turned towards us. We are thus able to say with certainty that, on that side of the moon at least, there can be no inhabitants like ourselves. The argument is where there is no atmosphere there can be no beings like men. But on the visible side of the moon there is no atmosphere. Therefore, on the visible side of the moon there are no beings like men. We have, on the other hand, strong reason to believe that in the planet Mars some of the conditions exist which render life possible on the earth. With regard to Mars, therefore, we may affirm that we cannot say that it is not inhabited by creatures like ourselves, but that we cannot say that it is, inasmuch as we have no knowledge of the conditions which are consistent with the absence of inhabitants from a heavenly body, and are altogether unable to prove whether in the case of Mars those conditions or any of them exist or not. With regard to many other heavenly bodies we are obviously altogether ignorant; and our belief that they are or are not inhabited, is, if it exists at all, a mere uncertified guess, suggested by our own fancy.

Perhaps it would be hard to suggest a case in which a lower degree of probability is proved as to any proposition than the degree of probability, if so it is to be called, which has been proved that Mars is inhabited. It is like a first step made upon a journey of which the length and the direction are utterly unknown to us; for, in order to prove, otherwise than by ocular demonstration, that Mars is inhabited by men, it would be necessary to disprove every hypothesis consistent with its being uninhabited by men. But we are utterly ignorant as to what these hypotheses are. We know that the absence of an atmosphere is one of them, and we have disproved that one; but there may be millions of others utterly unknown to us, and unaffected by any fact which is known to us. All therefore, that a reasonable person can affirm as to the inhabitants of Mars is, the absence of one condition which would be inconsistent with their existence.

To take an illustration from the other end of the scale, look at any criminal trial which attracts special attention. Dr. Newman refers to the trial of Müller the German who murdered a man in a railway carriage in London a few years ago, and it will do as well as any other. In this and in all similar cases the question was whether the facts proved excluded the hypothesis of the prisoner's innocence, as the phrase is, 'beyond all reasonable doubt.' The phrase assumes, as I have already observed, that some room is left for doubt, and that the testimony of others, although we may believe and act upon it, always leaves room for a possibility of error or deception, which is excluded in cases where we have the sustained continuous independent action of several of our own senses to depend upon. In a regular trial, such as Müller's, the various hypotheses of which the facts admit are carefully stated, and the reasons for rejecting all, except the hypothesis of the prisoner's guilt, are separately weighed and debated. The result usually arrived at when a man is convicted is, that every other hypothesis than that of his guilt is so improbable that twelve average men agree in thinking that for all practical purposes the possibility that any one of them may be true may be disregarded.

I may observe that it is at this point that Dr. Newman introduces his doctrine of an 'illative sense;' which as far as I can understand it appears to be this. The rules of logic cannot be applied to questions of fact, but as you can attain to certainty about facts, there must be a special faculty which warrants it in particular cases, and this faculty he calls the 'illative sense.' If it were not disrespectful to make such a supposition, I should have been led to believe by the *Grammar of Assent* that Dr. Newman had never read Mr. Mill's Logic. He never refers to it. He never shows the smallest acquaintance with any other sort of logic than the purely verbal one. Of the logic of facts, of the whole process of induction and deduction which Mr. Mill describes and of which all physical science, all history, all criticism, all rationally conducted judicial proceedings, are so many exemplifications, he may for aught that appears in the *Grammar of Assent* be altogether ignorant. If this were not so, I cannot understand how he could have found it necessary to invent a new faculty, the function of which appears to be to draw positive conclusions from insufficient premises. Surely the whole subject which he has contrived to spin into so strange and new a form is as plain and simple as any subject can possibly be. A man who clearly understands the process which I have stated can apply it to facts as they arise with the aid of no mental faculties other than those which are common to all mankind, and have been always acknowledged and described by well-known names. In all sorts of common matters, people apply the methods of agreement and difference without having ever heard of them, and a man of science conducting a scientific enquiry or a judge trying a complicated case simply applies the same process rather more accurately and with a more distinct appreciation of its character.

Twist the matter backwards and forwards how you will, you will never get out of it either more or less than this. A proper application of the inductive and deductive methods to the evidence relating to any given proposition, will enable a person who understands those methods to give to the proposition itself a degree of belief, proportioned to the degree of completeness of the proof; or if you prefer that form of expression, to give an absolute assent to the proposition that it is more or less probable that the matter proposed for belief is true—the degree of probability being proportioned to the completeness of the proof.

You may say that in theory this may be all very well, but that in practice people do believe unreservedly, and even passionately, in numberless cases in which the proof falls far short of the conditions required by the methods of induction and deduction, that such beliefs are often true, and that they are so useful that without them all the common business of life would come to a standstill.

If this were so, it would prove only that people's feelings about the truth of a proposition are no test at all of its truth—a matter of which I shall say mere hereafter—but I think it is an over-statement. The beliefs to which you refer are always or nearly always supposed by those who hold them to comply with the conditions of the method of difference, though not one person in ten thousand of those who hold them may ever have heard of such a method. This appears from the circumstance that as soon as their attention is drawn to the fact that the evidence respecting the facts so believed does not satisfy the conditions of that method, the belief ceases. The commonest and strongest of all such cases is that in which a person believes a fact because some one in whom he puts confidence directly asserts its existence. Such a belief, as I have already shown, satisfies the condition of the method of difference, because no other cause for the assertion can be assigned, except mistake or deception, which by the supposition are excluded; but admit either of these suppositions, show the person who believes the assertion any probable ground for supposing that his informant may have been mistaken or have wished to deceive him—show him, in other words, that the method of difference is not complied with—and his belief ceases at once. You will find it very hard to give a case of a man, who, on the one hand, is distinctly conscious of the fact that his premises are imperfect, and on the other is perfectly certain that his conclusion is true. I speak of common life and of the ordinary transaction of affairs. I am well aware that in religious matters the opposite is very often the case, and this is the reason why I and many others think that religious people are often dishonest upon principle. A juryman who returned a verdict merely because some one item of evidence struck his fancy, and although he was distinctly aware and admitted to himself in so many words that the evidence in question left untouched reasonable hypotheses as to the facts and inconsistent with the verdict, would perjure himself. A man of science who admitted that two theories were equally consistent with ascertained facts, and who nevertheless vehemently affirmed the truth of one to the exclusion of the other, would be laughed at. A person in common life who placed absolute confidence in the word of a man whom he admitted to have been frequently mistaken in reference to similar subjects, or to have an inclination to deceive him, would be called a fool; but if I understand Dr. Newman and his 'illative sense,' the sort of foundation on which religious belief should stand is this:—look out a few topics which as they stand render your creed probable, and then by the help of your 'illative sense' get a certitude of its truth before you have had time to consider any facts which look in the other direction. I can hardly be mistaken in supposing that this is Dr. Newman's opinion, for his 'illative sense' is a mere superfluity in cases in which the canons of inductive logic are satisfied.

V. This brings me to my fifth proposition, which is this: Whether belief is supported by evidence or not, there is no assignable connection between its truth and the degree of assurance or stability with which it is held.

In his *Apologia* Dr. Newman tells us that he learnt, when at Oxford, to distinguish between certitude, a state of mind, and certainty, a quality of propositions; this distinction would make it possible to express the proposition stated above very shortly as follows: 'There is no assignable connection between certitude and certainty.' Perhaps, however, such antitheses do more harm than good in speculative enquiries. It will therefore be better to attempt to prove the proposition given above, as it is stated. I have tried to show, in my third proposition, that belief may be the effect of a vast variety of causes, according to the temper and position of the believer; I have also argued that the intensity of this belief is often greatest where the cause which excited it had least to do with the truth. Different men at the same time, and the same men at different times, have believed contradictory propositions upon every sort of subject, with an ardour which torture and death only increased. That the Pope is Antichrist, that the Pope is the Vicar of Christ; that fifty different religious creeds are true, that those same creeds are false; that the Stuarts were rightful kings, that they were rebels or criminals; that there is a God and a future state, and that these doctrines are the foundation of all human society; that there is no God and no future state, and that these doctrines are a pernicious fraud, preventing the establishment of a rational condition of human society; all these and numberless other beliefs have inspired men in various ages with the most passionate conviction, and have turned them into persecutors, martyrs, heroes, fanatics, saints, monsters, what you will. If mere passionate ardour of belief could prove anything at all, it would prove each half of all these and numberless other contradictions. The inference is, that it proves nothing. It is an effect which may be produced by many causes, and therefore it is unsafe to infer any one of them for the fact of its existence.

There is one special class of cases in which this consideration is of much importance. These are cases in which belief is partly the effect of evidence and partly the effect of temperament. It is probable that Dr. Newman's theory about 'illative sense' would be applied principally to cases of this kind. He says, in substance, 'I cannot assert that the truth of Christianity is proved to such an extent that every other reasonable way of accounting for the facts before us is disproved: I can and do say that there are facts which point to its truth, and from those facts my "illative sense," draws a certitude.' If this were merely an obscure and peculiar way of saying, 'I think it probable that Christianity is true, and I am content to act upon that probability,' I, for one, should not have a word to say to the contrary. But it is something more than this. Dr. Newman's theory—and yours too, if I understand it correctly— seems to me to be that a certain feeling in your own mind can produce an effect upon facts outside of you; that your certitude can convert a probability into a certainty; that is, can cause a given set of facts to fulfil conditions which they would not otherwise fulfil. It seems to me just as rational to say that if you saw an object through a mist, which might be either a man or a bush, your conviction that it was a man could make it into a man. Let us suppose that three hypotheses, and three only, viz. A, B, and C, account for a given fact, and that A is inconsistent with fact 1, and B with fact 2, then C is certainly true, whether you believe it or not. Now suppose that fact 2 does not exist, then either B or C may be true. You may feel in your own mind quite positive that C and not B is true, and you may call that feeling a certitude or whatever else you please, and what is more your belief may be right; but if your certitude was caused by no facts at all, it was merely a lucky guess. If it was founded upon facts—forgotten, dimly perceived, incapable of being described or specified, if you please—then the case which I put has not arisen, because your belief in the truth of C as opposed to B was founded on facts which were inconsistent with the truth of B.

You, as well as Dr. Newman in his *Grammar of Assent*, are fond of insisting on the circumstance that certitude, the feeling in the mind, does not depend upon the strength of the evidence, and in this I think you are right. You say, and truly, that you believe in the existence of Moscow or Delhi as firmly as if you had seen them: that if a common fact is proved to be true by two credible witnesses, you believe it as firmly as if it was proved by three; that the broad outlines of history appear to you as certain as if you yourself had been present at Waterloo or Blenheim, or at the scenes of the first French Revolution. How came you not to see that this proves only what a very treacherous guide certitude is? A fact proved by many witnesses, as I have already shown, is far more difficult to disprove than a fact proved by few, and yet the mind feels towards the one fact just as it feels towards the other. If seventeen witnesses of undoubted credit and with ample means of knowledge asserted that they saw Mr. Gladstone in the House of Commons on a particular occasion, and twenty-three witnesses of the same order made a similar assertion as to another occasion, you would not feel more sure of the truth of the second than of truth of the first assertion. You would not find it easier or more difficult to lift a weight of three tons than to lift a weight of five tons, but it does not follow that three tons weigh as much as five, or that the evidence of twenty-three witnesses is not weightier than the evidence of seventeen. What follows is that your feelings are no test upon such matters, and that if you must resort to other means for arriving at a true conclusion upon them; you must suppose the witnesses to contradict each other flatly, or the weights to be placed in opposite scales. To try to weigh evidence by the feelings which it excites in minds agitated by a thousand conflicting interests and passions, often most imperfectly acquainted with the theory of evidence, and almost always unaccustomed to its application, is just like testing the strength of materials by touching them with your fingers. A deal board, an oak plank, an iron plate eight inches thick, and fifty other things are equally impenetrable to the finger-point; but the deal board may be pierced by small shot, the oak plank would turn an ordinary musket ball, the iron plate would resist all but the heaviest rifled cannon. It is just so with evidence. A person may feel equally positive as to the truth of some floating scandal which happens to gratify his spite; as to an ordinary fact stated to him by a credible witness of it; and as to a scientific truth, in the study of which great part of his life has been passed; but his certitude stands in no relation at all to the certainty of the various propositions which he believes. I have already illustrated the immense variety of contradictory propositions of which people have been perfectly certain. In the face of all this, I cannot understand how a reasonable man can say that the certitude felt by any person as to any proposition is any test of its truth.

Unquestionably it is often useful in the conduct of life to act upon a probable supposition as if it was true, and as I have already observed, it often happens that the mere fact that we have adopted a probability as a truth makes us think of it and feel about it as if it were true. Our intellectual processes are, as a rule, rough and summary; how can they well be other-wise? Few subjects are worth the trouble of the most complete investigation which it would be possible for an ingenious man to bestow upon them. We have to judge as well as we can and act for the best, and few intellectual defects are practically more mischievous than inopportune indecision and hesitation. Now when we have once considered a subject, and decided upon any practical course in reference to it, when, to use a most expressive phrase, we have 'made up our minds' about it, we naturally regard the conclusion at which we have arrived as true, and constantly forget the grounds upon which it originally rested, and accept it as a matter not to be disputed. No man can have mixed much in practical affairs without observing innumerable in-stances of this. No man, I think, can have seen much of the world without also seeing that in practice it is of the highest importance to steer between indecision and obstinacy; to avoid, on the one hand, the fault of being blown about by every wind of doctrine, and on the other the equally dangerous fault of refusing to disturb our convictions when once formed, whatever new evidence or alteration of circumstances may come to our knowledge. This is a practical problem on which I need say nothing except this: that though the feeling of positiveness, or the certitude which probabilities produce in the minds of persons who have determined for any practical purpose to act upon the supposition that the probability represents actual truth, is a natural, and in many cases, a useful state of mind, its existence forms no additional evidence, either to the person who feels it or to anyone else, that the probable hypothesis is actually true. To refuse to recognise a theory as merely probable, when the question whether it is probable or certain is brought up by circumstances, because you have acted on the supposition that it is true, is a mere weakness—the weakness of a person who does not like to be disturbed in matters on which he has decided. To refuse to act upon a probable proposition as true when such a course is necessary to effective action is also weakness—the weakness of a man who shrinks from acting for the best.

I must here recur for a moment to the implicit states of mind of which you say so much. Their value as evidence has nothing to do with the firmness of the conviction in which they result. If a very modest person, whose guesses were seldom wrong, said, 'I do not like that man's looks,' his remarks might carry more weight than the positive assertion of a self-confident person, frequently mistaken, that the man in question was an abandoned villain. In all cases in which we have to do with an estimate of probabilities, it is essential even to moderate correctness to know something of the temperament and circumstances of the person who forms the estimate. The eagerness with which a lover or a jealous person will fasten upon something which a person not in love or jealous would not perceive at all, is one of the common topics of fiction, and both the jealous man and the lover are often right; but then, also, they are often wrong; and no one, I suppose, would regard as otherwise than a weakness, amiable or not as it might happen, the certitudes engendered in them by trifles.

It would not be difficult to show that as the feeling of certitude produced by a mere probability is often disproportionately strong, so the feeling of certitude produced by the most complete evidence is often much weaker than it might have been expected to be. The strongest possible illustration of this is supplied by the case of a mathematical demonstration imperfectly mastered. Either Pascal or Fénelon, if I am not mistaken, compares Descartes' demonstration of the existence of God to a view of which you can just get a glimpse by drawing yourself up by your hands to a high window, but which is lost as soon as your muscles relax; and the image is a very expressive one. Till a demonstration is so completely mastered that the mind can retrace its step at will, with a complete understanding of each and all, the belief which it produces is rather a belief that a certain process is most probably a demonstration than a belief in the truth of the proposition demonstrated by it. There is much truth, too, in the old tag about convincing a man against his will. There is hardly any human passion which, if interested, in disputing a conclusion, would not enable a man to doubt in the face of demonstration.

Upon these grounds I conclude that no inference at all can be drawn from the warmth with which any belief is held, to the truth of the matter believed. A probability remains a probability and nothing else, though millions upon millions not only believe it to be true, but assert, however correctly, that if it were false their whole lives would lose their meaning, and become vain and useless dreams. The test, and the only test, by which its character as a truth or a probability can be measured is this. Is the evidence on which it rests such as to exclude every supposition, except that of its truth? If yes, it is proved to be true. If no, it is at most probable, in a greater or less degree according to circumstances. As to certitudes, people can if they please adjust their belief to the evidence before them, in which case they will usually believe what is true, but it is an idle dream to suppose that they can alter the effect of the evidence by their feelings about it. A good deal of what is written on the subject in the present day might be reduced to this form: 'Only love your evidence sufficiently, and you will get it to prove whatever you please.'

Having now completed the statement of my own case on this subject, I will proceed to make a few observations as to what I do not say, which will incidentally answer some of the things which you do say.

I do not say that it is expedient for all men always to believe the truth, the whole truth, and nothing but the truth, as far as it is accessible to them by the use of reasonable means, though I myself think so. I confine myself at present to the proposition, that if you wish to believe the truth you must act on certain principles, and not otherwise.

I do not say that it is wise in every man at all times to try to produce an equation (as you put it) between his opinions and the truth. I say that if he wishes to do so, he must take a certain course for that purpose. The question what enquiries is it wise for A B to undertake, and in what cases would A B do well to be satisfied with adopting the current opinions of his age, his class, or his country, without enquiry, is one which cannot be answered unless A B is, according to the expression attributed to Lord Eldon, 'clothed in circumstances.' You would advise a poor peasant woman with a large family of children and a husband to look after, to take one course, and a gentleman with full command of his time, a turn for intellectual pursuits, and an excellent education, to take another.

Truth may be good or bad. It may be attainable or not. It may be the common heritage of all men, or a remote treasure accessible only to a few. With all these matters, on the present occasion, I have nothing to do. I say only if you want truth, and intend to try to attain it, this is the road. A well-known and well-defined intellectual process based upon facts—upon the result, that is, of the joint action of reason and sensation—is a sure guide to truth, and nothing else is. So long as you allege that your religious belief is justified by this process, and that you are content to hold it if and in so far as, and so long as, that process continues to justify it and not farther, or longer, or otherwise, it is a question of detail whether your opinions are true or false. To assert any other truth than this, to set up any higher authority, no matter how sacred may be the subject under consideration, is to promote a delusion. If it is done consciously in order to work out a particular result, it is telling a lie.

This general principle supplies the foundation for all that I need say about the part of your article in which you speak of the evidence of the existence of God and the Infallibility of the Church. If you are willing to apply to these doctrines the test of all serious enquiry, if you will try the question whether there is a God, whether the Church is infallible, whether Jesus Christ rose from the dead, as men try the questions, Do heavenly bodies gravitate towards the sun? What is the nature of dew? Is a man accused of crime guilty or innocent? then I have nothing to say. But if you set up any other test of religious truth than such tests as these, and if you fail to show that the tests which you set up are in common use with satisfactory results in relation to other subjects, then I say you mean by truth in religion not what we men of the world mean by truth in common matters, but whatever happens to suit your own fancy.

I am, your obedient servant, F.

THE REASONABLE BASIS OF CERTITUDE
William George Ward

No one doubts that the cause of religion, whether natural or revealed, is just now going through a tremendous intellectual crisis, and that those who desire to uphold it must put their shoulders vigorously to the wheel. Out of the many anti-religious principles which are rife on every side, I take as theme of my present paper one which is not always at once recognised as an anti-religious principle at all. It is exhibited in the different shapes by different writers, but its substance is this. 'No one,' it is said, 'can reasonably hold any tenet with firm and absolute conviction, unless he have instituted an explicit and deliberate inquiry into its truth; unless he have examined the arguments adduced *pro* and *con*, and thus assured himself that reason warrants his conviction.' No doubt those who advocate this thesis may admit that 'reason' is a large word, including various and heterogeneous grounds of belief. The essence of their thesis is, that certitude, in order to be reasonable, must be preceded by explicit inquiry and logical examination.

Now when I admit, or rather affirm, that the acceptance of this thesis would inflict a fatal wound on religion, I must not be misunderstood. I am perfectly confident that in fair controversy, where the combatants on either side are pretty evenly matched, the advocates of religion will entirely vanquish their opponents. And I am confident also that the mass of believers possess super-superabundant reasons for accepting the great verities of their faith. But it is a simple matter of fact, that the enormous majority of mankind are entirely incapable of marshalling arguments or instituting a scientific inquiry into truth. It must follow therefore from the thesis which I oppose, that the enormous majority of mankind would act unreasonably by embracing the fundamental truths of religion with absolute certitude. But without certitude in religious conviction, no religious life is possible. 'Without certitude in religious faith,' says Fr. Newman, 'there may be much decency of profession and observance; but there can be no habit prayer, no directness in devotion, no intercourse with the unseen, no generosity of self-sacrifice.' 'Christian earnestness may be ruled by the world to be a perverseness or a delusion; but as long as it exists it will presuppose certitude as the very life which is to animate it.'[1]

There are other considerations also, leading me to regard the thesis which I oppose as subversive of religion. But I need say no more on this

[1]*Grammar of Assent*, 4th edition, pp. 220 and 238.

particular head, as most of the opponents with whom I have to deal will be only too happy to admit that I am so far right. And there is especial cause just now for discussing the question I have raised, because Professor Clifford's article on 'The Ethics of Belief,' which appeared in the *Contemporary Review* of January 1877, seems to have excited considerable attention. A Catholic writer, indeed, Mr. H. W. Lucas, has done good service, by three thoughtful papers on this article contributed to the *Month* (September, October, November, 1877); but he has hardly touched the particular point on which I wish mainly to insist.

I said at starting that the thesis which I oppose is exhibited by different authors in different shapes: by none other certainly in so extreme a shape, as by Professor Clifford. A writer, on whom I shall presently have to comment, asks this question, implying that an affirmative answer to it would be manifestly unfounded. 'Did any author of reputation,' he asks, 'ever maintain the proposition, that all persons ought expressly to aim at holding no proposition with absolute assent for which they do not possess evidence abundantly sufficient, whatever may be the nature of the proposition or the qualifications of the person concerned for undertaking the inquiry?' As far as I can possibly understand him, the Professor does maintain this precise proposition. In regard to the qualifications of the inquirer—'every rustic,' he says, 'who delivers in the village alehouse his slow infrequent sentences' is included in the general obligation. 'No simplicity of mind, no obscuring of station, can escape the universal duty of *questioning all that we believe*.'[2] ' "But," says one, "I am a busy man; I have no time for the long course of study, &c." *Then he should have no time to believe*.'[3] And as to the triviality of the questions which Professor Clifford would include under this obligation, his language is equally unmistakeable. 'No belief held by one man, *however seemingly trivial the belief*, is ever actually insignificant. . . . Belief, that sacred faculty, . . . is desecrated when given to unproved and unquestioned statements.'[4] 'If I let myself believe *anything* on insufficient evidence, *there may be no great harm done by the mere belief* . . . but I cannot help doing this great wrong towards man that I make myself credulous. . . . The credulous man is father to the liar and the cheat.'[5]

Let us apply this doctrine to a concrete case. Some agricultural labourer is sober, honest, chaste; and carefully educates his children in the same habits.[6] But he is very fond of cricket; and is quite confident that the eleven

[2] P. 293.
[3] P. 295.
[4] P. 292.
[5] P. 294.

[6] I need hardly say that if I were fully describing a virtuous man, there are other qualities on which I should lay even greater stress than on those mentioned in the text. I should represent him as living in the fear and love of God, and training his children in that fear and love. In argument, however, with Professor Clifford I cannot dwell on this, as he is not generally understood to hold Theistical doctrine.

of his own village are far superior to the eleven of another village whom they often encounter. This opinion is entirely unfounded; nor has it been engendered in his mind by any attempt at impartial inquiry, but exclusively by local prejudice and *esprit de corps*. According to Professor Clifford, this man is 'desecrating belief, that sacred faculty;' he is 'laying a stealthy train in his inmost thoughts which may some day leave its stamp on his character for ever;'[7] he is making himself 'father to the liar and the cheat.' I am slow to credit a writer of undoubted ability with such a position as this; but for the life of me I cannot see what else he means.

I suppose I may take for granted that he does not include young children in his theory: otherwise one might suppose him talking in this way to a boy of six years old. 'Your parents,' he might say, 'are very tender and affectionate towards you; for which reason there is all the great danger, lest you hold a higher opinion of their character than is warranted by the grounds of belief to which you have access. Observe carefully therefore all their faults, and take care to give every fault its due weight in your estimate of them.' I suppose I may take for granted he does not mean this, though I think we have a right to complain that he has not expressly disavowed it. But, at all events, there is some period or other in every one's life to which the Professor *would* apply his theory: the period of full maturity. At that period he must undoubtedly say that it is the youth's bounden duty—under pain of being 'father to the liar and cheat' and the rest of it—to weigh severely in exact balance his parents' character: and to examine it indeed the more stringently and severely, in proportion as his love for them and their unvarying acts towards him of tenderness and self-sacrifice might unduly bias his judgment and prejudice him in their favour.

So much as to our youth's parents. And now as to the lessons of morality which they have taught him: 'Thou shalt not steal;' 'Thou shalt not bear false witness;' and the rest. He should delay, I suppose, all recognition of these rules as authoritative, until he has carefully inquired what arguments are adducible whether in favour of their authority or against it; and until he has passed judgment on those arguments. To avoid this very awkward conclusion, the Professor adopts a singular expedient. 'Tradition,' he says,'[8] 'gives us the conceptions of right in general; of justice, of truth, of beneficence, and the like. . . . That it is right to be beneficent,' just, true, 'is matter of *immediate personal experience*.'[9] Had an unlucky *intuitionist* made

---

[7] P. 292.

[8] P. 303.

[9] It will be fairer to the Professor, if I quote the whole passage. 'Laying aside, then,' he says, 'such tradition as is handed on without testing by successive generations, let us consider that which is truly built up out of the common experience of mankind. This great fabric is for the guidance of our thoughts, and through them of our actions, both in the moral and in the material world. In the moral world, for example, it gives us the conceptions of right in general, of justice, of truth, of beneficence, and the like. These are given as conceptions, not as statements or propositions; they answer to certain definite instincts, which are certainly within us, however

such a statement as this, when would he have heard the last of it? It would have been crushingly replied, that we can have no *immediate personal experience*, except of mental phenomena; and that moral obligation is no mental phenomenon, though *belief* in it may be such. The intuitionist would of course speedily retrieve his blunder: he would explain that he appeals to immediate personal experience, only as testifying to that phenomenon which he calls an *intuition* of moral obligation. But he would add that in his view— for reasons assigned by him—this *phenomenon* suffices to establish the *objective existence* of moral obligation. Is this what Professor Clifford would say? Or if not, what is his meaning?

Not only however, according to Professor Clifford, is the rustic supposed to have this 'immediate personal experience' of 'right in general,' but he is also reasonably entitled to 'assume' the 'uniformity of nature.'[10] Professor Clifford indeed 'lays aside for the present' the 'question' what this uniformity precisely is, and how the rustic is able to assure himself of its existence. I hope he will satisfy a not unreasonable curiosity by treating this question at some early date. I hope he will explain what is the exact logical process, whereby every uneducated rustic can reasonably satisfy himself that nature proceeds universally on uniform laws.

And now, chiefly of all, what *reason* does he give for his amazing theory? I can really find no one reason assigned from first to last. That which to ordinary thinkers will appear the most incredible of paradoxes, he enunciates as a kind of truism; as what persons may culpably neglect indeed in practice, but what all will admit to be true in doctrine, as soon as they hear it propounded.

Professor Clifford's article then—I must really think—is so manifestly exaggerated and unreasonable, that I should be doing injustice to the general body of my opponents by taking him as in any sense their representative. On the other hand, it is far more satisfactory to deal, if possible, with some individual writer, than to invent for myself the details of an adverse position. Fortunately for my purpose such a writer exists, and one whom I have individually special reasons for considering. In the *Dublin Review* of April 1871 I published an article called 'Certitude in Religious Assent.' This was criticised in the *Fraser* of January 1872 by a distinguished contributor writing under the signature 'F.' Our next number was due in a fortnight; and I had only time therefore to signalise what appeared to me the two most fundamental fallacies of his argument. I was not without some notion that he might be disposed to continue the discussion. On the other hand, perhaps he

---

they came there. That it is right to be beneficent is a matter of immediate personal experience; for when a man retires within himself and there finds something, wider and more lasting than his solitary personality, which says, "I want to do right," as well as, "I want to do good to man," he can verify by direct observation that one instinct is founded upon and agrees fully with the other. And it is his duty so to verify this and all similar statements.'

[10] P. 206.

rather expected that in the following number I should develop my reply at greater length. However I could not hear that either my article or his criticism of it had attracted any general notice; and I proceeded therefore in the *Dublin Review* with other matters which then urgently pressed. At all events—however it happened—the controversy between 'F.' and myself has remained dormant from that day to this. Now that the question excites far greater attention than it did then, I will criticise 'F.'s' criticisms—not indeed thoroughly and exhaustively, because my prescribed limits do not permit this—but more at length than I had time to do in January 1872.

I have already quoted one passage of 'F.'s' in which he entirely repudiates what I understand to be Professor Clifford's position. 'F.' does not say[11] that 'all persons ought expressly to aim at holding no proposition with absolute assent for which they do not possess evidence abundantly sufficient.' He does not even say 'that it is expedient for all men always to believe the truth . . . as far as it is accessible to them by reasonable means; though he himself thinks so.' What he does say is, so far as I can understand his language, that those who on some given subject cannot (or at all events do not) 'undertake' explicit and deliberate 'inquiry'—who do not carry through in relation to it a certain 'well-known and well-defined intellectual process'—can have no assured knowledge on that subject. They have no right to any conviction of their own on it, but must slavishly 'adopt the current opinions of their age, their class, or their country.'[12] I will not consider his rhetorical exclamation, that those who differ from him 'promote a delusion,' or his insinuation that they are perhaps 'telling a lie.' I shall content myself with maintaining as a mere matter of reason, that his position (if I rightly understand it) is entirely destitute of foundation.

I contend then as for a most obvious matter of fact, that, on a large number of subjects, men arrive at a sure, certain, personal knowledge of

---

[11] P. 26.

[12] As 'F.' does not say all this in so many words, I am bound to cite his passage in full. I have italicised the parts to which I would draw especial attention, and taking it as a whole I find great difficulty in understanding it otherwise than as I have stated it.

'I do not say that it is wise in every man at all times to try to produce an equation (as you put it) between his opinions and the truth. I say that if he wishes to do so, he must take a certain course for that purpose. The question, *what inquiries is it wise for A. B. to undertake*, and in what cases would A. B. do well to be satisfied with *adopting the current opinions of his age, his class, or his country, without inquiry?* is one which cannot be answered unless A. B. is, according to the expression attributed to Lord Eldon, 'clothed in circumstances.' You would advise *a poor peasant* woman with a large family of children and a husband to look after, to take one course and a gentlemen *with full command of his time, a turn for intellectual pursuits, and an excellent education,* to take another.

'Truth may be good or bad. It may be attainable or not. It may be the common heritage of all men, or a remote treasure accessible only to a few. With all these matters, on the present occasion, I have nothing to do. I say only, if you want truth, and intend to try to attain it, this is the road. *A well-known and well-defined intellectual process* based upon facts—upon the result, that is, of the joint action of reason and sensation—is a sure guide to truth, and *nothing else is.*'

truth, often without instituting any kind of 'inquiry,' and almost universally without going through any 'intellectual process' whatever, which they deliberately intend or of which they are themselves even aware. This phenomenon is of course most conspicuously manifested in the uneducated class, though by no means confined to it. With the uneducated class then I begin. Take any ordinary mechanic or labourer, and consider how many truths there are, connected with his occupation, of which he has most certain knowledge, without any dependence whatever on 'the current opinions of his age, class or country.' He knows *e.g.* that certain materials, which he is continually using, may be depended on for certain results. He knows this without any kind of inquiry direct or indirect. He originally accepted the fact without question from those who instructed him; but he now knows it, by means of experience, with absolute certitude, and without any dependence whatever on the word of his teachers. Or I go to a competent shoemaker and recount to him the pain I suffer from the shoes he has sent me home. No doubt he thereon puts forth a mental 'inquiry' how he shall remedy the evil; but he arrives with certitude at an answer to this inquiry, without dreaming of any formulated 'intellectual process.' This supposed change—he says to himself—or that supposed change—would not remedy the evil; a third would do so, but at the expense of sightliness. Soon a good notion occurs to him; and he sees, with the certitude and precision of an instinct, that the plan will be thoroughly successful.

Nor is it necessary, in order to certitude, that the thing known be connected with matters of daily and unintermitting experience, such as is furnished by the exercise of a trade or habitual avocation. Let me give a very trivial, but not the less a very relevant, illustration of this. A butcher has bought a vicious horse, which he rides once a week, leaving it on other days to his boy. At first he is more than once thrown and often in danger of that catastrophe. But if he have the proper stuff in him, before very long he will have acquired a securer seat. He will know with absolute certitude, what is a sufficient response on his part to the brute's various eccentric movements one by one. Here no doubt there has been 'inquiry;' but most certainly no explicit intellectual process or formulated appeal to Mr. Mill's canons of induction.

Let us pass to graver instances. Shrewd rustics, entirely destitute of intellectual culture, not unfrequently can discern with absolute certitude the character of this or that man with whom they are brought into contact: that he is a sincere man *e.g.* or a humbug. They may know again with certitude whether he is friendly or bears them a grudge.

Again some pious parent in humble life—whose anxiety for his children's welfare quickens his faculties—will often see beyond the possibility of mistake that this or that child has this or that fault of character, and will be usefully visited by this or that method of correction. What can be more unmeaning than to say that—because he has not gone through any formulated intellectual process—he has nothing more sure to guide him in this consideration, than 'the current opinions of his age, his class or his country?'

Then again the certitude with which multitudes of uneducated men accept the fundamental principles of morality, is such that Professor Clifford (as we have seen) has been betrayed into saying that these principles are matters to each man of 'immediate personal experience.'

The results, obtained by entirely uneducated men in the absence of all explicit intellectual process, often imply that quite a complicated chain of reasoning has passed through their mind, without any reflection whatever on their part of there being such a process, and without any trace whatever of it being left on their memory. Consider the extraordinary quickness with which some mariner prognosticates on some fine evening that there will be a storm before morn. He fixes his attention on a certain assemblage of phenomena; accurately distinguishes them from others with which they have a greater or less resemblance; brings to bear on them the confused memory of innumerable similar occasions on which he has observed appearances more or less similar; and draws the one conclusion legitimately resulting from his premises. All will admit that there are many instances in which he is, on fully adequate grounds, absolutely certain of his conclusion; and that if on such occasions landsmen try to argue him out of his conviction—however ingenious their reasoning might be, and however incapable he might be of meeting logic by logic—his one reasonable course would nevertheless be, entirely to disregard logic and remain firmly fixed in his own conviction. A contemporary writer adds a parallel illustration, drawn from 'the power which a savage possesses of finding his way' by indications, which he would in vain attempt to communicate or even himself explicitly to recognise, 'through an apparently pathless forest.'

But, as was said a page or two back, the phenomenon before us is far from being confined to the uneducated. Take the case of medicine. A third-rate practitioner is one who forms his conclusions syllogistically: who derives universal propositions from his books, and deals no otherwise with each particular case than by classing it under one or other of these universal propositions. The physician of *genius*,—while availing himself to the utmost of past experiences as recorded in treatises,—at the same time studies each several case on its own merits, and forms a conclusion based on the whole symptoms before him. Now this physician is an educated man; and is as competent as any one to 'undertake an inquiry' and follow out explicitly a certain 'well-known and well-defined intellectual process.' But would he by such means increase the probability of his arriving at truth? Just the contrary. There would be imminent danger lest he calamitously misapprehend the balance of the reasons *pro* and *con* from the very probable circumstance, that those facts which tell on one side may be far more easily put into shape, or are far more precisely located in his memory, than those (legitimately preponderating) facts which tell on the other. And being by hypothesis a sensible well-judging man, we may rely on it that he will avoid this danger by steering clear of the logical method. Or take some accomplished scholar: he will pronounce with absolute certitude that some given passage is not the writing of Tacitus or Cicero, as the case may be. Will he be able to exhibit, even for his own inspection, the various subtle and impalpable premises which warrant his conclusion? Of course not. Again, every acute and intelligent person, who has lived an active life among men, possesses, stored within him, all sorts of miscellaneous convictions on the fit way of dealing with mankind, the result of his past experience. These are indeed among his most valuable possessions so far as this world is concerned; and yet it would be the merest child's play if he professed to remember the individual experiences which have gradually built them up. It is rather a hopeless task certainly for him to examine systematically the logical value of his various premises, when those premises (in their original and adequate shape) are no longer in his mind.

I wish I had space to quote, at the length I could wish, Mr. Leslie Stephen's testimony on the same side. I refer to an article on Newman which appeared in the *Fortnightly* of last December. 'When I form an estimate,' he says,[13] 'of a man's character, of the wisdom of a policy, of the truth of a creed, my mind is in fact determined by countless considerations, of which only a small part can be distinctly tabulated and drawn out into articulate logical order.' Again,[14] 'a man with an exquisite intellectual taste can recognise the flavour of Shakespeare as distinctly as the epicure recognises a special vintage;' and as regards himself, though not as regards others, 'his inference is conclusively proved.'[15]

Remarkably enough indeed, even 'F.' himself substantially admits what I have been saying. 'Who ever doubted,' he asks,[16] 'that an insurance board

---

[13] P. 795.

[14] P. 796.

[15] I may be allowed, perhaps, to express in passing a sense of the great ability and great fairness of intention exhibited by Mr. Stephen in this article; and also to make on it one comment. Certainly I have no right in any way to come forward as F. Newman's defender; though I am an enthusiast for large portions of his 'Grammar,' and read them again and again with ever increasing admiration and instruction. But in the general interests of truth, I would refer for a moment to Mr. Stephen's principal adverse comment on the work. He says (p. 793–4) that F. Newman's conclusions are purely psychological; that they are useful in discriminating between real and sham belief, but not between belief of what is true and belief of what is false. I think he has not sufficiently remembered F. Newman's repeated inculcations of the doctrine, that the laws of the human mind are in the last resort necessarily the supreme arbiters of truth. Those judgments are self-evident, which the intellect avouches as self-evident; those methods of inference are legitimate, which the intellect avouches as such. An appeal from the avouchment of our intellectual faculties is not only unreasonable but rather impossible; for we cannot appeal from our faculties except by using those very faculties themselves. 'We are as little able,' says F. Newman (p. 61), 'to accept or reject our mental constitution as our being. We have not the option: we can but misuse or mar its functions.'

[16] P. 31.

would do well to act on the advice of a physician, though the latter might be unable to analyse the grounds on which he gave it?' And it is 'F.' indeed who supplied me with my illustration, about the savage and the trackless forest. But he quite misunderstands the drift of my argument. He urges very justly that the physician's conviction is not reasonably sufficient to establish certitude in *another* man's mind. I was speaking however of the physician's own personal certitude.

These, and one or two other statements made by 'F.,' make me think it possible, that he does not definitely and distinctly intend the thesis with which I have credited him. If he does not—I am only too happy that so able a writer is not (so far) my opponent. But indeed—even if the facts on which I have hitherto insisted were admitted by every one to be true—it would be none the less important expressly to recount them; because they are forgotten by every anti-Christian writer, who alleges, as a fact obvious on the surface, that uneducated Christians can have no sufficient reasonable basis for their faith. So 'F.' himself[17] speaks of it—not merely as his own private opinion, but as 'notorious'—that, 'in a majority of cases, so great that no numerical proportion could express it, religious belief is produced not by evidence' [he means not by the legitimate dictate of reason] 'but by some other cause.'

I have been contending then (1) that a large number of very important convictions are established with certitude, by some process very different from that of systematically arraying evidence *pro* and *con;* and (2) that recourse to this latter method will often be far more unfavourable than favourable to the cause of truth. I have been freely using the word 'certitude' throughout; and have no misgiving but that my sense of the word will have been sufficiently understood. Now, however, it will be better, for more than one reason, briefly to treat this verbal question. 'F.' distinguishes[18] between two kinds of belief. I think there is another distinction of much greater moment: but I will first consider that of 'F.,' which has undoubtedly its own importance. He distinguishes between 'qualified belief,' that is, belief accompanied by present doubt,—and what may be called 'undoubting belief,' that is, belief *un*accompanied by present doubt. Thus, he says,[19] we have often an undoubting belief that a man is dead, when we see his death reported in the newspaper; and yet when that report is next day contradicted, we retract our belief of yesterday with the greatest ease. And here I make the obvious remark, that the mere *undoubtingness* of a belief does not at all imply any special *firmness*, but arises from pure accident. Yesterday I undoubtingly believed that A. B. was dead. The true analysis of this judgment was merely 'there is a certain *presumption* that A. B. is dead:' but as no

[17] P. 29.
[18] P. 24.
[19] P. 26.

particular motive for doubt occurred to me, I did not reflect on the true character of the belief which I entertained. The extreme facility, with which I abandon it to-day, shows how utterly weak was its hold on my mind yester-day. These 'merely undoubting' beliefs I will call 'simple' beliefs: and (as is evident) they vary indefinitely from each other in the firmness with which they adhere to the object believed.

But I maintain as very evident, that there are certain reasonable convic-tions, which are not only *unaccompanied* by doubt, but so firm as to be *incompatible* with the co-existence of doubt: and it is these convictions (as I understand the matter) which are commonly called 'certitudes.' For instance (to take the hackneyed illustration) my conviction that the cities of Paris and Vienna have existed, is so firm, that I cannot possibly bring myself to doubt the fact. Or take the physician who is certain on sufficient grounds that in this particular case such a treatment is appropriate. He can imaginably be *argued out* of that certitude, by some one who may be as much his superior in logical expertness as his inferior in medical insight. But so long as his conviction remained in its primitive firmness, the entrance of doubt was impossible. The entrance of doubt, in other words, shows, either that that special firmness of conviction never existed, which is called certitude—or else that it has now ceased to exist and is replaced by some weaker kind of belief.

We have arrived then at a threefold division of beliefs: 'qualified belief;' 'simple belief;' 'certitude.' Here, however, another consideration must be glanced at. It is a matter of everyday occurrence, that a man may be extremely confident and yet unreasonably so. He may hold some opinion with a firmness incompatible with the co-existence of doubt, and yet this opinion may be entirely mistaken. What shall we call this state of belief? Let us call it 'spurious certitude.' My present theme does not absolutely require any treatment of this very common phenomenon; though I wish space would permit me to enter on it at length. I will merely, in passing, express the humble opinion, that much oftener than not a careful psychial analysis would show a phenomenal difference *in kind* between these spurious certitudes and certitudes properly so called. There will be a word more on this subject towards the end of my article.

So much as to certitude. Now let me make, in passing, a brief remark on a very large subject. Against those who hold that inquiry is a necessary condition for genuine certitude, I maintain that in very many cases the most healthy and normal way of arriving at certitude, is to pass towards it through simple belief, without the entrance of any doubt whatever. So the mechanic, in learning his trade, begins with simple belief in his instructor; and in regard to many of the lessons which he has received, he arrives by experi-ence at absolute certitude of their truth, without having instituted any inquiry, conscious or unconscious. So we learn from our parents the great principles of morality; we accept them with simple belief, put them into practice, and by doing so arrive at secure knowledge of their truth, without once reflecting on the process we go through. This is a subject of great extent and extreme moment; and no kind of justice could be done it, unless an entire article could be devoted to its exclusive treatment. But what I wish here to point out, may be very concisely stated. As regards these simple beliefs—through which often lies the best path to certitude—it does not at all follow, because they are *undoubting,* that their *firmness* or *intensity* at any given moment is at all greater than is warranted by the grounds of belief which at that moment may be possessed.

The next question which has to be considered, may be thus exhibited. Reverting to those processes, which implicitly pass through the mind, and which lead men (uneducated or educated) along the path of true inference— what is the true *analysis* of those processes? I gave part of my answer to this question in April 1871, by saying that I accepted F. Newman's teaching on the existence in man's mind of what he calls the 'illative sense' or 'ratiocinative faculty.' On this 'F.' remarks[20] that the 'function' of this 'new faculty' 'appears to be to draw positive conclusions from insufficient premisses.' This remark and the general course of argument in which it is embedded imply a theory, that the mind has only a power (if I may so express myself) to *criticise* grounds of belief *independently* existing, and not itself to *supply* grounds of reasonable belief. This general theory I must regard as beyond all doubt a fundamentally mistaken one. And as the question is of great importance, I will briefly treat it.

Firstly, then, let us consider that absolutely necessary faculty which we call 'memory.' What is my ground for knowing my experiences of ten minutes ago? What is the work performed by my intellect, when it assures me that those experiences really befell me? Is its work the arranging and marshalling grounds of belief external to the intellect itself? On the contrary, there *are* no such grounds of belief, great or small. My one exclusive, and my entirely sufficient, means of knowing with certitude the past fact of those experiences, is the present avouchment of my intellect itself. Then secondly consider the power—which man's mind (as I hold) most indubitably possesses—of cognising as self-evident various 'à priori synthetical judgments,' as Kant calls them. I have set forth from time to time in the *Dublin Review* what seem to me conclusive proofs that the mind possesses this power; and I summed up the whole in an article contributed to the *Contemporary Review* of March 1875, on necessary truth. What happens again and again is this. The mind contemplates some given proposition, the idea of whose predicate is by no means contained in the idea of its subject: and the mind, by merely contemplating this proposition with careful attention, cognises as self-evident that the proposition is true. In discerning the truth of an *analytical* proposition, the mind no doubt performs a merely critical office. An ana-

[20] P. 36.

lytical proposition, as soon as its terms are understood, at once assumes the form 'A. is A.;' or 'A. is included in A. + B.': and certainly the intellect needs no originative power, in order to cognise the self-evidence of such propositions. But in avouching the self-evident truth of a *synthetical* proposition, the mind proceeds on no ground of belief whatever, beyond its own intrinsic illumination. Whereas, then, the intellect possesses (1) a 'remembering' faculty, and (2) what we may call an 'axiomatising' faculty,—so nothing can be more intelligible than to say that it possesses (3) an 'illative' faculty. Certain premisses—not as verbally exhibited on paper, but as personally apprehended in their concrete fulness by the individual,—tend with a converging and cumulative probability to some given conclusion. I certainly hold that each man possesses a faculty (whatever its appropriate name) whereby, at a given period of the cumulation, he possesses, with an assurance which is entirely reasonable, that the conclusion is now ascertained with absolute certitude. I am not here arguing for this doctrine. I follow with entire concurrence F. Newman's most masterly exposition of those psychical facts, which (to my mind) establish it beyond question. Here, however, I am only saying that 'F.' has no right to *assume* its erroneousness.[21]

'F.' is evidently one of those philosophers who deny the cognisableness of necessary truth as such; and though I differ from him *toto cœlo* on this, I will not here discuss the subject. But even as to truths which confessedly are contingent, I think he exhibits an entirely indefensible narrowness of view. He holds[22] that there is no valid method of inference, except the inductive process, as described by Mr. Mill. But Mr. Mill's canons are simply worthless, nay unmeaning, unless we begin by postulating the doctrine of *the uniformity of nature:* and this doctrine may be called the opprobrium of modern phenomenistic philosophy, so confidently is it affirmed and so inadequately established.[23] Now whenever 'F.' or any other phenomenist may exhibit the reasoning which leads him to accept this doctrine as sufficiently proved, we shall see what we shall see. I am curious to discover how

[21] As many readers of the *Nineteenth Century* know very little about Catholic domestic controversies, it is only fair to say that it is doubtful whether all Catholic philosophers would accept what I have said about synthetical axioms. F. Kleutgen indeed—than whom in modern times we have no greater philosophical name—says that the difference on this head between Kant and certain Catholic philosophers is a purely verbal one: viz. that they include, under the term 'analytical,' those judgments which Kant calls 'synthetical.' But it may be doubted whether all modern Catholic philosophers would here agree with Kleutgen. I discussed this domestic question in the *Dublin Review* of July 1869, pp. 159–166.

Much more is it doubtful how many Catholic philosophers would accept what has been above said on the 'illative sense.'

[22] P. 36.

[23] Of 'modern *phenomenistic* philosophy,' I am far from denying that the doctrine has been satisfactorily proved by introducing *metempirical* considerations. This word 'metempirical' is due to Mr. Lewes, and I agree with Mr. Lucas that it is a most useful addition to philosophical terminology.

he will even attempt to accomplish his task, without largely appealing to the certitude which results from cumulative probability. Mr. Leslie Stephen, for one, speaks somewhat airily on the uniformity of nature in his December article. 'The logician,' he says,[24] 'must accept the belief as an ultimate *fact*, while he leaves the problem of its *origin* to the psychologist.' But there is a question indefinitely more important than either the *fact* or the *origin* of this belief; viz. its *truth*. And on this Mr. Stephen is profoundly silent.

At all events, as regards the article I am immediately criticising, 'F.' is surely guilty of arguing in a mere circle. He thinks that all those, and only those, inferences can be admitted as certain, which are proved by Mill's canons of induction. Moreover, he holds that the uniformity of nature is itself a certain inference. A short dialogue then of the following kind may be imagined between him and an interrogator. Why do you hold the uniformity of nature as certain? 'Because it is proved by Mill's canons of induction.' But why are these canons valid principles of reasoning? 'Because of the uniformity of nature.' But why do you believe in the uniformity of nature? 'Because of Mill's canons of induction.' And so on *ad infinitum*.

In the course of criticising others, I have now almost sufficiently explained what I would myself affirmatively maintain. I will add, however, two explanations.

(1) Even as regards those many truths on which certitude may be obtained without inquiry or explicit argument, I do not at all deny the great and manifold advantages which may result, if highly trained thinkers exhibit as fully as they can the premises which (in their view) warrant this or that conclusion. It is obvious indeed that the incalculably predominant majority of mankind are utterly incapable of such a task. Even where this disqualification does not exist, there are cases in which—unless very great care be taken—the formulated application of logic (whether syllogistic or inductive) is far more likely to issue in false than in true conclusions. I refer to all those cases where those premises, which deserve to carry with them the greatest weight, are (for whatever reason) under imminent danger of being inadequately set forth by logical analysis. In such cases—I may refer to my illustration drawn a few pages back from the physician—there is a grave risk, lest the man of genius and keen perception be browbeaten (as it were) by the man of shallower but more logical mind, and bullied into abandoning a certitude which was entirely reasonable. But if this most serious peril be duly guarded against, great advantages (which I have here no space to enumerate) result from the logical analysis (even in that limited degree which alone is possible) of the implicit ratiocinative process.

(2) That special method of reasoning which proceeds by way of cumulative probabilities, I will call the 'cumulative method.' Now I by no means contend that the mode of inference whereby we arrive at concrete

truths is always of this kind. I implied *e.g.* a few pages back, that the weather-wise mariner seems to arrive at his conclusion through implicitly guiding himself by the regular canons of induction. And when an uneducated rustic believes (to his great grief) that his mother will one day die—this belief rests, I suppose, on a syllogistic process. 'All human beings die: she is a human being, *ergo, &c.*'

To sum up. What I maintain, in opposition to the thesis which I assail, is in substance this. There is a very large number of verities undoubtedly—theological, philosophical, historical, physical—which are obtained by logical process; by means of inquiry, methodical accumulation of facts, argument based on those facts, &c. &c., and which can be obtained in no other way. In regard to these I have been raising no question whatever. But putting aside these altogether—every adult (I contend), educated or uneducated, is constantly acquiring fresh certitudes by the healthy normal and spontaneous exercise of his intellectual faculties; the conclusions of to-day becoming premises of to-morrow, and so on day after day, without any reflection whatever of his on what is taking place. This process goes on again and again, where there has been no previous doubt; and in an incalculable majority of instances it is accompanied by no kind of scientific logic. Such is the healthy movement of the human intellect, proceeding on its own intrinsic laws. I do not of course deny that (as F. Newman points out) the normal working of these laws is with the mass of men more or less overlaid and hidden from sight by the superincumbency of prejudices, whims, fancies, caused (it may be) by cupidity, wilfulness, pride, or mere indolence;[25] but by patient observation it is generally possible, even for an external observer, with constantly increasing clearness and unmistakeableness, to distinguish those superficial excrescences from the solid and equable intellectual movement which takes place beneath.

And now in conclusion I would apply what has been said to a theological question of the most vital importance, which Professor Clifford also treats in his own characteristic way. Every Christian teacher, whether Catholic or Protestant, impresses as a sacred duty on the mass of believers, that they shall not read infidel books or otherwise allow themselves to doubt the truth of Christianity. We Catholics in particular not only are forbidden by the Church to read anti-Catholic treatises—unless we are exceptionally fitted to do so without peril to our faith—but we account it a mortal sin in any one who has really embraced the Faith to permit himself one deliberate doubt of its truth. On this unbelievers make a very obvious comment. Such precepts, they say, show that Catholics are bidden to renounce the use of their reason, and to decide the most momentous of possible questions by the dictates of blind prejudice. How do we defend ourselves against this plausible indictment? We reply that Catholic faith is a special gift from God, and that

[25] *Grammar of Assent*, p. 255.

rebellion against that gift is a grievous sin. In developing this reply, indeed, so as directly to meet the objection I have mentioned, there is naturally more or less mutual discrepancy among theologians. In the article of April 1871, which I have more than once mentioned, I set forth what seems to me the true explanation of this matter; following substantially F. Kleutgen's guidance, and in accordance with the philosophical doctrine which I have set forth in the present paper. I wish my readers would refer to pp. 262–272 of that article. Here I can but most briefly set forth what is there urged at greater length.

I consider, then, that (1) those who have been trained in the Catholic religion (brevity compels me to speak only of *them*), however otherwise uneducated they may be, have cognisance of various premisses which (according to the cumulative method of reasoning) are super-superabundantly sufficient to establish the truth of that religion; sufficient to prove that the Catholic Church possesses that authority which she claims. Several of these premisses no doubt are more or less subtle and impalpable, but for that very reason the more cogent and legitimately influential. Then I consider (2) that God, in imparting and upholding the gift of faith, specially illuminates the Catholic's mind, so that he shall give those premisses their due weight, and thus reasonably possess certitude.[26] Since then on one hand God commands firm faith in the dogmata taught by the Church, strictly forbidding all admission of doubt—and since on the other hand He gives Catholics abundantly sufficient proofs of their religion—it is an inexcusable and grievous sin to disobey His command.[27]

Perhaps it will be inconsiderately replied that I have been begging the whole question. I have assumed—it may be said—that God exists, that He has revealed the Catholic religion, and that He infuses the gift of faith: but these or some of them are the very doctrines which my opponents deny. On the contrary, I have assumed nothing whatever. Here are two propositions. (1) 'Catholics are strictly forbidden to doubt for a moment the truth of their

[26] An objection is not unfrequently urged, which is but indirectly concerned with the general theme of my paper, and which I will therefore briefly treat in a note. Since Catholics account an act of faith to be free and meritorious, they cannot—so the objector urges—hold that the doctrine believed is so exhibited as to be cognisable with absolute certitude. Cardinal Franzelin admirably replies (see *De habitudine rationis humanæ ad divinam fidem*, cap. 1, sec. 2) that a truth may well be exhibited to the mind, not indeed as 'evident,' but yet as absolutely 'certain.' Where a truth is exhibited as 'evident,' doubt is impossible; as in the instance of a demonstrated mathematical theorem. But where it is exhibited as 'certain' indeed but not as 'evident,' doubt is possible though most unreasonable, and belief therefore laudable. For a full exposition of this thought I must refer to the treatise itself, which is contained in the volume *De Traditione*. And I may be allowed to add that I think Cardinal Franzelin's treatment of the various questions connected with the 'analysis fidei' more satisfactory than that of any other author whom I happen to have read.

[27] I shall not be understood as implying that God—consistently with His attributes—could impose the precept of faith on any one in whom faith would not be intellectually reasonable.

religion.' (2) 'The Catholic's faith is entirely reasonable.' Objectors urge that these two propositions are mutually incompatible; and it is to this objection, not to some other, that I have been replying. Now it is demonstratively shown that two given propositions are not mutually incompatible, if any possible proposition can ever be imagined which shall harmonise the two. I have done in fact more than was needed by my argument. For the harmonising suggestion made by me—viz. that faith is a divine gift—is no gratuitous and arbitrary supposition, but the very doctrine held by all Catholics.

I have been speaking of the Divine prohibition imposed on Catholics, against their admitting a deliberate doubt on the truth of their religion. But one word should be added concerning the prohibition imposed on all but a very exceptional class against reading or listening to infidel arguments. The reasonableness of this prohibition however has been made, I hope, abundantly plain in the whole preceding part of this paper. Let it be supposed that persons, possessing no special intellectual qualifications or safeguards, choose to study the anti-Christian reasoning of some clever infidel. They are entering on a line of thought which can do them no possible good, because its true apprehension is entirely beyond their grasp; while on the other hand they wantonly expose themselves to be brow beaten and bullied by some ingenious logician out of the certitude infused into their mind by God Himself. To their own incalculable benefit, the Church earnestly denounces such unpardonable audacity and temerity.

But the Church has never shown any unwillingness whatever—emphatically the contrary—that those of her children whom she can trust in such matters shall study diligently and profoundly infidel writings and the general course of infidel thought, with a view to encountering opponents on the field of fair and frank controversy. And if I do not here enlarge on the vast benefit, or rather absolute necessity, of such controversy, it is merely because no one doubts it, and my space is limited. I will merely, therefore, make one remark bearing on my general theme.

Of course the individual Catholic's personal certitude cannot be offered to others, as by itself a reasonable ground for their belief. But on the other hand let us suppose some non-Catholic to be convinced on argumentative grounds—philosophical, historical, or the like—that Catholicity is true. On that supposition he ought reasonably to infer, that individual Catholics do possess that infused faith which we claim for them. Whatever arguments suffice to convince an educated man that the Catholic religion is *true*, should suffice also to convince him that individual Catholics, however uneducated, have reasonable grounds for firmly *believing* its truth.

RETROSPECTIVE ESSAYS

THE ETHICS OF BELIEF RECONSIDERED
Van A. Harvey

I

In the decades following the Enlightenment, it must have been particularly disturbing to the Christian intellectual to be told that faith itself is an irresponsible act. The assumption lying behind this accusation was, of course, that the genuine lover of truth is a person who does not entertain any proposition with a greater degree of assurance than the proofs it is built upon will warrant. Since Christian belief, by definition, is the entertaining of propositions incommensurate with the evidence, the Christian cannot also be regarded as a lover of truth. Moreover, if love for the truth be a virtue—and most Christians would have said that it is—then faith must be a vice. In short, it is immoral to be a Christian.

John Locke, who formulated so elegantly the assumption upon which this accusation rests,[1] did not himself draw the unkind conclusion about Christian believers since he thought that Christian belief could be rationally justified. It was only later, when it became a widely shared assumption that religious belief was unjustifiable, that Locke's criteria could be polemically turned against the Christian. One of the most powerful illustrations of this polemical use is to be found in W. K. Clifford's well-known essay "The Ethics of Belief."[2] Clifford argues that civilization itself depends upon the habit of forming only justified beliefs. Credulity, the readiness to hold unjustified beliefs, threatens the very foundations of society. Every belief, no matter how trivial, is significant because it prepares the mind to receive more like it. No one's beliefs are merely private matters because our modes of thought and belief are common property, "an heirloom which every succeeding generation inherits as a precious deposit and a sacred trust to be handed on to the next one. . . ."[3] Consequently, it is the bounden duty of every person in society, no matter how humble the station, to guard the purity of his/her beliefs. Whoever suppresses doubt or allows the quest for certitude to

[1]John Locke, *An Essay concerning Human Understanding*, abr. and ed. A. S. Pringle-Pattison (Oxford: Oxford University Press, 1934), bk. 4, chap. 29.

[2]Reprinted in *Religion from Tolstoy to Camus*, ed. Walter Kaufman (New York: Harper & Row, 1961), pp. 207–20.

[3]Ibid., p. 204.

overcome the critical spirit sins against mankind. Only when we arrive at our beliefs by patient investigation and testing are we entitled to the psychological pleasure that accompanies believing. If that pleasure attaches to unjustified belief, it is a stolen pleasure and we "should guard ourselves from such beliefs as from a pestilence, which may shortly master our own body and then spread to the rest of the town."[4] "It is wrong always, everywhere, and for anyone, to believe anything on insufficient evidence."[5]

In order to anchor this stark formal imperative in concrete existence, Clifford tells several stories to make his point. One of these concerns a shipowner who was about to send an immigrant ship to sea. Although the shipowner had received a troubling suggestion that the vessel might not be fully seaworthy, he had laid these anxieties aside and put his confidence in a Providence that would see these unhappy immigrants safely to their new homeland. Consequently, he acquired the sincere conviction that the ship was seaworthy, and he watched her departure with a light heart filled with good wishes for the immigrants. He also collected his insurance money when the vessel went down. "Now what shall we say of this shipowner?" asks Clifford, and he replies to his own question as follows: "Surely this, that he was verily guilty of the death of those men. It is admitted that he did sincerely believe in the soundness of his ship; but the sincerity of his conviction can in no wise help him, because *he had no right to believe on such evidence as was before him*. He had acquired his belief not by honestly earning it in patient investigation, but by stifling his doubts."[6] Clifford then proposes that the story be altered somewhat; that we suppose the ship had been sound after all and had completed the voyage safely. Would this happy fact have diminished the guilt of the owner? "Not one jot," he argues. "When an action is once done, it is right or wrong for ever; no accidental failure of its good or evil fruits can possibly alter that. The man would not have been innocent, he would only have been not found out. The question of right or wrong has to do with the origin of his belief, not the matter of it; not what it was, but how he got it; not whether it turned out to be true or false, but whether he had a right to believe on such evidence as was before him."[7]

One of the most interesting features of Clifford's essay is that the justification he gives for this ethics of belief is that persons are responsible for culture and society. He does not appeal to prudence—if you do not wish to be deceived, believe only thus and so—or to some ontic correlation between being truthful and self-realization. Rather, he argues that men are bound together by the formation of modes of thought and belief that have been established by "long experience and waiting toil, and which have stood in the

---

[4] Ibid., p. 205.
[5] Ibid., p. 206.
[6] Ibid., pp. 201–2.
[7] Ibid., p. 202.

fierce light of free and fearless questioning."[8] It is this cultural heritage that strengthens their common action. It is because his ethic is directed toward the preservation of a common and sacred heritage that Clifford can speak of virtues and vices and of believing as an awful responsibility. "Belief, that sacred faculty which prompts the decisions of our will . . . is ours not for ourselves, but for humanity."[9] Thus it is a sin against mankind that one should allow oneself to become credulous.

It is perhaps a measure of the psychic gulf that separates the modern intellectual from his Victorian counterpart that a contemporary critic of religious belief would never appeal to some universal duty of preserving the purity of the "sacred faculty of belief." In a permissive culture such as our own that seems committed to the relativization of all that Philip Rieff calls interdicts, the Victorian's call to duty and self-discipline can only seem quaint. Moreover, this psychic gulf between ourselves and the Victorian is paralleled by an even greater conceptual gulf because the epistemological assumption underlying Clifford's ethics of belief has largely collapsed; namely, the assumption that it is possible to justify all of our beliefs. If it is not possible to justify all of one's beliefs, then it is meaningless to argue that the believer has shirked a bounden duty to mankind because he does not do so.

The collapse of the justificatory principle might seem, then, to liberate the Christian from any concern with the problems posed by Clifford. Indeed, it is probably no accident that the three philosophies that have most influenced modern Christian thought—existentialism, phenomenology, and the philosophy of the later Wittgenstein—all seem to involve a rejection of the basic assumption upon which Clifford's ethic rests: that religious beliefs require to be justified. Although Michael Polanyi is not to be classified as an exponent of any one of the above philosophies, he speaks for them, in a sense, when he, too, argues in his influential book, *Personal Knowledge*, that all of our thinking and knowing rests on acritical beliefs, on what he calls a fiduciary framework.

Since I have in the past argued that the ideal of judgment cast up by the Enlightenment does pose the question of intellectual integrity for the Christian believer, I have frequently been asked how I can argue in this fashion, sharing as I do this basic postcritical assumption about the human cognitive situation. In reflecting on this question, I have been led to reread Clifford's famous essay, and in what follows I would like to share some of my reflections concerning it. To anticipate, I shall argue that there are some legitimate moral elements contained in Clifford's ethic of belief that he does not himself develop; moreover, that these elements are actually obscured by his own

[8] Ibid., p. 204.
[9] Ibid.

formulation of the moral imperative not to believe anything on insufficient evidence, which, he thinks, is the essence of his position. These moral elements, I will argue, can actually best be remade from a postcritical standpoint, that is, from just that standpoint that is alleged to have made Clifford's ethic untenable.

Before pursuing the main part of the argument, it would probably be useful to clarify somewhat how I shall use the rather general and rough-hewn term "belief." In the main and for purposes of this argument, I shall sidestep many of the difficult conceptual problems surrounding the analysis of believing and follow the suggestions of H. H. Price in his Gifford Lectures, namely, that to say "A believes that *P*" is to attribute a multiform disposition to A which is manifested or actualized in many different ways: not only in actions but in emotional states, feelings of doubt, surprise, confidence, and in inferences.[10] Some of these are public; some are private. I also think, with Price, that this dispositional analysis enables one to incorporate those elements stressed by so-called occurrence analysis, that is, the analysis of belief in terms of judgment and assent. Some of our beliefs, though not all, are arrived at through judgment and assents.

II

So far I have referred quite generally to what Polanyi calls the postcritical view of the human cognitive situation, by which I mean quite generally the view that what we call knowledge rests on acritical, nonjustifiable beliefs. But since philosophers as diverse as Quine, Polanyi, Wittgenstein, and Merleau-Ponty all agree on this general proposition but differ in important respects concerning the reasons for holding it, it is important for us to describe more specifically the merchandise that is being posted under this general label. For purposes of my argument, I have decided to follow the basic rudiments of the view set forward in Wittgenstein's posthumously published notes entitled *On Certainty*. I do this because even though there are some elements in that view that are, in my opinion, problematical, it has the virtue of providing a position sufficiently congenial to my own that I can both employ it for my purposes and make contact with those philosophers of religion who simply (and mistakenly) assume that Wittgenstein's view or something like it renders the kind of issue I am concerned with obsolete and even philosophically misguided.

Wittgenstein, as does Polanyi, argues that we do not acquire our beliefs by being dragged and screaming, as it were, out of skepticism. Nor do we carefully weigh the evidence for every proposition recommended to us. Rather, our culture teaches us to organize our own experience in certain ways by giving us conceptions, rules of use, names, and the like. We acquire

---

[10] H. H. Price, *Belief* (London: George Allen & Unwin, 1969), pp. 294 ff.

a picture of the world; that is, a loosely connected network of propositions in which the consequences and premises are mutually supporting.[11] It is against this background that doubt arises, either because what we expect is contradicted by our encounters with the world, or because we find ourselves entertaining propositions that are, or whose consequences are, contradictory. We begin by believing and we must have grounds for doubting.

In the systems of propositions we acquire, not every proposition stands on the same level. Not even every empirical proposition has the same status. Some propositions we believe are more fundamental than others; they "stand fast" and are relatively fixed. They are, Wittgenstein says, removed from the traffic and "shunted onto an unused siding."[12] It is not easy to generalize about these fundamental beliefs. Wittgenstein himself seems to have held that some of them are "fossilized empirical propositions" like "there is a brain inside of my skull," "water boils at 100° C," "the earth is part of a vast universe," etc. Some other propositions exist on the borderline of the empirical and logical. But all of these propositions constitute the inherited background against which we distinguish what is true or false. They are what we exempt from doubt. Just as the hinges must stay put if we want a door to turn, some beliefs must be exempt from doubt if we are to ascertain what is true. "When I am trying to mate someone in chess," Wittgenstein writes, "I cannot have doubts about the pieces perhaps changing places of themselves and my memory simultaneously playing tricks on me so that I don't notice."[13] We so take certain propositions for granted that if anyone were to deny these fundamental beliefs, were to question, say, whether there is a brain in my skull, we feel that they could doubt anything we say to be true. These beliefs constitute for us what it is reasonable to believe.

Wittgenstein, as was Polanyi, was prepared to say that many of our fundamental beliefs are literally groundless, and that this has nothing to do with stupidity or credulity. We do not acquire them through testing or investigation but simply by belonging to a community bound together by science and education.[14] One might say that at the foundation of well-founded belief is belief that is not well founded. "My *life*," writes Wittgenstein, "consists in my being content to accept many things."[15] Nevertheless, he maintains, we are and can be legitimately certain of many of these beliefs. Indeed, we hold that the reasonable man simply does not have certain doubts at all. "I, L. W., believe, am sure, that my friend hasn't sawdust in his body or in his head, even though I have no direct evidence of my senses to the contrary. I am sure, by reason of what has been said to me, of what I have

[11] Ludwig Wittgenstein, *On Certainty*, ed. G. E. M. Anscombe and G. H. von Wright (New York: Harper & Row, 1969), p. 21.

[12] Ibid., p. 29.

[13] Ibid., p. 44.

[14] Ibid., p. 38.

[15] Ibid., p. 44.

read, and of my experience. To have doubts about it would seem to me madness—of course, this is also in agreement with other people; but I agree with them."[16]

Now if one accepts the rudiments of this sketch of the cognitive situation, then it is not difficult to see why Clifford's view that it is immoral for anyone, anywhere, and at any time to believe anything on insufficient evidence seems so irrelevant because, on these terms, it is impossible to be moral. Just as Wittgenstein observes that he cannot mate anyone in chess and simultaneously have doubts that the chess pieces change places of themselves, so, also, the shipowner in Clifford's essay must assume many things for which he has no evidence and for which it would seem madness to ask for evidence: can he be sure that the ship about to embark today is the same ship that was in the yard yesterday? How does he know that someone has not systematically replaced the planking overnight? What justification is there for thinking that the words which the foreman uses to report his findings mean the same thing to all the other workmen? No, it is senseless to ask us to doubt systematically all that we have been taught to believe. Therefore, if we take the moral imperative not to believe anything on insufficient evidence seriously, we simply cannot observe it. To invert Kant's famous dictum we might say, "if one cannot, one ought not."

Since Clifford assumes that this universal moral imperative is the essence of the matter, to reject it seems to commit us to rejecting his entire argument. But, before we do this, we might ask whether there is anything to be salvaged from it that would enable us to talk meaningfully about an ethics of belief. I think there is, and we can best see this by reflecting initially on the story of the shipowner and his failure to inspect the ship that went down at sea. The first version of that story acquires its moral force from the assumption that the shipowner had, by virtue of his "station and its duties," a role-specific obligation to inspect the vessel upon which the immigrants had sailed. Because he did not, we can fairly say he is responsible for the death of these immigrants. As owner of the ship, all the lines of accountability terminated in his office. He had acknowledged this in a number of ways, not the least of which was accepting money in return for contracts of passage. It is just because we accept these lines of accountability that we can understand Clifford's conclusion that the shipowner is "verily guilty" of the death of those men.

It is also because we accept this role-specific obligation of the shipowner, however, that we find something fishy about the moral conclusion Clifford draws from the second version of the story. You will remember that in the second version the immigrants arrive safely at their destination even though, as in the first version, Clifford's shipowner had failed to inspect the ship. Clifford then asks us to conclude that this lucky happenstance in no way

16 Ibid., p. 36.

("not one jot") diminishes the guilt of the shipowner. "When an action is once done, it is right or wrong forever; no accidental failure of its good or evil fruits can possibly alter that . . . . The question of right or wrong has to do with the origin of his belief, not the matter of it; not what it was, but how he got it; . . . whether he had a right to believe on such evidence as was before him."[17] The reason this conclusion is fishy is because Clifford seems to be using two different models of ethical reasoning to talk about the guilt of the shipowner. In the first model, Clifford reasons back from the consequences of the shipowner's failure to inquire into the condition of the ship (the death of the immigrants) to the charge of murder. In the second version, however, the consequences are deemed to be irrelevant and the action said to be right or wrong without respect to them. Nevertheless, Clifford tries to have us believe that the shipowner is equally guilty in both cases. But if the shipowner's guilt in the first case is murder, he cannot be held guilty to the same degree in the second case where there were no deaths. Somehow the analysis is defective. Surely a less forced view would be that in both cases the shipowner did fail to fulfill his responsibilities, which led to the immigrants' death in the one case but, happily, not in the second. He is, to be sure, equally guilty of gross irresponsibility in both cases, but in the first of the death of the immigrants as well.

And how shall we specify this gross irresponsibility in both cases? Clifford naturally argues that it stems from a breach of the imperative never to believe anything on insufficient evidence. But this imperative is too sweeping and has all the difficulties noted above. On these grounds we might as well condemn the immigrants who trusted the shipowner because *they also believed on insufficient evidence* that the ship was seaworthy. We might as well say they too were guilty of their own deaths in the first version, and "equally guilty" in the second. But it would be senseless to argue in this fashion. No, it is not the violation of some universal imperative not to believe anything on insufficient evidence that constitutes the irresponsibility of the shipowner; it is that he failed to fulfill his role-specific obligation to inquire into the seaworthiness of his ship.

Some interesting lines of reflection are opened by this type of analysis, lines that should make it possible to see why a postcritical view of the human cognitive situation does not necessary make all of Clifford's concerns for an ethics of belief obsolete and untenable. These concerns are the duties and responsibilities of inquiry in given cases, the importance and duty of the justification of judgments, and the character traits requisite to the proper performance of these duties.

The first line of reflections begins with what may seem to be both obvious and trivial. A necessary though not sufficient condition of the shipowner being said to have a role-specific obligation to inquire into the

17 Clifford, p. 202.

seaworthiness of his ship is that there be some possible evidence bearing on his inquiry. It would make no sense to say he had a duty to inquire into the condition of his ship if there were nothing he could assess or come to a judgment about. Although obvious, this point is not trivial. In the first place, it throws into sharp relief the contextual nature of the object of the shipowner's responsibility to inquire, which is to say, it is *this* evidence bearing on *this* ship which he is to assess and come to a judgment about. He is not being asked to hold all of his beliefs on the basis of inquiry. He is responsible only for arriving at a specific range of critical judgments, judgments which will, of course, be made against the background of beliefs he will probably hold acritically. In the second place, it is the existence of such specific evidence that will enable Clifford (or any of us) to use the quasi-moral "right to believe." It is because the shipowner's inquiry will issue in a claim that this language of entitlement makes sense; because a claim is, as Stephen Toulmin has pointed out, "like a claim to a right or to a title. As with a claim to a right, though it may in the event be conceded without argument, its merits depend on the merits of the argument which could be produced in its support."[18] In the third place, it is because the question of "right" arises that we can distinguish one important difference between the shipowners saying "I believe" and "I know." One of the important contextual uses of the terms "I know" in contrast to "I believe," as J. L. Austin has pointed out, is to put forward a claim to speak with authority. "I know" implies one stands ready to give compelling reasons.[19] The words "I believe," "am confident," "am sure," on the other hand, are more ambiguous and are frequently used simply to report the state of one's mind, to indicate that one is aware that he lacks the accepted grounds for saying "I know." "I know," in short, lays claim to an entitlement in a way that "I believe" does not. "I believe" can sometimes even mean that one lacks justification for what one says. Now if all believing either has to be fully justified (screwed up to the standards authorizing "I know"), or is immoral, as Clifford's view dictates, then we could only say "I believe" without incurring some kind of moral guilt.

Clifford, of course, does not accept the view that some beliefs are legitimately untitled. The reason he gives is that to hold such beliefs, no matter how trivial, disposes the mind to accept others like it and leads to a careless attitude toward truth itself. But surely this is a dubious and over-simplified psychological generalization, as Ralph Barton Perry has shown in his discussion of William James's essay, "The Will to Believe." We can easily imagine, say, a type of education in which persons are taught to be very self-conscious about the nature of their beliefs—to distinguish among those which they hold on authority from those they hold because of the evidence

---

[18] Stephen Toulmin, *The Uses of Argument* (New York: Cambridge University Press, 1958), p. 11.

[19] Cf. Wittgenstein, p. 32. "'I know' relates to a possibility of demonstrating the truth."

and from those they know to be groundless. Would we say that such persons are credulous because not all of their beliefs are justified, or would we say that making just these discriminations is what we mean by noncredulous persons? Perry writes that "flat prohibitions of . . . [Clifford's sort] . . . are at best secondary rules, designed for weaker minds which cannot be trusted to grasp and wisely administer the first principles from which the rules derive their cogency."[20]

There is a second line of reflection that follows close upon the heels of the first. We may say that the shipowner not only had a role-specific duty to inquire into the state of the ship but also the duty to come to a judgment concerning it, a judgment which he is obligated to express truthfully. Moreover, this judgment should take the form of one of the following performatory utterances: "I know that the ship is seaworthy"; or "I know that the ship is unseaworthy"; or "I don't know whether the ship is seaworthy or unseaworthy."

Now some readers might object to this formulation of the shipowner's obligation. Thus, Polanyi might argue that the shipowner was only obliged to say "I believe this ship is seaworthy" not "I know this ship is seaworthy" on the grounds that to say "it is true that p" is equivalent to saying "I believe that p." I cannot accept this view, and the reason I cannot is implicit in the discussion of the differences between the uses of "I know" and "I believe." To say "I know that p" is to commit oneself to being answerable for the reliability of one's assertions in specific ways that "I believe" does not.

Wittgenstein makes this point in *On Certainty* when he argues, "If someone believes something, we needn't always be able to answer the question 'why he believes it'; but if he knows something, then, the question 'how does he know' must be capable of being answered."[21] To ask How does he know? is, as Toulmin also points out, to elicit the grounds, qualifications, and credentials of the person who has made the claim. In the case of the shipowner, if he were to say only "I believe the ship is seaworthy" it would not yet tell us whether he had made the necessary tests and, on the basis of the evidence, was putting his assertion "under seal," so to speak, or was merely expressing a hunch.

It is difficult, if not impossible, in the case of role-specific inquiry not to introduce terms like "authority," "necessary tests," and "proper procedures" in contrast to the broader and vaguer term "evidence." The reason is, of course, that a performative utterance like "I know" does imply expertise of a sort, which is to say, having mastered a particular repertory of procedures that justifies the "I know." In other words, the kind of answer one gives to the question How does he know? is likely to be context bound, calling for

[20] Ralph Barton Perry, *In the Spirit of William James* (Bloomington: Indiana University Press, 1958), p. 197.
[21] Wittgenstein, p. 72.

different kinds of appeals on different occasions. To the extent that one can generalize or justify "I know" in contrast to "I believe," however, one can say that the justification will make use of a network of propositions that, to use Wittgenstein's phrase, "stand fast." To say that they stand fast, as I have pointed out, does not mean they are themselves capable of being justified, although some may be such. It is only to say that for the moment these propositions have been shunted off on a siding, so to speak, and are accepted as all right, as true. Indeed, insofar as some of these propositions are bedrock and fundamental, it will be thought that no reasonable person will doubt them. If someone were to doubt them, then we would feel justified in thinking that they could doubt anything that we could say. "I know" in this sense operates within what Polanyi calls a fiduciary framework. This framework has a history to which science, philosophy, and what we loosely call our ordinary experience has contributed. It is now our common sense; not that it is the lowest common denominator—"common sense" is often uncommon— but is what we have come to think reasonable men informed by education and science do and should believe.

In the case of role-specific inquiry within such a culture, the restrictions on the use of "I know" are necessarily more delimited and circumscribed. The sense of entitlement to a claim is more precisely defined. There is a specific repertory of procedures that shipowners must follow that license, so to speak, the judgment "this ship is seaworthy." This procedure includes, among other things, specific tests made on the planks, the caulking, the chainplate fastenings, the windlasses, and the rigging. The public has an extraordinary interest in safe sea travel and therefore a stake in the specifica-tion of those procedures. Implicitly (and sometimes explicitly) it ties "I know" to the successful completion of those procedures. Consequently, when the culture asks for the judgment "I know," it is asking for the assurance that these procedures and standards of judgment have been satis-fied. So much so, that even if a shipowner believed he had a better (though more eccentric) way of testing the seaworthiness of ships the culture would probably still insist that "I know" be tied to its own public canons of assessment.

Now if we accept this line of reflection that stresses the role-specific nature of the shipowner's duty rather than some alleged duty to justify every single one of his beliefs, we can begin to see that it can make sense not only to argue in particular cases that a person has a duty to come to know certain propositions but that such an obligation implies a further obligation to justify this claim against the background of an accepted nest of propositions that "stand fast." This role-specific duty in the case of the shipowner is tied to his wider duty to the culture and to the safety of its citizens. One fulfills this wider duty by being responsible for one's narrower station and its duties.

I noted earlier in this essay that Clifford's concern for the ethics of belief contains two moral elements: the first is expressed in the language of moral obligation (one ought not to believe on insufficient evidence); the second is expressed in the language of virtues and vices (reverence for the truth, habitual care regarding one's believing). I have tried to make some sense out of the first of these moral elements; I should now like to try to indicate how one might see some validity in the second.

The first step is to understand that Clifford argues from one's duties to humanity to the obligation to form in oneself a certain kind of characterological trait regarding believing. Believing, he asserts, is a sacred faculty because it has its effects on the fate of mankind. It is "not for ourselves, but for humanity." It is properly at work when it is used to bind men together and to strengthen their common action. Consequently, "it is desecrated when given to unproved and unquestioned statements, for the solace and private pleasure of the believer. . . ."[22] Since no one's belief is a private matter that concerns himself alone, how one believes is an "awful privilege, and an awful responsibility."

This notion of Clifford's is best understood against the background of the Victorians' ideal of a healthy culture, or what they would have called "civilization." For the Victorian, civilization is an "area of intercommunication" and is possible only when the "clerisy," to use Coleridge's term for the literate classes, accept responsibility for knowledge as a whole. This responsibility, they also believed, will most effectively be exercised in the sphere of educational policy, for the aim of education is to create a certain type of citizen, with certain habits of mind and character. This educational aim will naturally generate a criticism of the school system just as it does, for example, in G. M. Young's scathing indictment of the schools in his own time, an indictment that could easily have come from the pen of one of Young's Victorians: ". . . our schools have for years been discharging into the world young people without the slightest capacity for, or the remotest interest in what, for brevity, one might call scientific thinking. And the proof is this, that whether they believe or disbelieve, the grounds of their faith or skepticism are purely emotional, traditional, or it might seem accidental. What the schools have failed to teach is that a man has no more right to an opinion for which he cannot account than to a pint of beer for which he cannot pay."[23]

Now, underlying this conception of education is the ideal of a person who has disciplined himself to believe responsibly, who has respect for sound judgment, who is not slothful or impatient in matters of the intellect, who prizes lucidity, who cultivates in himself the sense of entitlement. It would, I think, be a mistake to argue that these traits are skills or that they are acts to be brought under the rubric of rules. What is being talked about here are

---

[22] Clifford, p. 204.

[23] G. M. Young, *Victorian Essays*, ed. W. D. Hancock (London: Oxford University Press, 1962), p. 7.

dispositions that are a part of a moral outlook, an ideal of character; which is to say, they are virtues. In this respect the ethics of belief have to do not only with obligatory actions but ideal traits of personal being.

Such a dispositional trait has, of course, been an ideal of the intellectual classes in Western society since Plato. What seems necessary to explain is Clifford's universalization of this ideal trait. "It is not only the leader of men, statesman, philosopher, or poet, that owes this bounden duty to mankind. Every rustic who delivers in the village alehouse his slow, infrequent sentences, may help or keep alive the fatal superstitions which clog his race. . . . No simplicity of mind, no obscurity of station, can escape the universal duty of questioning all that we believe."[24] The explanation for this universalization, I suspect, lies in the fact that Clifford was witnessing the emergence of an industrialized and technological society that depends upon specialized knowledge and, hence, the intellectual classes. He must have intuited that the growth in the size of the intellectual classes was to be the single most striking feature of modern culture. They would become larger than ever before in history, both in absolute numbers and in proportion to the population as a whole. Moreover, these classes would live in a culture generated and sustained by academic institutions of all sorts. Consequently, the virtue of believing reasonably, which was once an ideal of the elite, becomes a virtue increasingly essential to a culture in which the crucial roles will be performed by engineers, doctors, journalists, lawyers, scientists, and educators of all sorts. The virtue of reasonableness is a part of this "form of life," to use Wittgenstein's phrase. It is an essential virtue for anyone that would participate in a rationalized civilization.

It is easy to see, then, why Clifford could so easily slip into the language of universal imperatives, that no one should believe anything ever on insufficient evidence, or that one had the universal duty of questioning all that he believes. What we can now see, however, is that believing reasonably can be intelligibly articulated as a virtue without entailing the duty to question everything that we believe. *What* we may reasonably believe can only be contextually determined, seen against the background of a fiduciary framework of a culture; but that we can and must believe reasonably as a role-invariant virtue of our culture.

III

In the brief space remaining, I would like to draw some implications for religious belief from this line of reflection, especially since Clifford thought that if one accepted his ethics of belief then religious belief would be seen to be immoral since, presumably, religious belief is not based on evidence.

---

[24] Clifford, pp. 204–5.

Now just as I cautioned against being taken in by Clifford's abstract imperative, I would also warn that we should not be bewitched by the umbrella-like adjective "religious" that qualifies belief in this case. It is doubtful whether there is one logical type of belief that we can label religious. Most religions, insofar as we speak of their intellectual content, contain a number of different logical types of claims. Some of these claims are anthropological (having to do with some view of human nature and its alleged potentialities and idea possibilities); some are cosmological (having to do with the nature of the universe); some are ontological and metaphysical; some are moral; some ecclesiastical; and some are historical, which is to say that claims are made about past events and how they are to be properly interpreted.

In any given religion, these various claims are related in complex and subtle ways. Sometimes the relationships are so interwoven that to alter or change one of the logical strands will put an intolerable stress or strain on a quite different but dependent logical strand. For example, a historical claim will be inextricably connected with an anthropological or a moral or a theological claim. Sometimes, however, the connections are surprisingly looser than seemed initially the case, and it will be possible to eliminate completely one type of claim without altering visibly the framework of belief. It is just because religions have this complex character that they can change imperceptibly through the course of history, adapting now to this culture and now to that. The so-called major religious traditions, including Christianity, have proved to be incredibly flexible and accommodating.

To understand this complex nature of religious belief is to understand something important concerning the phenomenon of contemporary religious doubt. As Alasdair MacIntyre once pointed out,[25] earlier generations of theologians debated the issues of faith and unfaith in rather wholesale terms: the opposition of faith to reason, arguments for the existence of God, and the like. The eighteenth-century philosopher, Hume, could question the truth of theism for reasons that are similar in kind though original in detail to those used for millennia, just as John Henry Newman in the nineteenth century could write an apologetics with similar arguments without anachronism. But the debates over theism in the late nineteenth and early twentieth centuries had to do with questions raised by new specialized forms of knowledge: by geology, evolution, social anthropology, psychology, and biblical criticism. Doubts arose in these spheres because the claims of Christianity impinged on some quite role-specific sphere of inquiry in which there were accepted rules of procedure for the making and adjudication of claims in that field. Insofar as these specific spheres have their accepted norms and procedures, a moral problem will arise if a claim is made in one of those spheres that

---

[25] Alasdair C. MacIntyre and Paul Ricoeur. *The Religious Significance of Atheism* (New York: Columbia University Press, 1969.

circumvents those procedures. Such a claim inevitably short circuits the process of inquiry, and, in effect, violates the general ideal of believing responsibly as related to that specific mode of inquiry.

It is understandable then, or so I argued in my book *The Historian and the Believer,* why, in the debates over the life of Jesus that wracked the last century and a half, the interjection of faith claims by traditional Christian New Testament scholars should have posed something like a moral issue for those historians and critics who felt such claims were unjustified. The historians and critics felt, to put the issue in terms of our analysis, that the role-specific duty of historical inquiry carries with it the commitment to certain modes of procedures, assessments, and arguments. To interject faith into historical inquiry is to set aside the warrants and backings that constitute the fiduciary framework of the historian, the common sense against which background the historian is able to make any claims at all. Only against such a background is it possible to properly qualify one's judgments, to conclude that a given report is likely or unlikely, probable or improbable, certain or uncertain, possible or impossible. This is what F. H. Bradley meant when, in his essay on critical historiography, he argued that the historian necessarily has to presuppose his own critically interpreted present experience in order to come to a conclusion about the past. We bring to any judgment, he wrote, the formed world of our existing beliefs.[26] Consequently, many historians and critics not only faced an issue of personal integrity when their historical work led them to conclusions incompatible with their faith, but they were morally outraged at what they regarded as the credulity, obscurantism, special pleading, and generally corrupted historical judgment of their more traditional and believing colleagues.

The difficulty with this sort of criticism, of course, is that it seems itself to be obscurantist because it interjects a moral element into scholarly discussion. Just as the interjection of morality into political affairs tends to force one's opponent into an untenable psychological situation (of being on the "immoral" side), so it is claimed that the interjection of an ethics of belief into historical work impugns the integrity of one's intellectual adversary.

There is, to be sure, this danger, but it is just because politics has finally to do with the formation of our culture that it is impossible to completely bracket the moral appraisal of policies. So, also, it is because the vocation of scholarship ultimately informs the spiritual substance of our culture that moral appraisal in historical reasoning cannot be completely eliminated. Historiography is a truth-telling profession, Clifford would have argued, as important as the shipbuilding profession. The corrosion of the sense of entitlement to speak in the one is ultimately as destructive of the general good as in the other.

---

[26] F. H. Bradley, "The Presuppositions of Critical History," *Collected Essays* (Oxford: Clarendon Press, 1935), 1:14–15.

The morality of believing arises most obviously and acutely, I have argued, when the ethos of a role-specific mode of inquiry is violated; that is, in situations in which we are usually dealing with matters of evidential belief. It would seem, therefore, an entirely different matter, as William James saw, when we are dealing with beliefs that are not evidential or where there is no accepted repertoire of procedures for their assessment and adjudication. Here our question is not whether certain procedures have been violated, but what kind of reasons can be brought forward for our beliefs; how these are related to evidential beliefs; what constitutes their "right" or "entitlement." What causes us to doubt such beliefs? These, I think, are the central issues for that type of religious belief (logical type) for which there seem to be no agreed upon forms of assessment and no background of knowledge that makes it possible for us even to say "I know."

INTELLECTUAL MORALITY IN CLIFFORD AND JAMES

George I. Mavrodes

In this paper I propose to discuss what are perhaps the two best known essays on the topic of intellectual morality, William K. Clifford's "The Ethics of Belief" and William James' "The Will to Believe."[1] I will argue that the position defended by James is *compatible* with Clifford's rule for morality in the cognitive life. In fact, I will claim, James could have presented his own view as a sort of long footnote to Clifford's article, a development and expansion of Clifford's point.

James himself might well be surprised (or perhaps dismayed) to hear of this thesis. He apparently thought of himself as separated from Clifford by a sort of intellectual chasm. For him, Clifford is the nay-sayer, the sceptical philosopher whose principles would shut us out from all that is most valuable in conscious life, preventing us from reaching out for the glorious possibilities that may lie hidden in the folds of reality. And Clifford, for his part, might well think of James as one of those soft-headed thinkers who have no respect for the austere beauty of a disciplined and rigorous intellectual life. My own investigation here, however, has little to do with what these philosophers thought, or might have thought, about each other. I am putting forward a thesis about the *logic* of the positions and principles which they actually expressed in these two essays. I defend a claim about how these principles themselves are related, regardless of what may have been in the hearts of their authors.

My essay here is historical, in the sense that it deals with texts which are now more or less classics. But my intention is not primarily historical, in the sense that it would be exhausted by achieving an understanding of these texts. It seems to me that the best thing we can do with the provocative thinkers of the past is to engage them, as well as we can, in our own philosophical conversation. I hope, therefore, that by considering what Clifford and James said we can advance our own understanding of the ethical aspects of belief.

I will begin by looking at Clifford's rule for intellectual morality, trying to

---

[1] William K. Clifford, *Lectures and Essays* (London, 1879) v. 2, pp. 177–211, and William James, *The Will to Believe and Other Essays in Popular Philosophy* (New York, 1897) pp. 1–31. Both of these essays, of course, have been reprinted many times.

see just what it says and what it does not say. And I will take some care to distinguish it from another rule with which it is often confused, a rule espoused, for example by John Locke and David Hume. Then I turn to James' defense of the will to believe, and make my case for construing it as a development of Clifford's rule. I conclude then with some observations about the reasons which might be given in support of the positions of both James and Clifford.

Clifford provides an admirable brief summary of his own thesis in the claim that "It is wrong always, everywhere, and for anyone, to believe anything on insufficient evidence." What does this come to?

We can begin with a point which is hardly likely to be controversial—or rather, while Clifford's claim itself may be controversial, the fact that he made this claim is not. And the point is that Clifford is here putting forward a *normative* thesis, or proposing a normative rule. He holds that a certain way of proceeding with respect to one's beliefs is "wrong." And evidently it is wrong, not in the sense in which we might say that a certain arithmetic procedure is wrong, i.e., mistaken, but in the sense in which stealing is wrong. Clifford believes that it is appropriate to talk about believing in moral, or quasi-moral, terms. His essay, in fact, is full of moral terminology, even the terminology of religious morality. He who believes with insufficient evidence, Clifford says, *steals* a pleasure, he commits a *sin* against mankind, and so on. And his essay is an attempt to explain the circumstances under which believing is wrong in this moral or quasi-moral sense.

That beliefs are properly subject to moral appraisal is not an uncontroversial claim. There is, for example, the troublesome fact that many beliefs do not seem to be sufficiently voluntary. But the moral approach is one which Clifford shares with his respondent, James. James too seems perfectly willing to talk about beliefs in moral terms, in terms of rights and duties. And so I will not explore here any of the objections which might be raised against the project at this level. I will take it for granted that moral language and moral appraisal are appropriate for this subject matter.

A second point is that sufficiency of evidence is here put forward as a *necessary* condition of the legitimacy of belief. Or (closer to Clifford's own way of making the point) an insufficiency of evidence is a sufficient condition of the moral wrongness of a belief. But what is the *sufficient* condition for a morally legitimate belief? If there is a morality of belief at all, then it is not immediately obvious that it is a function *only* of evidence. But so far as I know, Clifford expresses no opinion at all on whether a legitimate belief must meet some further condition beyond that of sufficient evidence. I do not expect to explore this point any further in this essay, and I will write the remainder of the essay as if there were no other *independent* factors (other than evidence, that is) relevant to the legitimacy of belief. That is, I will consider only those other factors which affect the morality of belief by affecting the level of evidence which is sufficient. But perhaps we should remember that no argument is given here, or by Clifford, that there are no other sorts of factors.

The third point to be noticed is that Clifford's normative rule is a *threshold* rule. It construes the wrongness of belief as a function of the evidence, but a function of a certain sort. Clifford apparently holds (as indeed do most of us, I think) that evidence is, or can be, a matter of degree in some way. We can have, in support of some possible belief, a certain amount of evidence. We might conceivably have had more evidence, or less. Our evidence might be increased or diminished. It could become stronger or weaker. Evidence is, in some way or other, a sort of continuum.

When Clifford talks about belief however, rather than about evidence, he does not at all use the language of degrees, of more or less. He evidently construes belief itself not as a continuum but as a yes-or-no affair. Either a person believes or he does not believe, and his belief status is either wrong or not wrong. Clifford talks about belief itself, in contrast with evidence, as a *discontinuous* phenomenon.

When a discontinuous phenomenon, such as the firing of a gun, is correlated with a continuous phenomenon, such as pressure on a trigger, then one gets threshold effects. There is a certain crucial pressure which is sufficient to trip the trigger and release the firing pin. Trigger pressures below that level result in no firing at all. But when the critical pressure level is reached, then there is a dramatic change in the effect—a threshold is crossed and the gun fires. Pressures exceeding the threshold level again produce comparatively little change in the effect. Pulling the trigger harder, for example, does not make the gun sound louder, nor does it make the bullet go farther.

Clifford thinks of there being a point or cut somewhere in the continuum of evidence. This is the point of sufficiency. If we believe when our evidence falls below this level, then our belief is morally wrong. Above this threshold, however, the moral status of belief is quite different—it is morally accept-able, at least so far as the evidence requirement is concerned.

So far as I know, Clifford says nothing at all about whether there is some degree of evidence which makes belief morally *obligatory*. One can imagine several different possible positions on this question. Someone could hold, for example, that in the realm of belief nothing is merely permissible. Every possible belief is either morally wrong or morally required. In that case a single point would be the threshold for both the prohibited beliefs (in one direction) and the obligatory beliefs (in the other direction). On the other hand, one might claim that no amount of evidence makes believing morally necessary. It is always permissible to withhold belief. And a third position would be that of holding that believing below a certain level of evidence is wrong, then there is a range of evidence within which belief is permissible but not required, and finally there is a second evidential threshold above which belief is obligatory. But Clifford says nothing about any of these possibilities. He concerns himself only with the circumstances under which believing is wrong.

It is important to distinguish Clifford's sort of normative rule from another kind which some philosophers have proposed. David Hume, for example, says that "a wise man proportions his belief to the evidence."[2] And he goes on to explain that the wise man matches the strength of his belief to the strength of his evidence. Although Hume puts the matter here in terms of what a wise man will do, it seems natural to interpret him as proposing, like Clifford, a normative thesis. I understand him, that is, to be claiming that this is how we *ought* to believe, or how it would be *good* to believe.

Like Clifford, Hume thinks of evidence in terms of more and less. But unlike Clifford, Hume also speaks of belief as a continuum which has degrees. One believes more or less strongly. And, since there are two continua here, Hume can speak of proportioning one to the other. More evidence more belief, less evidence less belief. And so Hume's rule, unlike Clifford's, is a *proportional* rule.

Hume does not, so far as I know, make clear anywhere just what proportional function he favors to relate these two continua. We do not know, for example, what level of evidence should correspond to the minimal belief (or zero belief?), to the mid-point on the belief scale, and so on. Consider a possible belief for which I have equal evidence pro and con. Is that a proposition which I should believe (according to Hume) with some minimal degrees of strength, or one which I should not believe at all, or one which I should believe with about 50% of maximum strength, or what? I think that Hume does not provide any clear answers to such questions. So he has not given us a complete version of the Wise Man's Principle. However, it seems plausible to suppose that the very minimum which we should take the proportionality rule to entail is the following:

If there are two propositions, p and q, such that I have more evidence in favor of p than in favor of q, and if I believe both p and q, then I should not believe q more strongly than p. It is hard to see how anything weaker than this could plausibly be said to consist of *proportioning* one's belief to the evidence. We could make this proportionality rule a little stronger by adding to it an additional clause, namely:

If I believe q then I should also believe p. Hume may, of course, have had something still stronger than either of these versions in mind. He might, that is, really have had some specific function in mind for relating the strength of evidence to the strength of belief. But I will not speculate any further on that here.

The difference between a proportionality rule and a threshold rule in this field depends on the difference between construing belief as a continuous phemonenon and as a discontinuous phenomenon. We need not, however, reject one of these ways of thinking about belief in order to accept the

---

[2] David Hume, *An Inquiry Concerning Human Understanding* (1748). Section X.

other. For belief may involve both continuous and discontinuous aspects. I myself believe that it does have both of these aspects, and that therefore both Clifford's rule and Hume's rule have some purchase on the reality of belief. (That is not to say, however, that I believe both of these rules to be morally correct.)

In this respect belief would be something like employment, or having a job. One question which a person might want to ask about me is that of whether I am employed by The University of Michigan. That is a fairly clear question, and it invites a straightforward yes-or-no answer. Either I am or I'm not. Thinking of employment in this way is analogous to Clifford's way of thinking about belief. And proposing that no one should be employed by the University unless he is at least 18 years old is analogous to what Clifford proposed about belief and evidence.

The question we have just mentioned, however, though it is perfectly legitimate, is not the only question we might want to ask about my employment. We might ask, for example, *how much* I am employed by the University. Do I have a full-time position, half-time, an 80% appointment, or what? In this respect employment has degrees, it can become more or less, and we can compare the degrees of my employment with that of someone else. This is, of course, the analogue of Hume's construal of belief. And we can make sense of the proposal that, taken in this sense, my employment should be proportional to some other continuum, such as perhaps my salary.

It seems to me that belief has both continuous and discontinuous aspects, and that consequently we can make sense out of both of these ways of talking about it. On the one hand, there are some things which I believe and some things which I do not believe. I believe that there is a God, for example, and I believe that Tokyo has a population larger than that of London. I do not believe that the forty-second digit in the decimal expansion of π is a 6.[3] There is a "yes-or-no" answer to questions (for me) such as "Do you believe that God exists?" "Do you believe that Tokyo is larger than London?", and so on. On the other hand, it also seems to me that, among the things which I believe, there are some which I believe more strongly than others. I believe that Tokyo is larger than London, but I do not believe it very strongly. I would not be much surprised to find that I was mistaken about Tokyo. I do not feel myself to be much committed to that belief. It seems to me that, though I have the belief, I do not believe it as strongly as I believe that God exists.[4]

[3] There is, of course, an ambiguity in expressions like "I do not believe that p." Sometimes we use the expression to mean that we believe in the negation of p, but sometimes we mean merely that we do not have a belief in p (and may not have a belief in its negation either). In this example I use it in the latter way. I do not believe that the forty-second digit is *not* a 6 either.

[4] I am not sure just what "strong" means in claims like this. I don't know, for example, whether the strength of a belief is an emotion or feeling associated with the belief, or a disposition to retain or abandon the belief under adverse circumstances, or something else. Nevertheless, there seems to be *some* continuous aspect of belief, for which expressions suggesting strength have appeared appropriate to many people.

It also seems to me to be useful to distinguish both of these aspects of believing that p from another belief we might have about p, namely the belief that p has a certain probability, or even that it is more probable than not. No doubt there are cases in which we believe a proposition and also believe that it is probable. Indeed, there are cases in which we believe a proposition *because* we believe that it is probable. Nevertheless, these are distinct beliefs. Or that, at least, is how they appear to me.

Some of the clearest illustrations of this distinction arise in gambling type games, perhaps because there we actually have some notion of how to compute a relevant probability. I may watch a dealer shuffling a deck of cards. I know, or at least believe, that this is a standard deck, etc., and that it has equal numbers of black and red cards. He begins to deal, turning up the first card, a heart. If I have time to do the relevant piece of reasoning I will readily conclude that the probability of the second card's being black is greater than 0.5 ($26/51$ to be more exact). I believe that probability claim—indeed, I would normally believe it rather strongly. And if I had to bet on the next card I would almost surely bet on black rather than red. But in these circumstances I would usually have *no belief at all*, weakly, strongly, or in any other way, that the second card will be black. (Of course, I would also not have the belief that it would not be black.) It seems to be a fact, a fact about me, anyway, that one can believe a certain proposition to be probable (and one can act on that belief) without believing the proposition itself to be true. And so, while probability beliefs may be reasons or causes for substantive beliefs, they are not identical with those beliefs, and the relation between them is not invariant.[5]

Well, if we can make sense out of both Clifford's rule and Hume's rule, then what is the relation between them? Perhaps the most important point is that they are logically independent, in the following sense. It is logically possible for a person to satisfy either one of these rules in his intellectual life without satisfying the other. There might, for example, be a person who never believed anything on insufficient evidence. He would be a model of Cliffordian virtue. But once he got above the level of sufficiency in evidence he might ignore proportionality entirely. He might, that is, hold some beliefs more strongly than others for which he had stronger evidence. He would thus violate Hume's rule. On the other hand, there might be a person whose strength or belief was invariably ordered in accordance with the strength of his evidence, but who held some beliefs (comparatively weakly, of course) on evidence which was insufficient to justify any belief at all. He would satisfy Hume's rule, but violate Clifford's.

Since these rules are logically independent, there might be reasons for

[5] For a somewhat fuller discussion of this point see my "Belief, Proportionality and Probability," in Michael Bradie and Kenneth Sayre (eds.), *Reason and Decision* (Bowling Green, OH, 1982), pp. 58–68).

accepting one of them as a genuine principle of intellectual morality which were not reasons for accepting the other. This is a point to which we will return later.

This excursion into a comparison between Clifford and Hume may have given us a somewhat better grip on Clifford's principal thesis. We can turn now to comparing that thesis with that of James in "The Will to Believe." He says, "The thesis I defend is, briefly stated, this: *Our passional nature not only lawfully may, but must, decide an option between propositions, whenever it is a genuine option that cannot by its nature be decided on intellectual grounds*" (Sec. IV). And in the introduction to his essay he describes it as "a defense of our right to adopt a believing attitude in religious matters, in spite of the fact that our merely logical intellect may not have been coerced."

We might reformulate the normative heart of James' thesis as follows, choosing a terminology which allows an easy comparison with Clifford:

There are some cases (e.g., some religious beliefs) in which it is morally legitimate to hold a belief even though you have no preponderance of evidence in favor of that belief.

A somewhat stronger version of the James thesis would be: There are some cases (e.g., some religious beliefs) in which it is morally legitimate to hold a belief even though you have some preponderance of evidence *against* that belief.

James' own reference to intellectual undecidability may seem to support the first, weaker, version of his thesis, and perhaps it does. He does not seem to me, however, to indicate clearly whether he holds that just any preponderance of evidence makes a matter intellectually *decidable*, or whether he requires some substantial preponderance for decidability. If the latter is his view, then it may be that the second, stronger, formulation represents the thesis of his essay.

In any case, this distinction, though important for some purposes, will not make much difference to my own argument here. For I maintain that *both* of these interpretations of James' thesis are compatible with Clifford's principle.

In making this claim, as I said, I do not intend to deny that James construed himself as disagreeing deeply with Clifford. Apparently he did think of things in that way. Nor do I deny that James and Clifford may have disagreed "in their hearts." I am claiming only that the positions which they actually put forward in these essays are consistent. And I will try to explain in just what sense they are consistent.

James thinks that, in some cases, it is morally legitimate to hold a belief even if your evidence is not so strong that your "logical intellect" is "coerced," not strong enough to make the case "intellectually decidable." Well, OK. Suppose that before coming upon this Jamesian thesis a person has read Clifford, and has been attracted by that vision of intellectual morality. He has resolved to follow Clifford's vision, to the best of his ability. And now some belief is proposed for his acceptance. Maybe it is a religious belief. He examines the evidence in support of this proposed belief, and perhaps he even undertakes to collect some more evidence. But it does not amount to much. There is not much preponderance of evidence in favor of this proposed belief, p. Maybe the evidence, such as it is, is evenly balanced, with no preponderance on either side. Or even worse, maybe it seems to him that whatever imbalance there may be lies against p. He does not find himself "logically coerced"; it does not seem to him that the matter is intellectually decidable. This looks like the sort of case with which James deals. But our hypothetical thinker has not yet read James. He has only resolved to follow Clifford's morality. What, therefore, is *he* to do?

Our initial inclination, I suppose, is to think that Clifford tells him not to believe p. James himself certainly seems to think of Clifford in that way. And it seems likely that there is where Clifford's heart lay. His treatment of the examples in his paper has that tone about it. But his principle, as he actually states it, and the arguments which he gives for it, do not at all have that consequence. They do not tell our hypothetical inquirer not to believe p. They simply do not tell him what he should do at all, what would be within the bounds of intellectual morality, in the case I have described.

The reason for this is that, while Clifford tells us that it is wrong to believe on insufficient evidence, he does not tell us *how much* evidence, in general, is sufficient for belief. And he does not tell us how to go about deciding how much evidence is sufficient. Clifford's approach invites us to think of a scale of evidence, and a cut somewhere in that scale, a cut which divides the sufficient from the insufficient. Clifford insists that this cut is very important, morally important. He who ignores it commits a sin against mankind, and all that. But Clifford's principle does not tell us *where* that cut is, or even how to go about looking for it.

James' essay, on the other hand, can be construed as an attempt to give an answer, and to provide a rationale for an answer, to just that question. He undertakes to tell us *how much* evidence is sufficient to make it morally permissible for us to believe, in certain important cases. James' project, therefore, is not at all incompatible with, or a denial of, Clifford's principle. It is, rather, a *development* of that principle. It attempts to provide a piece of machinery for applying Clifford's rule to a certain class of proposed and possible beliefs.

It is of course possible—indeed, likely—that Clifford would be dissatisfied with James' machinery, dissatisfied with the place where James locates the cut between the sufficient and the insufficient. But that would be an *additional* belief of Clifford's position which he holds along with his principle. It would need its own supporting arguments, its own refutation of James' arguments, and so on. And we might accept fully Clifford's claim that it is wrong everywhere. . . ., and so on, without accepting his opinions as to just where the level of sufficiency is. On that point we might accept James' views, or those of some third party.

Clifford, I say, does not tell us in his essay how much evidence is sufficient to allow for moral permissibility in believing. In fact, he does not tell us the answer to an important preliminary question. Does the line between sufficient and insufficient evidence come in the same place for all the different kinds of things which we might believe? James, of course, suggests that it does not. He holds that beliefs which are momentous, forced, etc., belong to a special class, and that the level of sufficiency in their case is different from that of other cases.

The general thesis that different sorts of belief involve different levels of evidential sufficiency has a lot of plausibility to it. Consider what we might call "The Meatloaf Factor." Imagine that you have some meatloaf in the refrigerator for several days. It occurs to you that it might have spoiled. But again, maybe it is still wholesome. Consider, then, the possible belief (a Jamesian "option") that the meatloaf is still OK. And assume that if you have this belief than you will eat the meatloaf, while if you do not have it, you will throw the meatloaf away. Under these circumstances, we may say that this belief is *valuationally asymmetrical*. If you have this belief, and it is true, then you get a good result (a wholesome meal at low cost). If, on the other hand, you have this belief and it is false, then you get a bad result (a serious illness). And the asymmetry involves the fact that one of these results seems to be much more serious, more weighty, than the other. In this case, the bad result (if the belief is false) seems much more serious and important than the good result (if it is true).

Under these circumstances (and especially if you are going to serve the meatloaf to someone else) it seems plausible to think that you *ought*, in some sense, to demand a fairly strong level of evidence in support of that belief. Or conversely, a comparatively small amount of evidence that the meatloaf is spoiled ought to be a barrier to the belief that it is OK.[6] It seems plausible, that is, to suppose that the Meatloaf Factor has a bearing on how much evidence is sufficient for a legitimate belief.

I think it is part of James' view—and it is well out in the open in Pascal's formulation of The Wager—that some religious beliefs involve the Meatloaf Factor. But they have the opposite asymmetry from that in my example. They are such that if we believe them and they are true, then we get very good results. If we believe them and they are false, then we lose comparatively little. And if there is anything at all in this claim, then probably the Meatloaf Factor applies to some other beliefs as well.

Clifford does not seem to recognize the Meatloaf Factor explicitly at all. He makes no mention of the way in which the consequential asymmetry of beliefs may bear on the level of sufficiency. But it is a striking fact—or so, at

[6]One might want to argue that there is a difference between belief and action, and that you could throw the meatloaf away even if you believed that it was OK. I think that there is some point to this distinction, though it does not have much significance for the issue being discussed here. At any rate, it is not a distinction in which either James or Clifford appears inclined to put much stock.

least, it seems to be—that some of his examples exhibit the Meatloaf Factor to a very marked degree. Think of Clifford's case of the unseaworthy ship. Perhaps the most insistent feature of that case is its valuational asymmetry. If the shipowner's belief is true, then a rather modest benefit is obtained. But if it is false, then a tragedy ensues. I, at any rate, cannot easily avoid the feeling that the force of this example in Clifford's essay derives principally from this asymmetry. But a Jamesian could welcome the example. He could agree wholeheartedly with Clifford's adverse judgment about the intellectual morality of the shipowner. And he would then go on to observe that the Meatloaf Factor is operative in many other cases as well, and that sometimes the asymmetry lies in the opposite direction. There would be substantial plausibility in his claim that in those cases the level of sufficient evidence is markedly different from that which applied to the shipowner.

Agreeing with Clifford's judgment about some particular case, then, such as that of the unseaworthy ship, does not commit us to rejecting James' proposal, unless we have some reason for thinking that the level of sufficient evidence must be the same for all cases. Clifford does not provide such a reason, and I do not think of one. For myself, anyway, this line of argument comes to an end.

That the level of morally sufficient evidence is different for different classes of belief does not of itself support James' judgment about just where that level should be set for the "Jamesian" class. It simply rebuts a counterargument from contrary examples, such as those of Clifford. But there is at least one powerful argument in favor of an assignment like that of James for belief options which are asymmetrical in the positive direction.

Assume that evidence is correlated with truth in a probabilistic way, so that what we call the "strength" of the evidence in favor of a certain proposition is identical with the probability of that proposition's being true, given that evidence. And assume too that a probability of this sort is associated with a frequency outcome—e.g., if one were to make a random selection of a large number of propositions, all of which had a truth probability of 0.6, then about 60% of them would turn out to be true. Now, if we construe James' proposal along the lines of my less radical summary of it earlier, then he defends our right to believe propositions whose truth probability is only 0.5. We would have a 50% chance of getting such a belief right, and presumably (unless we had unusually bad luck) we would get about half of them right. But if these propositions really are asymmetrical in the positive direction, then the likelihood is that those which we get right will confer a benefit on us greater than the loss we sustain on account of the others. The Jamesian proposal, then, can be seen as a strategy for increasing the *value* associated with our intellectual life. And, of course, there is a long and respectable tradition which associates moralilty with value.

The more radical interpretation of James' proposal can be supported in the same way. Even if the truth probability of a certain proposition, given the evidence, is somewhat lower than 0.5, its value asymmetry may be marked enough to compensate for that low probability. Belief in such a proposition would seem, therefore, to have a valuational justification, even though the belief is more likely than not to be mistaken.

This line of argument is, of course, a generalized form of Pascal's Wager. In this general form it makes no special reference to religious matters, nor to the special values which may be associated with religious belief. It simply proposes that we use values in trying to determine what the level of sufficient evidence is. And it can, I suppose, also be construed as issuing a challenge to critics: If you do not make use of *values* in this project, then how do you propose to determine how much evidence is morally sufficient?

Some objections to this line of argument are easily disposed of. I propose to mention some of these briefly, and then to bring this essay to a close with some observations about a line of objection which has more substance to it.

Clifford disparages beliefs which are adopted "for the solace and private pleasure of the believer," those whose function is "to add a tinsel splendour" to life, and so on. But the line of argument which I have sketched out need not appeal to cheap and tawdry values. It is applicable to *any* value, even the most profound or austere, provided only that there are belief options which have the required asymmetry relative to that value. We can therefore reject some particular application of this argument, because we reject the values to which it appeals, without rejecting the general propriety of this approach.

In a similar way we need not, in appealing to this argument, restrict ourselves to the external consequences of a belief. It may be that there are beliefs which have *intrinsic* values, values which are independent of the consequences to which the beliefs lead. If there are any such beliefs then there may be some which are intrinsically asymmetrical, having a large intrinsic value if they are true and comparatively little intrinsic disvalue if they are false. (For that matter, may there be beliefs which have a positive intrinsic value regardless of their truth?) Intrinsic asymmetries will function in this argument just as well as external (consequential) asymmetries.

Clifford also suggests in some places that what is crucial to the morality of believing is not so much the truth of the belief, or the nature of its consequences, but the moral character to which it leads. So he says:

> If I let myself believe anything on insufficient evidence, there may be no great harm done by the mere belief; it may be true after all, or I may never have occasion to exhibit it in outward acts. But I cannot help doing this great wrong towards Man, that I make myself credulous. The danger to society is not merely that it should believe wrong things, though that is great enough; but that it would become credulous, and lose the habit of testing things in inquiring into them; for then it must sink back into savagery.[7]

---

[7] Clifford, p. 189.

Well, may be there is something to this after all. But there is nothing in it which a Jamesian might not accept and assert with even more "robustious pathos" than Clifford himself. To make myself credulous is to develop the habit of believing on insufficient evidence. And to make society credulous, I suppose, would be to engender this habit in the populace at large. But Clifford does not tell us here, any more than elsewhere in his essay, what the level of sufficient evidence is. If James is right about where that level is, then believing in the Jamesian way is not an exercise in credulity and does not develop the habit of credulity. A concern with this character defect provides us with no clue as to how much evidence is morally sufficient for belief. Instead, it would seem, we cannot identify the defect of credulity until we have determined where the cut between sufficient and insufficient lies.

There is, however, an objection to the Jamesian procedure which has more bite than these. Or so, at least, it seems to me. This objection does not reject a valuational approach. It holds, however, that believing is a special activity to which only a single value is relevant. And that value is truth. A person who holds this view need not believe that truth is a value which exceeds all others. He may simply hold that believing (or perhaps some other wider class of cognitive activities and attitudes) is a teleological enterprise which has only a single natural end or goal—the grasping of a truth. If that is so, then the introduction of other values would be a distorting irrelevance. The asymmetries to which I have been appealing should be ignored when it is a question of the ethics of belief.

I think there is a powerful appeal in this claim. There seems to be something deeply right in the suggestion that truth is in some way the *special* business of the cognitive life, and not merely one among several values at which it might aim. And if that is so, then the argument which I have been defending is, at least, not yet rightly put.

If we are attracted to some version of this "primacy of truth" claim, then we will have at hand a ready way of settling a question to which we alluded earlier. For we will have a reason for preferring, in connection with the ethics of belief, a threshold rule, such as that of Clifford, rather than a proportionality rule, such as that of Hume. An evidential threshold has a regular relation to truth. It gives us beliefs with a certain probability of truth, and therefore will tend to give us (over the long haul) the corresponding ratio of truths and falsehoods in our beliefs. The proportionality rule, on the other hand, seems to have no regular relation to truth at all. That is because it does not make *believing* a function of evidence. Rather, it makes the *strength* of belief a function of evidence. But how one is to decide whether to believe at all is left unspecified. Consequently, a pure proportionality rule has no bearing on the extent to which our beliefs achieve truth.

Some version of a threshold rule, therefore, could be defended and advocated on the basis of the way in which it could be expected to yield truth in belief. A proportionality rule would have to be defended, if at all, in some other way.[8]

Some versions of a proportionality rule might, of course, incorporate a threshold at the lower end of the scale. These "mixed" rules would have a regular relation to truth. But it would be the threshold element, and not the proportionality element, which would generate that relation.

Well, as I say, some version of a threshold rule might be defended on the basis of its relation to truth. But which version? Different specifications of where the cut comes between the sufficient and the insufficient generate different probabilities of being correct in adopting a belief on the basis of sufficient evidence. And when we try seriously to pick one specification rather than another—to decide for or against James' proposal, for example—then we find that the way in which belief aims at truth seems more problematic than it did at first.

We can think of a variety of ways of formulating the ideal goal of the cognitive life, putting them, if we wish, in the form of "commands" for our conduct in believing. Each of these commands can then be associated with a specification of the proper level for sufficient evidence, that level which will give us the best chance of satisfying the command and achieving the goal. Each of these commands has something attractive about it, and may even be initially plausible. But each, I think, becomes implausible on reflection.

We may think of our goal as that of believing the maximum possible amount of truth (or the maximum number of truths). "Believe every truth you can!" This goal, which takes no account of falsehood, can best be achieved by setting the level of sufficient evidence so low that it excludes nothing at all. For if we believe *everything,* or everything which we possibly can believe, then we will believe all the truths we can believe. An equally extreme alternative, taking account of falsehoods but not of truths, is "Believe as few falsehoods as possible!" And the safest way to go after this goal is to set the level of sufficient evidence so high that nothing can satisfy it. For if we believe nothing then we believe no falsehoods.

Few of us, I think, will find either of these ideals attractive. Evidently something more complex is needed. How about, "Believe the greatest *preponderance* of truths over falsehoods which you can manage!" Curiously, our best chance of approximating this goal is provided by adopting the "modest" version of James' proposal. (James, of course, did not defend his proposal on these grounds. Perhaps he did not recognize this as one of its consequences.) If we set the level of sufficient evidence at just 0.5 (i.e., at that level which yields a truth probability of 0.5), and if we apply this level to *all* belief options (to the trivial as well as the momentous, etc.), then we will

---

[8] For a more extensive discussion of proportionality rules, see my "Belief, Proportionality, and Probability".

accept all possible beliefs whose probability on the evidence is 0.5 or greater. On those whose probability is just 0.5 we should more or less "break even." On all of the remainder we have a better than even chance of being right. Thus this strategy gives us our best chance of amassing a favorable balance of truth over error.

Well, maybe this too lacks some plausibility upon reflection. We can try the similar sounding, but substantially different, rule "Aim at believing the maximum possible *ratio* of truths over falsehoods!" Our best shot at this goal would be provided by setting the level of sufficient evidence at the highest point which will allow us to believe anything at all. We will have very few beliefs, but the few we have will have a high probability of being right. (This is analogous to the case of a baseball player whose sole ambition is to have as high a batting average as possible. Such a player should bat very seldom, against only the weakest of pitchers. In fact, if he is lucky enough to get a hit on his first trip to the plate, then he should never bat again. He will thus have a batting average of 1.000 forever. But, of course, no manager is likely to hire him.)

Well, the project of formulating the goal of the cognitive life in terms of truth begins to look more and more difficult. it is not that we cannot think of formulations. We can. But we do not readily think of a formulation with which we are willing to live. I, at any rate, have not been able to do so. And this difficulty may be connected with another fact. While there is something attractive in the claim that truth is the special business and goal of cognition, it also seems that it is not truth *per se* which serves this function. Rather, it must be truth in connection with something else.

The local newspaper has just been delivered. How many separate sheets of paper are included in today's edition? It would take me only a few seconds to spread the paper on the floor and count the sheets. I would thus acquire a belief, very likely a true belief. In a couple of minutes I could do the counting several times, thus acquiring a highly reliable belief, one of the most reliable in my repertoire. But I do not do it, and not many of us would do it. If truth is all that central to the cognitive enterprise then why do we not immediately seize upon this truth, so readily and easily available?

In contrast, we may spend days, months, even a whole lifetime, searching for the truth about some profound matter. And we may commit time, effort, and resources to the project even though we believe, from the very beginning, that we are unlikely to achieve anything more than a very tentative conclusion. Why does it make sense to struggle at great length for a shaky grasp of one truth, when we could have instead, with almost no pain or effort, a practically certain grip on a different truth?

At one level, of course, we know the answer to that question. Some truths are important, and some are not.[9] And we know, too, *some* of the

---

[9]These facts, of course, are person-relative. The number of sheets in today's newspaper may very well be important to the publisher or to the printer. It would make good sense for *them* to count them carefully.

things which go into making a truth important. A truth is important if it has important consequences for our practice and our life. But one has the feeling that maybe that isn't the whole story. Maybe there are truths which have an *intrinsic* importance, an importance apart from their consequences. And we don't have at hand a ready and satisfying account of intrinsic importance for beliefs. And (some moods at least) we may also feel that there is still something more unaccounted for in this area.

Once we recognize that not all truths are created equal, as it were, then it seems evident that we cannot express the goal of the cognitive life simply in terms of truth. The importance of what we believe must somehow be worked into it, and maybe some other (and even more obscure) elements as well. And the formulation of the goal must make room for the fact that a year of work for a tentative opinion about some things makes more sense than a minute spent for practical certainty about other things.

All of this, however, seems to lead us back in the direction of James. Perhaps not precisely to James, but in that direction. or so, at least, it seems to me. Perhaps James' characterization of the relevant class of beliefs in terms of liveness, momentousness, etc., is not entirely accurate or complete. But he seems to be probing there for something profound in the structure of the cognitive life, something which bears deeply on the evaluation of cognitive strategies and procedures. Much more than with most epistemologists, one has the feeling that James is sensitive to the complex reality of the human cognitive situation in the world, and to the profundity (and obscurity, too) of the human cognitive enterprise. Perhaps we can, in the end, do better than James. But we can do so only be going deeper than he went, not by withdrawing to a simpler and shallower analysis.

For the moment, however, our position (as we see it) is this. In Clifford we have an attractive, but radically incomplete, rule for the conduct of intellectual life. In James we have a proposal for one way of completing Clifford's threshold rule, along with a suggested line of powerful supporting argument. We are then faced with a challenge. If we are attracted by Clifford's proposal, but dissatisfied with that of James, then how do *we* propose to specify and complete Clifford's criterion? And what argument can we put forward to compare in power with that which the Jamesian can marshal?

BELIEVING FOR PROFIT
James F. Ross

I. INTRODUCTION

"Moral principles sometimes require our believing for profit." "Beyond that, some volitional believing is a regular necessity of nature that yields knowledge." Both statements contravene saying "wantings and choosings cannot produce belief" or saying "whether they can or not, they *ought* not to." They epitomize two versions of "the profit of believing" doctrine, St. Augustine's and St. Thomas Aquinas' (which incorporates St. Augustine's). Both reject the "empiricist" keystone of the English "ethics of belief" debate.

Any view, except that believing for profit is impossible, presupposes that we can give up or take up (some) belief(s) we find relevant to fulfilling our wants. At the pathological extreme, undoubtedly belief can be caused by wishful thinking (illusions), though at that extreme, belief-selection is not genuinely volitional, because its *content*, as well as its occurrence, seems to be "internally" programmed. At the other extreme, it is entirely impossible, and is certainly not part of any theory under discussion here, that one can, be mere willing, believe just anything.

Freud called belief-pictures (like belief in monotheism) that result from wish-fulfillment, "illusion"; even when they are not at the psychotic extreme, he regarded them as pathological (cf. his *The Future of an Illusion*). The pathology supposes there is no conforming reality to make the beliefs true, or, if they happen to be true, to cause, in an appropriate way, their being believed. He thought that when a belief would be held, granted a certain internal cause for believing it, entirely irrespectively of whether it is true or not, it creates an "illusion."

Whatever the merits of that point, Aquinas rejects a related one: that all beliefs caused by wantings and choosings, and not merely by the accumulation of evidence, are cases of illusion. Augustine and Aquinas argue, instead, that belief caused by the will, going beyond the "weight of the evidence," may and regularly does, yield *knowledge*. That's because the will, an ability of the rational appetite, is appropriately *biased* to the good of the person, where "appropriate bias" requires a successful adaptation to reality. In a word, it is not true that beliefs that arise from the will, an "internal cause," arise irrespectively of whether they are true or not. They are not, therefore typically illusory.

In consequence, volitional conviction is not always, not even typically, pathological, irresponsible, irrational or immoral. That some believing is meritorious, even salvific, commits them, too, to an ethics of belief, but not, in Aquinas' case, to ethical appraisal of all "volitional cognition" (as I call it). That's because important ranges of it are compelled. Aquinas attributed much "volitional cognition" (I think most ordinary empirical knowledge) to the structure, actually the bias, of the cognitive system, beyond self-control and moral appraisal. That is clear from "the devils' case" (See III, 5, below.).

The classical English debate about the ethics of belief, from the seventeenth to the nineteenth and twentieth centuries, premised that rationality can be "offended" by wishful thinking, but without offering any explanation of *how* belief is produced by the will. Instead, whether belief that lies beyond the warrant of the evidence, "believing for what you can get out of it," can belong to the *rational* and morally responsible range of human activity, seemed to be at issue. I say it *seemed* that way; yet, though that was what the "liberals" denied, it was not actually what Newman, et. al., affirmed. They found a way of bringing one's assent *within* the warrant of the evidence one has. So the issue really turned on whether certain kinds of claims (like key religious ones) fall outside the warrant of experience; that was argued in terms of whether there is an "accumulator" of empirical evidence not acknowledged by earlier emp;iricism, with Newman arguing that there was, and had to be, in order for us to explain the very human abilities both sides recognized. That is why I think the framework of the English dispute was far narrower than Aquinas or Augustine would accept. It was restricted to the experiential warrant for belief.

1. John Locke offered some of the most conservative general restraints on belief, for instance, that the firmness of one's belief ought to be directly proportioned to the evidence one has for it: "viz. the not entertaining any proposition with greater assurance than the proofs it is built upon will warrant. Whoever goes beyond this measure of assent, it is plain receives not the truth in love of it; loves not the truth for truth's sake but for some other bye-end."[1]

He also offered tight restrictions on the realm of faith: "Light, true light, in the mind is, or can be, nothing else but the evidence of the truth of any proposition; and if it not be a self-evident proposition, all the light it has or can have is from the clearness and validity of those proofs upon which it is received."[2] And he insists that in matters handed to us by *tradition* reason "is that only which can induce us to receive them."[3]

T. H. Huxley, George Eliot, W. K. Clifford, and in some of his writings,

[1]*An Essay Concerning Human Understanding* (Oxford, 1894), Book IV, pp. 428–429.
[2]*Ibid.*, pp. 437–438.
[3]*Ibid.*, pp. 422.

John Stuart Mill formulated the idea differently, but stood for the same principles: it is dishonest and/or irrational to "accept a belief on evidence not proportional to the confidence we accord it, or for any reason that is *not* evidential," where "evidence" has to be sensory or reducible to sense impressions.

Because the fault to be avoided is "confidence that exceeds the warrant of the evidence," they presuppose that belief and/or firmness of belief can arise from, or at least, be effectively restrained by the will.

It was no novelty to attribute error in belief to the will, as Descartes did in the Sixth Meditation, or, indeed, to say error arises from the fact that common sense, though it fits our wanting well enough, does not fit reality.[4]

Furthermore, Augustine, Aquinas, Luther, Calvin, Pascal, and every other major theologian I know of, not only attributed errors about religion to the will (How else could heresy be damnable?), but also made right willing, under the assistance (causation, in some cases) of grace, the *means* by which faith brings salvation (How else could faith be meritorious?).

So, despite the fact that no Christian was disputing that the will might cause belief, even true, possibly salvific, belief, *both* sides in the English controversy seemed to think *knowledge* can be generated only by the accumulation of evidence into conviction. (I have some hesitation concerning Newman here, because his complex analysis seems to assign a role to the will in illative thinking.[5])

The English dispute flared up, fuelled with complex convictions that reflected the intricacies of the wrangle within the Church of England over the moral conditions for affirming the Thirty-Nine Articles, *apparently* over whether a person whose confidence exceeds the sensible evidence for his belief, assessed inductively and deductively, could be acting rationally and morally. (The converse applied more particularly: was a person, whose conviction, accumulated from the evidence he had, fell short of confidence that the Articles were "agreeable" to the word of God, obliged to refrain from publicly affirming them?)

Locke, and others who opposed obedience to authority in belief, were called "liberals" because they stood for "freeing" thought from the bonds of religious-political authority, particularly in the Church of England.[6] For instance, Sir James Fitzjames Stephen, a nineteenth century "liberal" who

[4] For this essay, I omit discussion about how to distinguish reasons, grounds, evidence, motives and motivations for belief, because the only range of data considered by the "empiricists" to warrant belief is entirely sensory or reductively so. In fact, at the level from which the debate first issues, both sides agree that one's expectation of good to be achieved or a profit to be gained from believing is not "evidence," though on deepest analysis it turns out for the Aristotelan cognitive scientist like Aquinas, such considerations are as "evidential" as anything short of *insight* into truth.

[5] On this point, see M. Jamie Ferreira, *Doubt and Religious Commitment: The Role of the Will in Newman's Thought* (Oxford, 1980).

[6] For a discussion of the ecclesiastical context of these discussions see James C. Livingston, *The Ethic of Belief: An Essay on the Victorian Religious Conscience* (Tallahasse, Florida, 1974).

followed Locke and Mill, argued that to accept "tradition" as having any
authority in religion, rather than on the basis of rational evidence, "is like
keeping a corpse above ground because it was the dearest and most beloved
of all objects when it was alive."[7]

Foremost among the opponents of the liberals was J. H. Newman who
argued that we have an "illative sense," an interior reasoning ability that is
cognitively and functionally prior to our inductive and deductive abilities,
and which patterns reality into coherence and into streams of evidential
convergence. (That is a distinctively British way of finding a functional
equivalent for Kant's *a priori* conditions for the unity of experience.) The
illative sense is the "originator" of "formal reasoning," yet more powerful and
more comprehensive; it is the "patterning" ability from which the other
"forms of reasoning" differentiate and attain contact with reality.

Newman tried to show that people have a general ability to arrive, from
evidence basically sensible, at rational conviction, *beyond* the tramways of
deduction and induction. Still, the outcome of his account is that rational
conviction is caused by accumulation of the evidence. He does not attribute
rational belief to any other ability, like the will, for instance.

The issue metamorphoses within the treatments of Augustine and Aquinas, unconfined to how (and how extensively) sensible data is transformed
into rational belief (and by what kinds of "accumulators," sensory or rational);
instead, widening into how rational belief is caused in the absence of compelling evidence. That is, how is rational belief caused in the absence of enough
evidence to accumulate automatically into rational conviction? I think neither Newman nor his opponents seriously thought rational belief might come
about under such conditions.[8]

2. The "empiricist" pictures of Clifford, Locke, Mill, Bentham, Huxley,
and others, not all of a piece to be sure, *focused* on limiting responsible belief
to "evidence" (ultimately sensory) that deductively or inductively warrants
beliefs. Newman thought that too restrictive and, as I said, insisted we have
additional abilities to accumulate evidence into "warrant," even warrant

---

[7]Cited in Leslie Stephen, *The Life of Sir James Fitzjames Stephen* (London, 1894), p. 370.

[8]Implicitly the "intuitionists" were accused of endorsing kinds of thinking, "illative sensing,"
that lie beyond deduction and induction and, therefore, are basically unreliable and irrational.
Thus, a great deal of Newman's analysis was toward showing how natural (and habitual) such
patterns of accumulation are, and how indispensable they are as *foundations* for induction and
deduction. They were also charged with somehow denying that sensory data are the evidential
bedrock of rational thought, even though Newman proposed a cognitive ability that does not
have its own primary or secondary sense qualities but operates, at bottom, on the same primary
qualities, arising from the five external senses, recognized by the empiricists.

Still, they represented a conservative, anti-scientific, proreligious tendency, even though
they opposed the philosophical "establishment" of the time. Nowadays, our appraisal of those
who improvidently restricted the range of rational thought and "free conscience" would probably reverse the labels, making Newman, Ward, James and Kierkegaard "liberals" because they
were hospitable both to the accomplishments of science and sensitive to the other successful
cognitive reaches of the human spirit.

"beyond a reasonable doubt." But even this, with Newman's important addition, is not the whole of the basis in reality for human cognition, as St. Augustine and St. Thomas Aquinas explain the matter.

(i) St. Thomas Aquinas, following Aristotle's *De Anima*, offered "black box" explanations of cognition. The idea is to figure out, from the input of sensory stimuli publicly observable and from the range of rational, and irrational (output) behavior, what internal, even constitutive, "software" and "hardware" actually transforms the sensible input into the distinctively human output. From that the intervening cognitive system is "constructed."

For a while, including the heyday of British Empiricism, that kind of psychology was vilified, derided as "faculty psychology" and dismissed as falling short of science. Its twentieth-century successes in automata theory and cognitive science rehabilitated the approach (both Aquinas' and Aristotle's). Once it is established that belief does result from the will, the question whether it is morally permissible to acquire beliefs that way boils down to how much the activity is within our control and how reliably the promptings of desire and the products of election generate cognition. The issue refines into "when" such beliefs are permissible, not "whether."

That's the more reinforced when we recognize that whether or not to *have* volitional convictions is not itself within one's free choice or even to a significant degree modified by intellectual cultivation and moral exercise (though social conditioning, particularly toward delayed gratification, seems to have a detectable effect on the "volitional" generation of childish beliefs). One can inhibit one's imprudence, one's credulity, one's *incredulity*, for that matter; but one cannot "turn off" the cognitive system that operates automatically when the evidence for belief does not cause insight into the truth, but the satisfaction of relying for one's "good" on believing is very great.[9] Aquinas describes how that system works.

(ii) St. Augustine of Hippo insisted that the will, motivated by gain, "goods," is fundamental in the psychology of rational belief, over and beyond the "evidence" and the clarity provided by divine illumination. He argued that the foundation of our understanding *could* not lie in things already proved (as Aristotle had also argued) and that in the most embracing, important matters one cannot begin from insight, but can reach understanding only from a starting point of faith.

I outline their views, not just for the historical interest of their balking at the constraints of the English debate. Rather, I think they are substantially right, and for the reasons they offer, too. Together with Newman, they knock the "empiricist ethics of belief" off the pedestal of its misshapen psychology. Moreover, their differences are deeper than Newman's, I think.

Ingenious and profound, Newman was, nevertheless, a native in the

---

[9] Of course, I do not mean that there is not a significant question about what "reliability" of the warrants for belief has to do with whether a person acts morally in taking up or rejecting a belief. It is merely that in the dispute, both "empiricists" and their opponents share "enough" common ground on those issues.

British Empiricst contention, mostly unsympathetic to scholasticism, without roots in the psychology of Aquinas. English temperamentally, he opposed, with the introspective analysis used by his opponents, a "narrow gauge" rationality that requires all responsible thought to distill to sense impressions exclusively by deduction and induction. He recognized that human versatility displays a broader, deeper cognitive power to enable us, as we do, to reach conviction from converging evidence which, piece by piece, is not compelling and, only together, has "force" "beyond a reasonable doubt." And, that, not explicable deductively or inductively.

He was right about that, no doubt. But notice how much he differs from the cognitive theory of Aquinas, where certainty is *not* only generated by *evidence* that becomes compelling, but far more broadly, by what one can gain from one's so believing (See III, below).

Newman shared with his opponents the project of supplying a "transformation" device by which sensible evidence causes rational belief. They disagreed over "accumulators." Aquinas worked outside that restriction, explaining that rationality and cognitive force also come from the *finality of the cognitive system*, from the way its biases root in reality.

Faith, as I mentioned, for all the Christian thinkers is essentially a matter of assent caused by the will of one who relies upon God for some good, for instance, truth or eternal life. How similar reliances produce ordinary knowledge is explained by *the rooted finality of the human cognitive system*. That is what Aquinas adds to Augustine's argument that understanding broad enough for human fulfillment, cannot, given the human condition, be generated from an *outset* of understanding alone.[10]

Moral appraisal of a person's gaining and changing beliefs as virtuous or vicious is apt. No one disputed that, neither Augustine nor Aquinas. But that volitional cognition is the natural outcome of the rooted finality of the human cognitive system is just a fact, supporting no moral appraisal whatever. Its manifestations by "natural exaction" are insulated from moral appraisal, too. It is just a fact that experiential knowledge is woofed with believing for profit, directed to gains from believing (and disbelieving, too).

II. St. Augustine on the Profit of Believing

Augustine's *De Trinitate* was written "as the reader ought to be informed," "to guard against the sophistries of those who disdain to begin with faith.[11] Augustine commits himself to a *rational* process, grounded not in proofs, the self-evident, or other infallible or incorrigible grounds, but faith."

---

[10] I do not mean that Augustine rejects Aristotle's notion that real science is bottomed in the self-evident. Augustine had no knowledge of that theory and would not have considered it in opposition to his own, anyway. For the knowledge he has in mind is what he later calls "wisdom," and that does not come from science; neither does our ordinary knowledge of the experienced world.

[11] "On the Trinity," II, 667. The quotations from St. Augustine are taken from W. J. Oates (ed.), *Basic Writings of St. Augustine*, 2 vols., (New York, 1948).

He offers to explore Scripture and to consider reasons for and against (the position that there are three persons in God), to remove obstacles to belief created by "the overbold affirmation of their own presumptuous judgments," that "preclude them from entering the very path of understanding," in order that "they may return and begin from faith in due order."[12]

"Beginning from faith in due order" is the only way to understanding, to satisfy the craving of the convalescent mind, nourished by God, for a grasp of the means of human fulfillment. He applies the idea to the unfortunate Honoratus, a Manichee, to whom *De Utilitate Credendi* is addressed.

Augustine diagnoses Honoratus, who seeks undoubtable reasons from which to begin an examination of the faith, as sick in spirit, whom God alone can cure. Symptomatic is the perverse liking of one's own condition, reason-seeking, in which the evil replicates itself, and, thus, mimics the self-renewing attraction of the good. Reason-seeking creates a desire for reasons and, where the seeking of reasons is inappropriate, makes one sicker than ever.

"So vast a difficulty, God alone can remedy." The crisis is caused by the fact that "the very extreme of the difficulty of discovery of the truth" about God's being and care for us, and of the wisdom, which "to have is nothing else than to see," is "an exercise of the mind which requires a light."[13] But as *De Trinitate* puts it, "the human mind being weak, is dazzled in that so transcendent light, unless it first be invigorated by the nourishment of the righteousness of faith."[14]

Augustine's is a daring objective: to use reasons to disclose that the condition of a person inquiring without faith is one that reason cannot satisfy: first because the inquirer is ill and in need of something to restore his impaired understanding; secondly, because the needed inner light, illumination, is not only beyond the inquirer to create, it is beyond the inquirer's ability to tolerate. Thus, what is necessary for seeing (on one's own) is unbearable to begin to see in.

Augustine argues that for the mind even to engage to reach understanding in some matters, *belief has to precede proof.* Thus, far from being morally defective, faith on incomplete evidence is meritorious, even rationally demanded. Moreover, there is a very important good to be gained by faith, a good not otherwise attainable, yet the very same good to which the rational enterprise as well is directed, *wisdom:* "But now I call wise, not clever and gifted men, but those in whom there is, so much as may be in a man, the knowledge of man himself, and of God most surely received, and a life and manners suitable to that knowledge."[15]

Wisdom, he says, is the gift the having of which consists in one's seeing (the truth about man and God and embracing a suitable life and manners).

---

[12] *Loc. cit.*
[13] "On the Profit of Believing," II, 420–421.
[14] "On the Trinity," II, 670.
[15] "On the Profit of Believing," II, 420.

"For I not only judge it most healthful to believe before reason when you are not qualified to receive reason, and by the very act of faith to cultivate the mind to receive the seeds of truth, but altogether a thing of such sort, that without it, health cannot return to sick souls."[16]

Augustine tries to convince Honoratus (i) that the profit from believing without having proof first is knowledge you cannot have otherwise, and (ii) that the same good, understanding, is the objective of both our unassisted rational inquiry and our having faith, but is accessible only by faith.

The rational basis for certain beliefs is unattainable to someone who *won't* hold them unless he first possesses the rational basis for holding them. How would an "empiricist" convince us that there cannot be, or simply are not, any (life-basic) truths so related to humans?

The "profits" of accepting the "holy authority of the church," for Augustine, are (1) "understanding of the things that have to be believed in order to be understood at all"; (2) the health of spirit that results from that believing without which the sick soul stays ill; and (3) cultivation of the mind, to appreciate, accept and understand what is otherwise inaccessible and unintelligible.

Augustine clearly stands for the rational necessity of our believing some things whose rational basis is not accessible to us at the time of first unwavering assent, and holds that it is *morally required* that we go far beyond the empirical evidence available to achieve minimal human wisdom.

In the gestalt of his *whole* theory, it is not only rationally necessary that we establish a bridgehead of faith to construct human understanding, the failure to do so, under the invitation of grace, is morally reprehensible.

III. AQUINAS ON BELIEVING FOR PROFIT

1. FAITH CAUSES KNOWLEDGE. Despite sloppy construal to the contrary, St. Thomas Aquinas is explicit that faith causes *knowledge (cognitionem)*. In the *Summa Contra Gentiles* he says rational investigation and faith both yield *knowledge (cognitionem)* of God. This is contrasted with "mere belief" (credence) as we use the term now and with what Aquinas calls "opinion" (*De Veritate*, 14,1) "an adherence not intense enough to suppress all fear that an opposed proposition may be true." The term "believe" (*credere*) never occurs where "knows scientifically" or "sees it to be so" can be substituted in St. Thomas' text, and means, roughly, "willingly assents that p, without insight that p." "Believes" is not coapplicable with "*scientia*" but is coapplicable with "*cognitio.*"

In Chapter 3 of the *Summa Contra Gentiles*, I, Thomas says, "the *way* of making truth *known* is not always the same," and distinguishes faith and reason. In Chapter 4, after arguing that truths one can in principle uncover

---

[16] *Ibid.*, p. 421.

through rational inquiry are "fittingly" proposed for faith, he said that was so "all men would easily be able to have a share in the *knowledge* of God, and this without uncertainty and error" (emphasis added). In Chapter 5, he explains that some truths men are *not* capable of attaining by inquiry, supernatural truths, are proposed for faith so men "may have a true *knowledge (cognitionem)* of God" (emphasis added).[17]

In the *Summa Theologiae* (1a, 12, 13, ad 3) he says:

> We must say that faith is a certain kind of *knowledge (cognition)* inasmuch as the intellect is determined by faith to something knowable *(cognoscibile)*. But this determination to one (proposition) does not proceed from the insight *(visione)* of the believer but from the insight of the one in whom he believes. And so, in so far as insight is lacking, it falls short of the conditions for cognition in science; for science determines the understanding to one (proposition) through insight and the grasp of first principles (Emphasis added).

In a word, faith yields knowledge; it makes things evident, not in themselves, but to us: "Faith is the evidence of things unseen," as the Apostle says. Reliance turns (some) propositions into knowledge. To deny this is Aquinas' view simply contradicts the text.

2. FAITH'S ASSENT COMES FROM THE WILL. Faith and reason contrast, not in the nature or status of their products; both yield cognition. Not in the matter about which we believe: anything we know by inquiry can be an object of faith for someone (*Summa Theologiae* IIa, IIae 1, 5: "It can happen that what is 'seen' or known scientifically by one person is believed by another.") The root difference is in the cause of assent. When you find something out for yourself (and that's what "reason" is, "finding out either by looking or figuring it out and checking"), the evidence causes the assent, in fact, compels it. When you find something out by reliance, by being told or by accepting it because of a good enjoyed or to be gained, the *will causes assent*, as Aquinas says repeatedly. For example, in *Summa Theologiae* IIa, IIae, 5, 26: The understanding of the believer assents to the thing believed not because it sees it to be so, either in itself or through resolution to self-evident first principles, but *because of a command of the will* (Emphasis added).

Throughout two major treatises on faith, *De Veritate*, q. 14 and *Summa Theologia*, IIa IIae, 1, 1–5, science (and knowledge of first principles) is said to involve *insight (manifestam visionem veritatis)*, while the rest of cognition, the outcome in various ways of faith, is said to result from "a command of the will" *(imperium voluntatis)*, also described as "election voluntarily" *(elec-*

---

[17] See similar remarks in *Summa Theologiae* Ia, 109, 1c; Ia, 12, 13, ad 3; IIae, 172, 2 ad 3; Ia, 94, 3c and Ia, IIae, 76, 2c.

tionem voluntarie). (That does not exclude the assent's being compelled but in another way than by insight, as we shall see. See 5, below.)

Thus there are two kinds of cognition, scientific and volitional. Scientific knowledge (and the knowledge of the self-evident principles that generate science) involves assent compelled by the evidence, actually, insight caused by the evidence. Volitional knowledge, (to which I gave this name—Aquinas has·no special name for cognition that is not *scientia*), requires the evidence be insufficient to cause insight and that there be an election "to push the believe-button" (in modern metaphor), election of assent, because of reliance upon some good (enjoyed, or) to be gained.

The *act* of faith, that is, volitional assent because of one's reliance on some apprehended good (even a person loved), an assent that cancels all fear of error, is found throughout the fabric of knowledge (and error as well).

Aquinas does *not* think coming to believe things willingly requires the ability to believe just anything someone might propose; you can't believe "at will"; neither can you believe "unwillingly." Whether volitional assent is just "wishful thinking" or "illusion," depends entirely on how the reliance that moves the will is rooted in reality.

Questions about the mechanism and the cognitive reliability of faith are not confined to religion because Aquinas made faith central to a general account of empirical, as well as religious, knowledge.

He explains that the *act* of believing (of coming to believe) is the act that:

(1) *punctuates* consideration of a matter (thinking-it-out) with assent,
(2) in the absence of a completing insight,
(3) without, necessarily, stopping the consideration that may run on "in parallel" with the achieved assent,
(4) as a result of considerations insufficient to move the intellect to insight but strong enough to motivate the will to command assent (to push the "believe-button").

In *Summa Theologiae* Ia, IIae.1, 4c, Aquinas says that in cognition by faith the intellect "assents to something not because it is sufficiently moved by its proper object (insight) but through a kind of voluntary election, tilting it to one outcome, rather than the other, with certitude and no fear at all; that's faith." And in IIa, IIae, 75, 12c, he says, "the believing intellect assents to the thing believed not because it has insight into it either in itself or by resolution of it to first principles which are grasped in themselves but because of a command of the will."

In another treatment (*De Veritate* q.14, written about 1257, ten years or so before the treatment in the *Summa Theologiae*, Aquinas differs in detail[18]

---

[18] As I explain in "Aquinas on Belief and Knowledge," in *Essays Honoring Alan B. Wolter*, ed. by Gerard Etzkorn (Franciscan Institute Publications, 1984).

with some of the important elements explained more comprehensively. He says the person who gets scientific knowledge:

(1) gives assent,
(2) employs discursive reasoning (thinks-it-out)
(3) it is the thinking-out that *causes* the assent by creating insight,
(4) thereby terminating the thinking-out.

But "in faith the assent and the discursive thought are more or less parallel. For the assent is not caused by the thought but by the will, as has been said." So, "the assent does not terminate the thought (automatically), rather the believer still thinks discursively and inquires about the things he believes, even though his assent to them is unwavering."

So, as he explains, a conflict can arise despite the believer's unwavering commitment: "Because the intellect is determined to its assent (from without), a movement directly opposed to what the believer holds most firmly can arise within him, although this cannot happen to one who understands or has scientific knowledge." Because voluntary assent doesn't automatically terminate thinking about the matter, and because the cause of the assent is external, that is, is *not* understanding, but volition, there is room for a conflict between considerations yielded by the thinking-out and one's unwavering volitional assent.

3. FAITH IS THE ENGINE OF EMPIRICAL KNOWLEDGE. In ordinary knowledge. as contrasted with "idealized" scientific knowledge (to which even the best of physics and chemistry does not conform), there is a gap because the evidence on which assent is based is not sufficient to cause insight. Yet there is knowledge. What fills the gap? St. Thomas says, something sufficient to move the will to command assent, but not sufficient to cause insight. What could that be? It has to be "a good" either enjoyed or sought. And that, to account for knowledge, supposes the rooted finality of the cognitive system: that the goods relied upon stand in appropriate relationships to reality.

4. FAITH OPERATES THROUGH SATISFACTION. We need to explain the principle: "Faith does not work by love *(per delectationem)* instrumentally but as by its proper form" (*Summa Theologiae* IIa, IIae 23,6 ad. 2). First, I think *"delectationem"*, "love" is better rendered "satisfaction" for present purposes, even though the issue arises from St. Paul's saying "faith . . . works by charity." Secondly, "satisfaction from reliance" is not to be regarded as an instrument or *means* by which volitional knowledge is achieved; rather, it is the very activity (the "mechanism" if you like older metaphors) that causes volitional cognition.

What "fills the gap" is a motivation. What moves the will to cause assent is the satisfaction-in-reliance (on an apprehended good, even a person loved) that things are as proposed (as the proposition formulates).

The gap between grounds for believing that do not cause insight and the causing of assent by which we, in effect, say "OK; it's that way," is filled by satisfaction-in-reliance (on people, coherence, completeness, veracity, etc.) that things *are* as proposed. "Faith works through love as through its proper form."

Reliance on *someone* is distinctive of faith (*fides ex auditu*), but is not its distinctive activity. The distinctive activity is *satisfaction-in-reliance* that things are as proposed.

In *De Veritate*, 14,1, Aquinas says:

And in this situation our understanding is determined by the will which chooses to assent to one side definitely and precisely because of something which is enough to move the will though not enough to move the understanding, namely, *since it is good or fitting to assent to this side*. And this is the state of one who believes. This may happen when someone believes what another says *because it seems fitting or useful to do so*.

Thus we are moved to believe what God says because we are promised eternal life as a reward if we believe. And *this reward moves the will to assent* to what is said, although the intellect is not moved by anything which it understands (Emphasis added).

In Article 2, he says: "[the believer's] 'Intellect is determined to something through the will and the will does nothing except insofar as it is moved by its object, which is the good to be sought and its end. In view of that, *faith needs a twofold principle*, a first which is the *good that moves the will*, and a second which is that to which the understanding gives assent under the influence of the will."

Furthermore, he says, "the will, under the movement of this good, proposes as worthy of assent something which is not evident to the natural understanding. In this way it gives the understanding a determination to that which is not evident, the determination, namely, to assent to it."

Nothing could be more appropriate, in the very context where we are explaining how "faith works . . . through love," than Sir James Fitzjames Stephen's caustic indictment of Newman's (and company's) explanation of the way "probabilities and strong feelings" convert into certitude. He said they increased "the bulk and weight of the evidence by heating it with love."[19] That applies rhetorically and hyperbolically to Newman's theory, which doesn't explain how it is *not* love that does the job. It applies literally, quite unhyperbolically, to St. Thomas' theory which says love does do the job—not increasing the evidence, of course; but motivating willed assent. Whether the assent "should" be so commanded is exactly a question about how the motivation, and its system, is based in reality. Such considerations would be

---

[19] James Fitzjames Stephen, *Liberty, Equality and Fraternity* (London, 1894), p. 344.

strange, horrifying and completely irrational to the British liberals (and very probably the intuitionists too). That indicates just how revolutionary and different Aquinas' cognitive psychology really is.

5. THE TEST CASE: THE FAITH OF THE DEVILS. Why is this case important? To establish that willed assent can arise from natural necessity. The devils have to *know*, but without scientific knowledge, certain supernatural truths in order that both their rebellion and their damnation be complete. There is no option but that they must have faith; it is the only way to achieve cognition without insight. And yet, their faith cannot be meritorious or, through it, they will have been saved.

In *Summa Theologiae* IIa IIae 5, 2, on whether devils have faith, he says:

> The intellect of the believer assents to the thing believed not because he has insight into it either in itself or through a resolution to first principles which are self-evident but because of a command of the will. That the will should move the intellect to assent can be caused by two things. First, the will's being directed toward a good; and thus, to believe is a praise-worthy act. Secondly, because the intellect is convinced that it ought to believe what is said, even though it is not convinced by the evidence of the things themselves. Thus, if a certain prophet predicted something future as the word of the Lord and supported it by raising the dead, the intellect of those seeing this would be convinced through this sign so that they would see that this was said by a God who does not lie; as long as that which is predicted is not self-evident, the basis of belief is not obviated.

Aquinas has to block "merit" from the devil's believing: he does that by reasoning: "The belief of the devils is somehow exacted by the evidence of the signs." So, volitonal assent can be both from the will and compelled. In the second and third answers to objections, he says that "they are forced *(coguntur)* to believe because of their natural intellectual acumen *(perspicacitate naturalis intellectus)* "and that "the signs of faith are so evident that, because of them, they are compelled *(compellantur)* to believe." The devils are "forced" *(coguntur)* and "compelled" *(compellantur)* to believe by the "perspicacity" of the natural intellect and by the evident *sign-relationship* of what they can see (e.g., miracles).

The exaction, the compelling, of willed assent is compatible with one's assenting by election voluntarily, even though, because it occurs with natural necessity, merit is denied it. In the same way, we seek happiness necessarily but voluntarily. Such exactions are different in their cause from the compelling of assent by scientific insight or the plain sight of the truth *(visum)*. Those results are not voluntary because they do not come about *because* we want them, and, no matter how willingly we assent, we *would* have assented under conditions of insight even if we had not wanted to. Thus the assent of insight, however willing we are, comes about willy-nilly. Whereas, an "*im-*

perium voluntatis" comes about only willingly, yet inevitably in some cases, given that the rational appetite (even of devils) has biases. So the faith of the devils is compelled, but willing, yet without merit. Augustine's principle "no one believes unless he's willing" is preserved without the devils' becoming redeemed.

Certain biases of the rational appetite, e.g., for the truth, are from its nature; others, like one's interest in coherence, simplicity and beauty may be, at least in degree, cultivated and subject to moral appraisal. Aquinas does not develop his views in that kind of detail. Rather, he seems to think that, typically, our empirical knowledge is "exacted" from us by "signs" and goods that compel us to assent, whereas our religious assent is coaxed from us by less immediate and ubiquitous signs and by an inner invitation: "the believer has sufficient motive for believing; for he is moved by the authority of divine testimony, confirmed by miracles, and what is more, by the inward instinct of the inviting God" (*Summa Theologiae* IIa IIae, 2, 9 ad. 3).

In a word, little of our knowledge comes from insight. The largest portion comes from willed assent motivated by our satisfaction-in-our-reliance on some good. A vast range of such assent, including our experiential knowledge, is both willing and compelled by the biases of the rational appetite. Such judgments are no more subject to praise or blame than are our insights.

Thus belief that goes beyond the warrant of the available evidence is not only not irrational and immoral, automatically; it may, if fact, be in no way even suitable for such praise or blame. That is, of course, to be understood so that particular acts, typically, fall within habits of thought subject to moral appraisal.

A comparably large range of cognition is the result of willing election in reliance upon goods to which we have committed ourselves, like seeking the reward of eternal life. Such belief is voluntary, can be meritorious or deleterious, and can exhibit various virtues and vices: it can be provident or improvident, lazy or thoughtful, credulous or incredulous, responsible or irresponsible.

IV. Conclusion

Augustine and Aquinas stood for the view that belief that goes beyond the sensible evidence, or any evidence at hand, may be both rationally and morally required. Aquinas went further, holding that quite typically assent (with resulting cognition) is actually compelled by the biases of the rational appetite, biases rooted in our environment and "toward our good."

Of course, unfavorable environments might lead things, thus biased, into extinction; others would leave us "truth" machines, but not knowers, because of merely accidental relations between our beliefs' being true and the conforming reality. So Aquinas implicitly supposed the suitability of our cognitive adaptation to our environment. Thus there is a key empirical question to which Aquinas, following Aristotle, presupposed, generally, an affirmative answer: "Granted that there is a *bias* to the cognitive system, is it so based in reality that the volitional convictions it creates are knowledge?"

Most of the usual discussions of the "ethics of belief" concern when the evidential supply is enough for us to avoid reckless, irrational, frivolous or immoral believing. Whatever the merits of the best considerations in such discussions, there is something left out: rational and moral believing can gain the status of knowledge, even though the "evidential supply" does not provide insight.

The psychological make-up of humans is viewed myopically, overlooking that faith is a *reliance-device* for producing cognition. Aquinas' cognitive psychology puts the issues in fairer perspective, incorporating Augustine's view that human cognition cannot be founded only on the self-evident, or on what we find out for ourselves or arrive at by the evidence-accumulators acknowledged by the empiricists.

We do not, as Fitzjames Stephen charged, "increase the weight and bulk of the evidence by heating it with love." Instead, we command assent, motivated by satisfaction, by love. Augustine and Aquinas offer different options, with new issues about when believing is responsible and rational, and when immoral.